Commercial and Economic Law in Denmark

Commercial and Economic Law in Denmark

Third Edition

Peter Møgelvang-Hansen

In co-operation with

Jane Bolander
Jesper Lau Hansen
Søren Friis Hansen
Marie-Louise Holle
Camilla Hørby Jensen
Bent Ole Gram Mortensen
Sandie Nøhr Nielsen
Hans Viggo Godsk Pedersen
Andrej Savin
Jan Trzaskowski
Christina D. Tvarnø
Grith Skovgaard Ølykke
Kim Østergaard

This book was originally published as a monograph in the International Encyclopaedia of Laws/Commercial and Economic Law.

Founding Editor: Roger Blanpain
General Editor: Frank Hendrickx
Volume Editors: Jules Stuyck & Evelyne Terryn

Wolters Kluwer

Published by:
Kluwer Law International B.V.
PO Box 316
2400 AH Alphen aan den Rijn
The Netherlands
E-mail: international-sales@wolterskluwer.com
Website: lrus.wolterskluwer.com

Sold and distributed in North, Central and South America by:
Wolters Kluwer Legal & Regulatory U.S.
7201 McKinney Circle
Frederick, MD 21704
United States of America
Email: customer.service@wolterskluwer.com

Sold and distributed in all other countries by:
Air Business Subscriptions
Rockwood House
Haywards Heath
West Sussex
RH16 3DH
United Kingdom
Email: international-customerservice@wolterskluwer.com

ISBN 978-94-035-1621-9

e-Book: ISBN 978-94-035-1622-6
web-PDF: ISBN 978-94-035-1623-3

This title is available on www.kluwerlawonline.com

The Authors

Peter Møgelvang-Hansen is Professor emeritus at CBS LAW, Copenhagen Business School. His research mainly concerns contract, consumer protection and civil enforcement law.

Jane Bolander (born 1965) obtained a Master of Law at Aarhus University in 1990, and a practising certificate as a lawyer in 1994. In 1999, she obtained a PhD. Since 2010, she has been employed as Professor in Tax Law. From 2011, at the Law Department of Copenhagen Business School. She teaches and researches in different areas of tax law.

The Authors

Jesper Lau Hansen (born 1965) is a Professor of company law and financial regulation at the Faculty of Law, University of Copenhagen. He holds a Law Degree (Cand.Jur., 1989) and a Doctorate Degree (Dr. Jur., 2001) from the University of Copenhagen and a Masters of Laws (LLM, 1993) from the University of Cambridge. He has served as a government-appointed expert on many Danish law committees, including the one that prepared the present Companies Act (2006 – 2008), and he has served in several capacities at the European Union level, such as an academic member and chair of the Stakeholder Group connected to ESMA (2011 – 2016) and on the European Commission's expert groups on company law: the Reflection Group (2010 – 2011) and the ICLEG (2014 – 2019). He also chairs several Danish UCITS and AIF and serves as an arbitrator in private arbitration cases.

Søren Friis Hansen obtained an MSc of Law at Copenhagen University in 1991 and a PhD in 1995. He was Professor of company law from 2001 to 2011, at the University of Southern Denmark, and from 2011 at the Law Department, Copenhagen Business School. His research includes company law, tax law and EU law.

Marie-Louise Holle holds a Master's degree of Law (DESS) from Université de Paris V-René Descartes, France, and a Master's degree of Law (cand.jur.) from the University of Copenhagen, Denmark. She earned her PhD degree at the University of Copenhagen in 2012. Since, she has been a researcher at CBS LAW, Copenhagen Business School, currently as an associate professor. Her research areas are commercial law, especially tort and contract law as well as private-public cooperation.

Camilla Hørby Jensen (born 1979) obtained an MSc of Business Administration and Commercial Law at University of Southern Denmark (SDU) in 2004 and a PhD degree from SDU in 2007. Since, she has been employed at the Department of Law at University of Southern Denmark; from 2010 as an associate professor. Since 2016 Camilla has been acting as head of department. Her main research areas are law of banking and finance, commercial law and consumer law.

Bent Ole Gram Mortensen (born 1962) obtained an LLM Law degree in 1986 and his PhD in 1998. He holds a chair in 'Commercial Law, including especially Environmental and Energy Law' at the University of Southern Denmark. Since 1995, he has been working at universities. Previously, he has been working at law firms (was admitted as solicitor 1989), The Danish Ministry of Justice and The Maersk Group. Since 2000, he is a member of the Danish Energy Board of Appeal, since 2017 as a vice chairman and since 2009 Chairman of the Valuation Authorities in the Region of Southern Denmark in compliance with the Renewable Energy Act. He has written and contributed to a large number of articles and books in English, Danish and German, having dealt with legal matters on both national and EU level not only dealing particularly with energy law matters but also within the field of environmental law, polar law, marketing law and administrative law.

Sandie Nøhr Nielsen (Born 1985) is MSc in Business Administration and Commercial Law from Copenhagen Business School (2014) and a PhD fellow at CBS LAW. Her research topic is Contractual conditions for efficient application of Public-Private Partnerships – in a social infrastructure perspective. The PhD dissertation seeks to analyze the scope of potential benefits of Public-Private Partnership (PPP). Specifically, to what extent contractual conditions in a PPP can optimize the value of collaboration among the public and private contracting parties. The dissertation focuses on the intersection between private law and public law. In particular, the research centres its attention towards social infrastructure PPPs and the contractual relation. The aim of the dissertation is to propose a mutually optimizing perspective for both parties in which sectoral collaboration is promoted along with a general enhancement of collaboration value as well as the PPP contract itself.

Hans Viggo Godsk Pedersen (born 1947) is Professor at the Department of Law, University of Southern Denmark. He obtained his cand. jur. in 1975 and his PhD in Law in 1985. From 1975 to 1982, he worked at the Århus School of Economics, from 1979 on as an Associate Professor. From 1982 to 1997, he worked at the Law Department of the Copenhagen Business School as an Associate Professor. He did research within the field of credit security law. Among the books he has published are: *Kaution* (Guarantee), 11th ed., 2016; *Om ejerpantebreve & skadeløsbreve* ('On Mortgage Deeds & Letters of Indemnity'), 1990; *Bankgarantier* (Bank Guarantees), 2nd ed., 2003; and on subjects as domestic relations and right of inheritance, amongst others *Familie-og arveret* (Law of Domestic Relations and Inheritance), 10th ed., 2018 in cooperation with Anitta Godsk Pedersen.

The Authors

Andrej Savin (born 1973) gained an LLM in International Business Law from Central European University in 1996 and a PhD from Cambridge University in 2001. He worked as a lecturer at Cambridge University from 2001 to 2007 when he took a post as Associate Professor at Copenhagen Business School. He teaches International Business Law, EU law and Information Technology Law.

Jan Trzaskowski is Professor, PhD at CBS LAW, Copenhagen Business School. He specializes in internet law with particular focus on consumer and data protection. Author or co-author to many books, articles and reports covering these subjects.

Christina D. Tvarnø (born 1969) is MSc of Business Administration and Commercial Law from Copenhagen Business School (1994) and obtained her PhD degree at CBS in 2001. Since, she has been employed at the Law Department of Copenhagen Business School, since 2011 as Professor. Her main research area is private partnering contracts in the Danish construction industry and thus contracts based on trust, corporation, open books, joint utility and incentives between the parties. She has focused her research on the economic influence on the Danish partnering contract, e.g. strategic alliances, optimal contracts, relational norms and social contracts, and Christina has investigated the legal effects of contracting on those economic terms. Christina Tvarnø has also investigated the difference between public-private partnering contracts and privately financed PPP contracts and the effect of the EU-procurement rules. Furthermore, she writes books and articles on legal theory and legal method.

Grith Skovgaard Ølykke (born 1976) obtained an MSc of Business Administration and Commercial Law at Copenhagen Business School in 2006, and a PhD in 2010. She was employed at the Law Department of Copenhagen Business School, from 2010 to 2017, most recently as Professor (wsr). Since 2017 she has been employed as Commerical Law Consultant at the law firm Kammeradvokaten in Copenhagen. Her areas of expertise are public procurement law, State aid law and competition law.

Kim Østergaard (born 1960) obtained an M.Sc. of Business Administration and Commercial Law at Copenhagen Business School in 1990, and a PhD in 2003. Since 1990, he has been employed at the Law Department of Copenhagen Business School, now CBS LAW. Kim Østergaard is a professor (WSR). His research and teaching include strategic contracting, general contract law, intermediaries, and transport law, especially maritime law.

The Authors

Table of Contents

The Authors 3

List of Abbreviations 19

General Introduction 21

§1. General Background of Denmark 21
I. Geography 21
II. Cultural Composition 21
III. The Political System 22
IV. Population and Production Statistics 25
V. Social and Cultural Values 29

§2. The Economic System 31

§3. The Legal System 32
I. Historical Development 32
A. General Development 32
B. Denmark and the European Union 33
C. The Home Rule of Greenland and the Faroe Islands 34
II. Constitutional Law 34
III. Administrative Law 36
IV. The Ombudsman 36

Part I. Commercial Law 39

Chapter 1. Concepts and Sources of Commercial Law 39

§1. Concepts And Sources in General 39

§2. Statutes 40

§3. Administrative Rules 41

§4. Other Sources 42

Chapter 2. The Economic Operators 44

§1. Personal Status of Merchants 44
I. Minors and Incompetents 44
II. Foreigners 45
III. Right to Exercise Trade 47
IV. Legislation on Equality of Men and Women 47
V. Married Persons and Registered Partnership 48

§2. Partnerships and Companies 48
I. Partnerships 49
A. Unlimited Partnerships 49
B. Limited Partnerships 50
II. Associations and Cooperative Societies 51
III. Foundations 51
IV. Mortgage Institutions 52
V. Investment Associations 53
VI. European Economic Interest Groupings 53

Chapter 3. The Economic Institutions 54

§1. Professional Organizations 54
I. The Danish Chamber of Commerce 54
II. The Confederation of Danish Industry 55
III. The Danish Federation of Small and Medium-Sized Enterprises 55
IV. The Organizations of the Labour Market 56
V. Specialized Organizations 57

§2. Administrative Authorities and Advisory Bodies 57
I. The Ministry of Industry, Business and Financial Affairs 57
II. Standardization, Technology and Energy Bodies 60
III. Administrative Recourse 60
IV. Local Bodies 61

§3. Commercial Courts and Arbitration 61
I. Commercial Courts 61
II. Arbitration 62
A. Regulatory Framework 62
B. Arbitration Institutions 63

Chapter 4. General Obligations on Economic Operators 64

§1. The Act on Business Enterprises 64

§2. The Registration System 64
I. Registration in General 64
II. Registration of Enterprises and Companies 65

§3. Name and Procuration of the Enterprise 66

§4. The Duty to Keep Books 66

§5. Requirements Concerning Bank Accounts 67

§6. Requirements Concerning the Local Situation 67

Chapter 5. Business Assets, Goodwill and Commercial Property Rights 68

§1. Business Assets 68
I. Trade Names 68
A. Legislation 68
B. Registration 69
C. Scope of Protection 69
II. Goodwill 70
A. Legislation 70
B. Scope of Protection 70
III. Know-How and Trade Secrets 71

§2. Intellectual Property Rights 72
I. Trademarks 73
A. Legislation 73
B. Registration 73
C. Scope of Protection 75
D. Transfer 76
E. Duration 76
F. Employee Rights 76
II. Copyrights 76
A. Legislation 76
B. Registration 77
C. Scope of Protection 77
D. Transfer 78
E. Duration 79
F. Employee Rights 79
III. Protection of Photographs 79
A. Legislation 79
IV. Patents 80
A. Legislation 80
B. Registration 80
C. Scope of Protection 82
D. Transfer 82
E. Duration 83
F. Employee Rights 83
V. Utility Models 83
A. Legislation 83
B. Registration 84
C. Scope of Protection 84

D. Duration 85
E. Employee Rights 85
VI. Design Protection 85
A. Legislation 85
B. Registration 86
C. Scope of Protection 86
D. Duration 87
VII. Computer Chips 87
A. Legislation 87
B. Registration 87
C. Scope of Protection 88
D. Duration 88
E. Employee Rights 88
VIII. Biotechnical Inventions 88
IX. Plant Breeders' Rights 90

Chapter 6. Bankruptcy and Related Institutions 91

§1. GENERAL SURVEY 91

§2. RECONSTRUCTION 92
I. Reconstructor and Mandatory Person 92
II. Dispositions During the Reconstruction 93
III. Relations with the Creditors 94

§3. BANKRUPTCY 94
I. Petition in Bankruptcy: Terms of Bankruptcy 95
II. The Disposal of Property 95
III. The Assets of the Bankruptcy Estate 96
IV. Voidance 97
A. Terms of Voidance 97
B. Voidance of Preferential Treatment of Creditors 98
C. Legal Proceedings 100
D. Reducing Dispositions 100
E. The Effects of Voidance 101
V. Claims on the Estate 102
A. The Order of Priority of Creditors 102
1. Preferential Claims 102
2. Secondary Preferential Claims 103
3. The Wage Privilege 103
4. Claims for Purchase Taxes 103
5. Ordinary Claims 104
6. Secondary Claims 104
B. Joint and Several Debts 104
C. Set-Off 104
D. Fulfilment of Secured Rights 105
E. Winding-Up of the Estate 105

§4. Composition Scheme Under Reconstruction 105
I. The Progress of a Compulsory Composition Scheme 105
II. The Contents of the Composition Scheme 106
III. The Effects of the Composition Scheme 107

Chapter 7. Negotiable Instruments 108

§1. Promissory Notes 108
I. Promissory Notes in General 108
II. Debtor's Claims Against the Creditor 108
III. Rules of Transfer 109
A. The Relation Between the Assignor and the Assignee 109
B. The Relation Between the Assignor's Creditors and the Assignee 110
C. Transfer to Different Assignees 110
IV. Release of the Debt 110
V. Dematerialized Instruments 110

§2. Bills of Exchange and Cheques 111

Chapter 8. Stock and Commodity Exchanges 113

§1. The Primary Trading Venues 113

§2. Admission to Trading 114

§3. Rules on Stockbroking 116

§4. Obligations on Issuers and Parties Related to the Issuer 117

§5. Takeovers 119

§6. Market Abuse 121

Chapter 9. Commercial Contracts 123

§1. General Principles of Contract Law 123
I. Formation of Contracts 123
A. General Rules 123
B. Standard Terms 124
C. Electronic Transmission 125
II. The Form of the Contract 125
III. Interpretation of Contracts 125
IV. Validity of Contracts 126
A. General Rules 126
B. Incapacity 126

C. Declarations of Will 127
D. Implied Terms 128
E. Unfair Contract Terms 128
V. Authority 129

§2. SALE OF GOODS 130
I. Legislation on Sale of Goods Contracts 130
II. Types of Sale and Product Description in the SGA 131
III. Delivery 131
IV. The Price 133
V. Breach of Contract 133
A. Regulation in General 133
B. Late Performance 134
C. Examination of the Goods 135
D. Regulation of Defects 135
E. Regulation of Payment 136
F. Anticipated Breach of Contract 137
G. No Obligation of the Purchaser to Take Delivery 138
H. Differences Between the SGA and the CISG 138

§3. COMMERCIAL SERVICES 139
I. Distribution 139
A. Distribution in General 139
1. Definition and Concept of Distribution 139
2. Legal Regulation 139
3. Validity and Effects of Exclusivity Clauses 140
4. Obligations of the Parties 140
5. Termination of the Distribution Relationship 141
B. Contracts on Distribution of Petrol 142
C. Franchise Contracts 142
D. Selective Distribution 142
II. Middlemen or Intermediaries 143
A. General Survey 143
B. Commercial Agents 143
1. Definition of a Commercial Agent 144
2. Obligations of the Parties: Right to Commission 144
3. Termination of the Commercial Agency Contract 146
4. Right to Goodwill Indemnity 146
5. Competition Clauses 147
C. Commercial Travellers 147
D. Commission Agents 147
1. Obligations of the Parties 147
2. Termination of the Commission Contract 148
E. Brokers 148
F. Forwarding Agents 149
III. Insurance 149
IV. Financial Services 151

A. Leasing 152
1. The Leasing Concept 152
2. Relation Between the Lessor and the Lessee's Creditors 152
3. Obligations of the Parties 152
B. Factoring 153
1. The Concept of Factoring 153
2. Relations to the Clients 154
V. Carriage by Land, Sea and Air 154
A. General Survey 154
B. Sea Transport Agreements 155
C. Agreements on Transport by Road 157
1. Legislation 157
2. The Transport Contract 158
3. Liability 158
D. Contracts on Transport by Railway 159
E. Contracts on Air Transport 161
F. Other Contracts on Transport 162
VI. Other Services: Construction Contracts 163

Chapter 10. Commercial Securities 164

§1. Types of Securities 164

§2. Surety or Guarantee (Kaution) 164

§3. Pledge and Mortgage (Pant) 166
I. Pledge and Mortgage on Movable Property 167
A. Pledge 167
B. Mortgage 167
II. Mortgage on Real Property 168
III. Negotiable Securities and Promissory Notes 168

Part II. Economic Law 171

Chapter 1. State Intervention in Economic Activities 171

§1. Institutional Framework 171

§2. Planning 172

§3. State Shareholdings 174

§4. Basic Principles of Economic Law 176
I. Import and Export of Goods and Capital 177
A. General Regulation 177
B. Foreign Exchange of Capital 177

II. Labour Forces 178
III. Facilities for Development 179
IV. Global and Local Planning 179
V. Means of Communication 180
A. Railways 180
B. Aviation 181
C. Roads 181
D. Postal Service 181
E. Telecommunication 182
F. Radio Communication 182
G. Building Regulation 183

Chapter 2. Law of Establishment and Supervision of Commercial Activities 184

§1. Requirements for Professional Qualifications and Exercise of Trade 184
I. General Requirements 184
II. Liberal Professions 185
A. Advocates 185
B. Auditors 186
C. Real Estate Agents 186
III. Self-Employed Trade 187
IV. The Health Sector 188

§2. Quantitative Limitation of the Number of Enterprises 188

§3. Supervision of Credit Institutions, Insurance Companies, etc. 189

Chapter 3. State Incentives for Economic Activities 190

§1. Subsidies 190
I. The Agricultural Sector 191
II. The Sector of Fisheries 191
III. The Environment 192
IV. Trade and Industry Subsidies 193
A. Protection of Trade and Industry in General 193
B. Subsidies for New Enterprises 193
C. Export Credit 193
D. Regional Measures 194
E. Measures Relating to Compensation of Loss 194
F. Other State Subsidies 195
V. Subsidies for Vocational Training and Education 195

§2. Tax Incentives 195
I. Tax Relief Concerning Enterprises 196

II. Tax Reliefs Concerning Persons 197

§3. The State as Shareholder 197

Chapter 4. Competition Law 198

§1. Introduction 198

§2. Regulation of Anti-competitive Practice 198
I. The Danish Competition Act in General 198
II. The Purpose of the Competition Act 198
III. The Scope of the Competition Act 199
IV. Institutional Provisions 199
V. Substantive Provisions 201
A. Market Transparency 201
B. Measures Against Harmful Effects of Anti-Competitive Practice 201
C. Appeal 202
D. Penalty Provisions 202

§3. The Law of Unfair Competition and Trade Practices 203
I. Introduction 203
A. European Marketing Law 204
II. The Danish Marketing Practices Act 205
A. Scope of Application 205
B. The Average Consumer and Children 206
C. Substantive Provisions 206
1. The General Clause 206
2. Misleading and Aggressive Marketing 207
3. Identification of Commercial Intent 208
4. Comparative Advertising 208
5. Unsolicited Communication with Specific Customers 209
6. Price Indications 210
D. Administration: The Danish Consumer Ombudsman 211
E. Sanctions 212
III. Specific Regulation 213
A. Particular Products 213
B. Particular Media 214

Chapter 5. State Regulation of the Conditions of Commercial Transactions 215

§1. Price and Supply Regulation 215
I. Price Regulation 215
II. Supply Regulation 216
A. Public Supply 216

B. Supply Regulation Within the Private Sector 217

§2. Consumer Law 217
I. Institutional Aspects, General Principles and Representation of Consumer Interests 217
A. Consumer Law in General 217
B. Institutions and Consumer Representation 219
II. Consumer Information 219
III. The Safety of Goods and Services 221
A. Regulation of Safety 221
B. Product Liability 223
IV. The Quality of Goods and Services 225
V. Consumer Contracts 225
A. General Survey 225
B. Unfair Contract Terms 226
C. Sale of Goods 227
D. The Act on Consumer Contracts 227
E. Credit Contracts 228
F. Real Estate Transactions 228
VI. Sales Promotion and Commercial Practices 229
VII. Consumer Redress 229

Selected Bibliography 233

Index 235

List of Abbreviations

AC	Danish Confederation of Professional Associations
B2C	Business-to-Consumer
BA	Bankruptcy Act of 1977
CAA	Act on Commercial Agents
CISG	Contracts for the International Sale of Goods
COTIF	Convention concerning International Carriage by Rail
CSDR	Regulation on Central Securities Depositories
DA	Confederation of Danish Employers
DCMA	Danish Capital Markets Act
DI	Danish Industry
DFEA	Danish Financial Enterprises Act
DFSA	Danish Financial Supervisory Authority
DS	Danish Standard
DSB	Danske Stats Baner
EC	European Community
ECPA	EU Patent Agreement
EEA	European Economic Area
EEIG	European Economic Interest Groupings
EKF	Denmark's Export Credit Agency
EPC	European Patent Convention
EU	European Union
FH	Danish Trade Union Confederation
FTF	The Salaried Employees' and Civil Servants' Confederation
GDP	Gross Domestic Product
KL	Local Government Denmark
LO	Danish Confederation of Trade Unions
MA	Maritime Act
MiFID2	Directive on Markets in Financial Instruments
MiFIR	Regulation on Markets in Financial Instruments
MTF	Multilateral Trading Facility

List of Abbreviations

OECD	Organisation for Economic Co-operation and Development
PCT	Patent Cooperation Treaty
PPP	Public-Private Partnership
SGA	Sale of Goods Act
SKAFOR	Danish Association for Non Life Insurance
TFEU	Treaty on the Functioning of the European Union
UPC	Unified Patent Court
VAT	Value Added Tax

General Introduction

§1. General Background of Denmark

I. Geography

1. Denmark is situated in the northern part of Europe and stretches along coast of more than 7,300 km.[1] The total population is approximately 5.7 million inhabitants.[2] The self-governing areas of Greenland and the Faroe Islands is a part of the Kingdom of Denmark. Geographically, the territory of Denmark is composed of a total of 391 islands. To the east lies the largest island Zealand including the islands of Lolland-Falster (9,194.8 sq.km), and further east is the remote island of Bornholm (5,884 sq.km). To the west is the peninsula of Jutland (29,663.3 sq.km) and in the middle the island of Funen (3,479 sq.km).[3] Copenhagen, the capital of Denmark, is situated on Zealand and has a population of 783,323[4,5] and including the suburbs (The Greater Copenhagen) there is a total of 1,295,686 inhabitants as of the 1 January 2017.[6]

II. Cultural Composition

2. The population of Denmark had on the 1 January 2017, 2,860,178 males and 2,888,591 females.[7] Demographically, Denmark has a homogeneous population of which 741,572 persons (immigrants and descendants) or 12.9% comprise the total Danish population with direct foreign origins.[8] The total population of immigrants and descendants from western countries constitutes 264,845 individuals and from

1. Authors: Christina D. Tvarnø & Sandie Nøhr Nielsen.
2. Danish Statistics, *Statistical Yearbook 2017*, Jun. 2017. 121rd ed., p. 457.
3. Danish Statistics, data extraction, *AREALDK1: Land by land cover, region and unit (Geography, environment and energy)*, Feb. 2019.
4. Danish Statistics, *Statistical Yearbook 2017*, Jun. 2017. 121rd ed., Table 1 Population in Denmark, p.21 (Population and elections).
5. Including the core of Copenhagen City, Frederiksberg and Gentofte municipalities.
6. Danish Statistics, *Statistical Yearbook 2017*, Jun. 2017. 121rd ed., Table 2 Urban and rural population, p.21 (Population and elections).
7. Danish Statistics, *Statistical Yearbook 2017*, Jun. 2017. 121rd ed., Table 4 Population by sex and age, 2017, p.23 (Population and elections).
8. Danish Statistics, *Statistical Yearbook 2017*, Jun. 2017. 121rd ed., Table 9 Immigrant population by country of origin, 2017, p.28 (Population and elections).

non-western countries 476,727 individuals.[9] By the beginning of 2017, approximately 62,700 individuals of Turkish origin lived in Denmark.[10] Turkey is the country outside European Union (EU) that most immigrants and descendants originate from followed by Syria with 37,880 individuals and Iraq with 31,902 individuals[11] Within the EU, Poland and Germany have the largest number of nationals in Denmark with approximately 45,000 and 33,000 individuals, respectively.[12] The language is Danish, which is closely related to the other Scandinavian languages. The dominating religion in Denmark is Protestantism. The Evangelical Lutheran Church is organized as a State church, according to the Danish Constitution section 4, with extensive independence on the local level.[13] In accordance with the Constitution section 66, the administration of the National Evangelical Lutheran Church is laid down by statute. The share of the Danish population with membership was 75.9% on 1 January 2017.[14] Denmark has a strong relationship with the surrounding Scandinavian countries and the other Nordic countries, the EU, their allies in North Atlantic Treaty Organization and globally the United Nations.

III. The Political System

3. The Danish Constitution of 1849 (*Grundloven*),[15] abolished the absolute monarchy and made Denmark a constitutional monarchy in accordance with section 3 of the Constitution.[16] In accordance with this section, the power is divided into three powers in the legislative, the executive and the judicial power. The legislative power is wielded collectively by the King (Queen) and the Parliament.[17] According to section 13, the King (Queen) has no legal responsibility; legal power rests solely in the Ministers. This means that the Parliament votes on and adopts the acts and the King (Queen) signs the acts. The executive power is vested in the King (Queen) and his ministers due to section 3 in the Constitution. Hence, the ministers and the government hold the executive power to implement and enforce the laws, establishes orders and other legally binding administrative regulations. The courts hold the judicial power, both now and in 1849.

4. The Constitution was amended in 1953. Before this amendment, the monarchy could only be inherited by men, but after 1953 both men and women can inherit

9. Danish Statistics, *Statistical Yearbook 2017*, Jun. 2017. 121rd ed., Table 9 Immigrant population by country of origin, 2017, p.28 (Population and elections).
10. Danish Statistics, *Statistical Yearbook 2017*, Jun. 2017. 121rd ed., p. 12 (Population and elections).
11. Danish Statistics, *Statistical Yearbook 2017*, Jun. 2017. 121rd ed., Table 9 Immigrant population by country of origin, 2017, p.28 (Population and elections).
12. Danish Statistics, *Statistical Yearbook 2017*, Jun. 2017. 121rd ed., Table 9 Immigrant population by country of origin, 2017, p.28 (Population and elections).
13. Act 169/1953 (*Grundloven*).
14. Danish Statistics, Statistical Yearbook 2075, Jun. 2017. 121rd ed., p. 161 (Culture and National Church).
15. Act 169/1953 (*Grundloven*).
16. *See* further *infra* section 3.
17. In Danish, the Parliament is called *Folketinget*.

the Throne.[18] By the same amendment, the parliamentarism, which in its essence had been followed since 1901 was written into the Constitution by the 1953 amendment, the previous two-chamber system was abolished and the Parliament expanded to 179 members. Two of these members are elected in Greenland[19] and two in the Faroe Islands.[20] Elections to the Parliament take place every four years, according to section 32 in the Constitution, but may be more frequent under certain circumstances, for example, in cases where the Government has not obtained the majority on an important bill in the Parliament, for example, the annual State budget. The Government forms the top of the hierarchy of the administration. Each Minister in the Government is chief executive within his/her field. Each Ministry is divided into several departments, which are divided into subsections.

5. The administration of Denmark is divided between the State, five State Counties (regions)[21] and ninety-eight municipalities. The five State Counties are: The Capital Region, Region Zealand, Region of Southern Denmark, Region of the Mid-Jutland and Region of North-Jutland. The regions' main task is to manage the Danish healthcare system, but they are also responsible for parts of the social sector and development of the regions.[22] The council of the State Counties has forty-one elected members,[23] all elected for four-year terms.[24] At the head of the Regional Council is the regional chairman, elected by the Regional Council.[25] The latest elections to Regional Councils took place in 2017.

6. The five State Counties are funded through contributions from State and local authorities and the economy is divided into three areas: (1) Health; (2) social services and special education; and (3) regional development.[26] The three areas are funded separately and must each be in balance.[27]

7. The ninety-eight municipalities are funded by tax payments and rates from the government. A defining characteristic of this organization of the administration is the considerable extent of local self-government within the ninety-eight municipalities.[28] These resources of income are spent on the functions in which the municipalities engage, for example, local services such as schools, teaching, public assistance, social security, health, recreational areas and infrastructure. According to section 82 of the Constitution, the municipalities are entitled to manage their own affairs independently; however, they are still under the supervision of the State. This

18. Consolidated Act 847/2009 (*Tronfølgeloven*).
19. Consolidated Act 916/2018 (*Folketingsvalg i Grønland*).
20. Consolidated Act 25/2019 (*Folketingsvalg på Færøerne*).
21. Consolidated Act 1032/2018 (*Regionsloven*), Section 1.
22. *Ibid.* Chapter 2.
23. *Ibid.* 1032/2018 (*Regionsloven*), Section 8.
24. Act 138/2019 (*Kommunal- og regionvalgloven*), Section 6.
25. Consolidated Act 1032/2018 (*Regionsloven*), Section 9.
26. Executive Order 1019/2018 (*Regionernes budget- og regnskabsvæsen, revision, m.v.*), Section 3.
27. *Ibid.* Chapter 2.
28. Consolidated Act 47/2019 (*Kommunestyrelsesloven*), Chapter 5 and Executive Order 128/2019 (*Kommunernes budget- og regnskabsvæsen, revision m.v.*).

right to self-administration is restricted to a certain geographical area and is managed by the municipal council, composed of representatives elected among the citizens in the area for a period of four years.[29]

8. Denmark has relatively many political parties represented in the Parliament, in the five State regions and in the ninety-eight municipalities. The formation of a new party that wishes to participate in the parliamentary election must collect a statement from a number of voters, which at least corresponds to 1/175[30] of all valid votes at the last parliamentary election held.[31] At the parliamentary elections on 18 June 2015, 3,518,987 valid votes were cast in Denmark (23,364 in The Faroe Islands and 20,206 at Greenland).[32] A new Danish party must, therefore, currently collect at least 20,109 voter declarations in order to participate in parliamentary elections in 2019. However, a correctly notified party is not sure of being represented in the Parliament, as the rules on election by method of proportional representation lay down certain conditions which normally require a greater number of votes to obtain a seat in the Parliament.

9. At the election to the Danish Parliament in 2015, nine political parties were elected. The parties elected in 2015 were (from left to right wing): Unity List (*Enhedslisten*), the Socialist People's Party (*Socialistisk Folkeparti*), the Social Democrats (*Socialdemokraterne*), the Social Liberal Party (*Det Radikale Venstre*), the Alternative *(Alternativet*), the Conservatives (*Det Konservative Folkeparti*), the Liberal Party (*Venstre*), the Liberal Alliance (*Liberal Alliance*), and the Danish People's Party (*Dansk Folkeparti*) (Figure 1).

29. Consolidated Act 138/2019 (*Kommunal- og regionsvalgloven*), Section 6.
30. A total number of 175 members of Parliament are elected in Denmark, 2 members are elected on the Faroe Islands and 2 members are elected in Greenland, cf. Danish Statistics, Statistical Yearbook 2075, Jun. 2017. 121rd ed., p. 19 (Population and elections).
31. Consolidated Act 137/2019 (*Folketingsvalgloven*), Section 12.
32. Danish Statistics, Statistical Yearbook 2017, Jun. 2017. 121rd ed., Table 42 Elections to the Folketing (the Parliament), 2017, p.48 (Population and elections).

Figure 1 Distribution of seats (mandates) in the Parliament. Danish election 18 June 2015.[33]

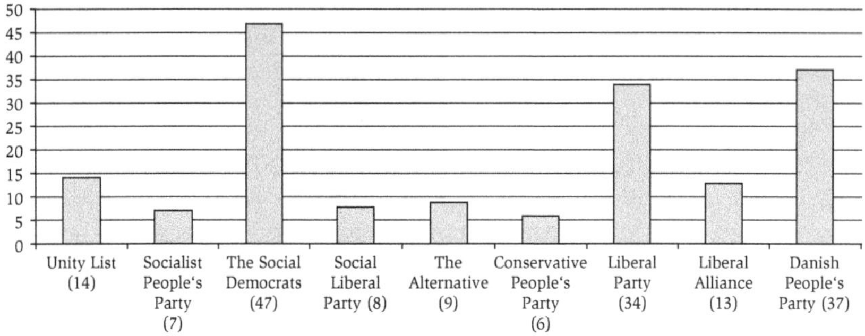

10. Currently, the government is formed by the Liberal Party, the Liberal Alliance and the Conservative People's Party and supported by the Danish People's Party.

IV. Population and Production Statistics

11. Formerly, the Danish economy was based on agriculture. A change has taken place together with other developments of society since the Second World War. Today it is the industrial activity, where services[34] are the dominant activity in terms of employment, is the most important sector in the Danish economy.[35] According to Danish Statistics, there were 299,800 active enterprises in Denmark in 2014.[36] The divisions of enterprises are 22% in trade and transport, 17% in business services where 10% of the enterprises have their main activity in agriculture, forestry and fishery and 7% in manufacturing, mining and quarrying and utility services.[37]

12. The number of new active enterprises created was 29,911 in 2015, of which 24% were established within business services, 20% within trade and transport and 5% within manufacturing, mining and quarrying and public utilities. There were 297,235 active enterprises altogether in Denmark in 2015.[38]

33. The figure 1 is created with data from: Danish Statistics, Statistical Yearbook 2017, Jun. 2017. 121rd ed., Table 45 Elections to the Folketing (The Parliament), distribution of votes and candidates, 2017, p.52 (Population and elections).
34. Services include private services in the form of trade, transport, finance, knowledge-based services and personal services as well as public services.
35. Danish Statistics, *Statistical Yearbook 2017*, Jun. 2017. 121rd ed., p. 386 (Business sectors in general).
36. Danish Statistics, *Statistical Yearbook 2017*, Jun. 2017. 121rd ed., p. 387 (Business sectors in general).
37. *Ibid.*
38. Danish Statistics, *Denmark in figures 2018*, Apr. 2018, p. 28.

13. In 2016 the totals of real active companies[39] in the private sector were almost 298,000. It is more than 10,700 more companies than in 2015, which corresponds to an increase in growth of 3.7%. The three industries with the largest relative growth in the number of companies were financing and insurance, information and communication and culture, leisure and other services. With an increase of 10.1%, financing and insurance had the highest relative growth in the number of companies from 2015 to 2016.[40]

14. Danish enterprises had a total turnover of DKK 3,595 billion in 2014. Trade and transport account for the largest share of enterprises as well as the largest share of turnover with 46%. Manufacturing, mining and quarrying was ranked second on the share of turnover with 29% and accounts for only 7% of the total number of enterprises in Denmark.[41] In 2015 almost 6,400 enterprises in Denmark were owned by foreign entities, corresponding to 2% of the total number of enterprises. Turnover was DKK 845 billion, equivalent to 23% of total revenue in the private sector.[42]

15. The total growths in the enterprises' turnover were 42% until 2008, but following the financial crises in 2008 the level decreased to 25% above the 2001-level[43] in 2009. In 2016 the level of the enterprises' turnover in all the industries shown was 64% above the level of 2001, [44] though there are great differences from one industry to another; Business services have increased by 82% in the period until 2009, and fell to 78% above the level of 2001 in 2011 where after it rose to a level of 150% above the 2001-level in 2016. Construction experienced a considerable growth of 52% in turnover until 2008 followed by a marked slowdown in 2009. Up till 2010, there was a large decrease in turnover inside construction to a level of 9% above 2001-level in 2010. And up till 2012 a part of the lost turnover inside construction has been regained, and the industry in 2016 is 65% above the level of 2001.[45]

16. The total labour force was in 2017 approximately 3,686,000 individuals; 1,863,000 men and 1,824,000 women.[46] In 2015 the largest industry groups were thus public administration, education and health employing 874,000 persons (corresponding to 31.3% of persons employed) and trade and transport, etc. employing

39. Registered enterprises, with an obligation to registration with respect to the tax law or with respect to company law, irrespective of the level of activity.
40. Danish Statistics, *NYT FRA DANMARKS STATISTIK*, *Generel firmastatistik* 2016, *Erhvervslivet på tværs* (English: NEWS FROM DANISH STATISTICS, General company statistics 2016), no. 262, 29 Jun. 2018.
41. Danish Statistics, *Statistical Yearbook 2017*, Jun. 2017. 121rd ed., p. 388 (Business sectors in general).
42. Danish Statistics, *Denmark in figures 2018*, Apr. 2018, p. 28.
43. Index 2001-level = 100.
44. Danish Statistics, *Statistical Yearbook 2017*, Jun. 2017. 121rd ed., p. 387 (Business sectors in general).
45. Danish Statistics, *Statistical Yearbook 2017*, Jun. 2017. 121rd ed., p. 388 (Business sectors in general).
46. Danish Statistics, *Denmark in figures 2018*, Apr. 2018, p. 15.

685,000 persons (24.5% of persons employed). Primary industries, e.g., agriculture, forestry and fishing, accounted for a substantially lower share employing 74,000 persons (2.7% of persons employed).[47] After the first oil crisis in 1973–74 began an increase in unemployment that came to last more than 20 years – only interrupted a few times. Partly in 1979, when the early retirement scheme was introduced, and partly during the short economic boom in the mid-1980s.[48]

17. From 2008 (mid) to 2010 (mid) the unemployment increased sharply from 2.4% to 6,2% - more than a doubling of the total level of unemployment.[49] This increase in unemployment had a particularly great impact on men.[50] From 2010 to 2012 the total gross unemployment has largely remained unchanged. From 2012 there has been a trend of a slight decrease in the total gross unemployment from around 6.0% of the labour force to 4.2% in 2016.[51] In 2017, the unemployment rate for men was 5.7% and for women, it was 6.0%.[52]

18. Since the economic crisis began in late 2008 and on to late 2011, the male unemployment rate has been higher than that for women.[53] Subsequently, the unemployment rate for men and women remained at the same level, and in April 2012 both men and women have an unemployment rate of 6.2% (Figure 2).[54,55]

47. Danish Statistics, *Statistical Yearbook 2017*, Jun. 2017. 121rd ed., p. 182 (Labour, earnings and income).
48. Danish Statistics, 60 år i tal – Danmark siden 2. Verdenskrig, (English: 60 years in numbers – Denmarks since World War 2), Dec. 2008, p. 12.
49. Danish Statistics, *Statistical Yearbook 2017*, Jun. 2017. 121rd ed., p. 184 (Labour, earnings and income).
50. Danish Statistics, *Statistical Yearbook 2017*, Jun. 2017. 121rd ed., Figure 10 Gross unemployment in per cent of the labour force, seasonally adjusted, p. 185 (Labour, earnings and income).
51. Danish Statistics, *Statistical Yearbook 2017*, Jun. 2017. 121rd ed., p. 184 (Labour, earnings and income).
52. Danish Statistics, *Denmark in figures 2018*, Apr. 2018, p. 15.
53. Danish Statistics, *Statistical Yearbook 2017*, Jun. 2017. 121rd ed., Figure 10 Gross unemployment in per cent of the labour force, seasonally adjusted, p. 185 (Labour, earnings and income).
54. *Ibid.*
55. Danish Statistics, data extraction, Table AKU300 Labour, income and wealth. Feb. 2019.

Figure 2 Unemployment compositions by status for unemployment, sex and time

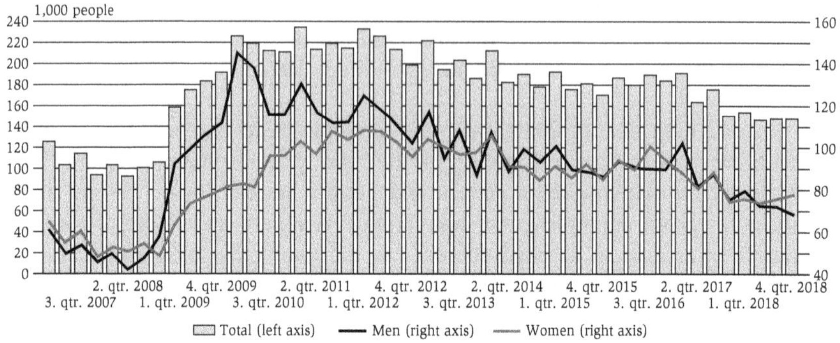

19. In the first quarter of 2012, unemployment was at its highest level since the financial crisis in 2008 with 234,000 unemployed persons. Since then there has been a downward trend with only slight fluctuations and in the fourth quarter of 2018, the rate has fallen to 148,000 persons.[56]

20. There is a high degree of unionization in Denmark. The Unions are: The Danish Confederation of Trade Unions (LO); The Salaried Employees' and Civil Servants' Confederation (FTF) – in 2019 LO and FTF merged by formation of The Danish Trade Union Confederation (FH); The Danish Association of Managers and Executives; Danish Confederation of Professional Associations (AC); and membership of associations outside the common organizations.

21. In 2017, 1,821,045 million workers belonged to a labour union.[57] In 2017 the Danish labour unions had an increase of 6,820 (approximately 0.4%) members compared to the year before (1,814,225 million members in 2016).[58] The largest labour union, LO, lost 2.25% of its members,[59] while the AC and membership of associations outside the common organizations both increased with 4.2% each. Simultaneously, the members of the Managers and Executives Union and FTF both increased by 0.3%.[60]

---

56. Danish Statistics, data extraction: Table AKU300 Labour, income and wealth. Feb. 2019.
57. Danish Statistics, data extraction: Table LONMED1: Member per 31.12 by member of organization and sex. Feb. 2019.
58. *Ibid.*
59. Danish Statistics, data extraction: Table LONMED1: Member per 31.12 by member of organization and sex. LO members (2016: 806,500 individuals) (2017: 788,377 individuals). Feb. 2019.
60. Danish Statistics, *NYT FRA DANMARKS STATISTIK, Lønmodtagerorganisationernes medlemstal* (English: NEWS FROM DANISH STATISTICS, Employees' organizations' number of members) 31 Dec. 2017, no. 202, 24 May 2018.

V. Social and Cultural Values

22. The Danish tax rate is relatively high and both the overall tax burden and the tax structure in Denmark differ from that of the EU – and Organisation for Economic Co-operation and Development (OECD) – average. Total taxes can be divided into four main types: Income and property taxes, production and import taxes, capital taxes and compulsory contributions to social security schemes.

23. First, more than half of the total tax revenue in Denmark comes from personal income taxation (income and property taxes).[61] Second, social security contributions are not widely used in Denmark in contrast to most OECD countries.[62] The development in the tax rate in the last decades is shown in Figure 3 from the Danish Ministry of Taxation.

Figure 3 The Tax Burden (% of GDP) in Denmark 1971–2017.[63]

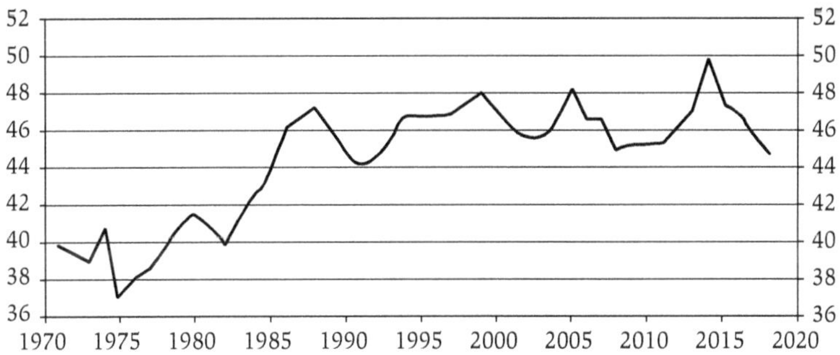

24. The national accounts in 2016 in current prices in billion DKK are shown in Table 1 below.

Table 1 National Accounts for Denmark[64]

Gross domestic product (GDP)	2,060.9
Imports of goods and services	9,526
Resources = Final Demand	30,135
Exports of goods and services	10,943

61. Danish Statistics, *Statistical Yearbook 2017*, Jun. 2017. 121rd ed., Figure 22 National accounts distribution of total taxes and duties, p. 270 (National accounts and government finances).
62. OECD, Tax Policy Reforms 2018 OECD and Selected Partner Economie, OECD 2018, p. 45, Figure 3.1. PIT, SSCs and payroll taxes as a share of total tax revenues by country, 2016.
63. Figure 1 is copied from the Danish Ministry of Taxation (Facts and figures), www.skm.dk. Feb. 2019.
64. Danish Statistics, *Statistical Yearbook 2017*, Jun. 2017. 121rd ed., p. 268 (National accounts and government finances), Table 243 National Accounts for Denmark.

Household consumption expenditure	9,486
Government consumption expenditure	5,256
Gross fixed capital formation	4,125

25. The Danish social security system is generally financed through tax revenues and most of the public expenditure is used for social protection (47.7%) and health (16.1%).[65] The national expenditure in 2016 on social and health services are shown in Table 2 below.

Table 2 Expenditure in 2016 on social and health services in billion DKK[66]

Health care	129
Disability and rehabilitation	82
Senior service (old age)	233
Survivors benefits	35
Families	71
Unemployment	29
Housing	14
Other social expenditures	32

26. In 2016 the total social and health expenditure amounted to DKK 653 billion inclusive of administration costs.[67] A visit to the doctor or hospital is free of charge, and the State pays a limited amount of, for example, dental treatment, chiropractic treatment and physiotherapy.[68] Municipal institutions take care of children to a considerable extent if and when parents go to work, and there are also possibilities for parents to obtain leave within a certain period to take care of the children.[69]

27. Expenses for old age represent the largest share of social spending in 2016 by DKK 233 billion. This is primarily due to the expenditures for old-age pensions (DKK 1,119 billion), disability pensions (DKK 208 billion) and early retirement payments (DKK 70 billion).[70]

65. Danish Statistics, *Statistical Yearbook 2017*, Jun. 2017. 121rd ed., p. 269 (National accounts and government finances).
66. Danish Statistics, *Denmark in figures 2018*, Apr. 2018, p. 9.
67. *Ibid.*
68. *Ibid.*
69. *Ibid.*
70. Danish Statistics, *Denmark in figures 2018*, Apr. 2018, Table Recipients of temporary and permanet public benefits, p. 9.

§2. THE ECONOMIC SYSTEM

28. In 1970, the number employed by the general government sector amounted to 14.9% of the total number of employed. In 1994 the share was at its highest level with 30.5%. In 2008 the share had fallen to 27.8%, and after an increase to 30.4% in 2010, the share in 2016 is 28.4%.[71]

29. Total number of employees in the public and the private sector in 2015 were 2,562,731 persons, divided into 875,139 in the public sector and 1,687,592 in the private sector.[72] From 2010 to 2015 employment in the private sector[73] has been increasing by an average of 13,900 persons (0.7%) per year, while employment in the public sector[74] has been declining by an average of 4,900 persons (0.6%) per year.[75] Employment has risen steadily since 2013 and in fourth quarter of 2018, nearly 2,773,800 individuals had a salaried position (in the public or private sector).[76]

30. The Danish economy is facing significant challenges and tightens requirements to lead responsible and credible economic policies. In the Government's plan *Med Danmark i arbejde - udfordringer i dansk økonomi frem til 2020,*[77] the Government introduced a budget act setting out the future framework of cooperation between the State and municipalities, where the latter are obliged to take more responsibility. The budget act sets a fixed upper limit on spending in the State, regions and municipalities, and the limit is set by Parliament and is valid for four years.[78]

31. Danish economy has increasingly become a part of the global economy which is reflected by the fact that the Danish Foreign Trade represents a growing share of the overall Danish economy. Since 1987, Denmark's total exports of goods and services have exceeded total imports. In 2011 Danish exports had reverted to the same level as that of 2008 (before the financial crises), for imports that were the case in 2012. In 2016 there was a DKK 25 billion decrease in total exports of goods and services and a DKK 17 billion decrease in imports.[79] Between 1955 and 1986,

---

71. Danish Statistics, *Statistical Yearbook 2017*, Jun. 2017. 121rd ed., p. 268 (National accounts and government finances).
72. Danish Statistics, *Statistical Yearbook 2017*, Jun. 2017. 121rd ed, Table 183 Employees by sex and sector – Nov. 2015, p. 198 (Labour, earnings and income).
73. The private sector includes private corporations, public corporations, private non-profit organizations and international organizations.
74. The public sector includes central government, regional government, municipal government and social security funds.
75. Danish Statistics, *Statistical Yearbook 2017*, Jun. 2017. 121rd ed, p. 183 (Labour, earnings and income).
76. Danish Statistics, data extraction: LBESK21 Employees (quarter) by sector, time and unit. Feb. 2019.
77. English: With Denmark in work – Challenges for the Danish economy towards 2020.
78. Budget Act No. 547 of 18 Jun. 2012.
79. Danish Statistics, *Statistical Yearbook 2017*, Jun. 2017. 121rd ed, p. 359 (External economy).

the annual deficit on the trade balance averaged 4.3% of GDP. The average surplus in the recent period (including 2016) is 3.2% of GDP.

32. Businesses are free to choose the legal foundation of the structure of their enterprise. Public limited companies are typically used as a legal framework for the large firms, whereas private limited are used by small or medium enterprises. *See* an example of the Danish company structure in Table 3 below.[80]

Table 3 Danish company structure (2014)[81]

Public limited companies	39,671
Listed companies	194
State-owned public limited companies	22
Private Limited Companies	202,431
Branches of foreign public limited companies	526
Branches of foreign private limited companies	381
Limited partnership with shares (kommanditaktiengesellschaft)	576
Companies with limited liability according to Act on Commercial Undertakings, section 3	2,597
Entrepreneurial companies	3,243
Business foundations	1,362

33. The infrastructure in Denmark is highly developed with regard to railroads, roads, ferries, bridges, and air and seaport facilities. Telephones and other kinds of telecommunication systems as well as postal services are also highly developed. Electricity and water supply is of high quality and the water is supplied by public as well as private suppliers.

§3. The Legal System

I. Historical Development

A. General Development

34. The first Danish Constitution from 1241 was called The Jutland Law (*Jyske lov*).[82] The first section is a preamble pronouncing that the 'Society shall be founded on Law', and lays down the principle that no one shall judge contrary to the law

80. The authors have obtained the figures through *Erhvervsstyrelsen* (The Danish Business Authority).
81. *Lov om visse erhvervsdrivende virksomheder*, consolidated Act 1295/2013.
82. Authors: Christina D. Tvarnø & Sandie Nøhr Nielsen.

issued by the King and adopted by the people. The chosen king and the nobles jointly held the formal power in government affairs in a so-called aristocracy.

In 1660, the Danish legal system was changed by King Frederic the III to absolute monarchy. The evening of the 13 October, Bishop Hans Svane officially offered Frederick the III the throne and the right to inherit the Danish Kingdom. This decision was, in fact, achieved through a military coup. During the previous legal system, every king had to sign an intergovernmental agreement (*håndfæstning*) with the nobles. After the introduction of the absolute monarchy, the Kings inherited the crown of his predecessor's death and ruled with absolute power, which meant that the supreme legislative, judicial and executive power lay with the king.

This dramatic change of political and legal system was adopted by the King's Act – Lex Regia, signed by Frederick the III on 14 November 1665. Lex Regia was the legal foundation of the king's power – *jura majestatis*. This regime lasted until 1849. *See* below under The Constitution. The King's Act was a constitutional act and is the only written constitution for an autocratic regime in Europe.

As a direct result of the absolute monarchy in 1660, King Christian V initiated the national unification of law implementing the absolute monarchy in the substantive law, accomplished in 1683 by the Danish Code of King Christian V (*Danske Lov*). Important principles of the Danish Code are still in force, for example, fundamental rules of the law of contract and principles of liability for damages.

35. As mentioned above in §1, the Danish Constitution of 5 June 1849 abolished the absolute monarchy and introduced the present democratic constitutional system. About the same time, the cooperation between the Nordic countries was initiated, which formed the basis of the current cooperation on legal matters. For example, the 1880 Bill of Exchange Act, the 1897 Cheque Act and the 1917 Contracts Act constitute common Nordic acts. On the constitutional basis, a modern legislation has been elaborated, consisting of single statutes issued within the different areas of law. Apart from the 1683 Danish Code, it has not been attempted to establish civil code books like the French and German civil codes. Constitutional amendments have taken place several times. The rules in force are laid down in the Constitution of 5 June 1953 and are applied in all parts of the Kingdom of Denmark.

B. Denmark and the European Union

36. Denmark signed the accession to the European Communities on 22 January 1972. The accession entered into force on 1 January 1973 in regard to Denmark and Greenland. The Faroe Islands chose not to join the EC. By the Treaty of 13 March 1984, Greenland withdrew from the European Communities. Upon withdrawal, Greenland obtained an agreement on fisheries and the adhesion to the Overseas Countries and Territories associated with the EC. The treaty on the relationship of Greenland with the European Communities entered into force on 1 January 1985.

The Danish government signed the Maastricht Treaty and by that entered into the EU on 7 February 1992; however, it was rejected by a referendum on 2 June 1992. Consequently, the European Council agreed on a set of arrangements in Edinburgh on 12 December 1992 concerning the problems raised by Denmark. By a Danish referendum on 18 May 1993, Denmark adopted the Treaty on European Union supplied by the Edinburgh Agreements. Denmark has signed the Nice Treaty, the Amsterdam Treaty and the Lisbon Treaty. Denmark is not a member of the EURO, but did agree on the EURO PLUS pact 2012 and has by that agreed on a budgetary discipline and economic coordination to ensure the public finances in a long run perspective to avoid similar debt in the future. The EURO plus pact requires that Denmark and the other participating countries must have a government budgetary position in balance or surplus.

C. The Home Rule of Greenland and the Faroe Islands

37. As a result of the abolishment of the colonial system after the Second World War, the home rule system was introduced in the Faroe Islands in 1948. In 1978, a similar system was established in Greenland.

In May 2009, Denmark and Greenland set up a new agreement implemented by the law of self-determination in Greenland.[83] The law must promote equality and mutual respect in partnership between Denmark and Greenland. The Act is based accordingly on an agreement between *Naalakkersuisut* and the Danish government as equal partners. In accordance with section 1 in the Act, Greenland has the legislative and executive power within the matters entrusted to Greenland.

Inatsisartut (the Parliament) holds the legislative power, *Naalakkersuisut* (the government) holds the executive power and The Courts hold the judicial powers.

The Home Rule of the Faroe Islands is a different system. According to section 1 in the Home Rule Act, the Faroe Islands is an autonomous community within the Kingdom of Denmark.[84]

Thus, the home rule and self-determination system have converted the Danish Kingdom into a 'Kingdom Community' consisting of three independent territories with delimitation of powers for each of them on material and geographical levels. Greenland has independently entered into binding agreements with third countries, for example, on fisheries. Although the home rule systems of Greenland and the Faroe Islands are very similar, they differ because the system of the Faroe Islands does not distinguish between areas which are self-financed and financed by subventions. In Greenland, the area of raw materials is submitted to a particular common Danish-Greenlandic administration, whereas this area is completely transferred to the Faroe Islands as a special area.

II. Constitutional Law

38. The Constitution regulates the constitutional organs and their functions based on a system of mixed monarchy. It separates the legislative, executive and

83. Act 473/2009 (*Grønlands Selvstyre*).
84. *See* further Act 137/1948 (*Færøernes Hjemmestyre*).

judicial power, and lays down provisions on civil rights which include personal freedom, protection of property and habitation, freedom of speech, the right to establish legal associations and to assemble, free access to exercise trade, and the right to work, as well as certain social rights.

According to the Constitution section 13, the King has no legal responsibility; legal power rests solely in the Ministers. The limited power held by the King in international matters is part of the so-called prerogatives. Submitted to this designation are also the rights of the King to denominate ministers and to divide the particular sectors between them, the right to introduce bills through the ministers and the right to coin money. The prerogatives do not directly influence economic life, but they confer in particular the administrative power with 'a fourth power of State' which may be of importance for the regulation of economic aspects of law.

Under the 1953 amendment to the Constitution, rules on change of constitutional powers have been adopted. Rules on change of constitutional powers shall be more definitely specified and must be adopted by a statute. According to the Constitution, section 20, change of constitutional powers requires a majority of five-sixths of the members of the Parliament (*Folketinget*). In cases where this majority cannot be obtained, the bill proposing a change of the Constitution shall be submitted to a referendum. According to the Constitution section 42 paragraph 5, the bill shall obtain a majority of the participants of the referendum. The majority shall constitute at least 30% of the electorate.

The courts have an independent position. According to the Constitution section 62, judicial procedure must be regulated by statute and shall be separated from the executive power. The Constitution section 64 provides that the judges shall be directed only by the law concerning the performance of their duties; judges may be removed only for misconduct.

The courts decide private conflicts and impose punishments. According to section 63, they also control the limits of the competence conferred to the administration. Furthermore, they are competent to decide the compatibility of a statute with the Constitution. Special courts with judicial power are illegal. Courts only entitled to screen may be established.

Legislation can be initiated by a bill introduced by a member of the Folketing in accordance with the Constitution section 41, paragraph 1. Most commonly, the relevant minister will introduce a bill. Before being passed, the bill must be read and negotiated three times in the Parliament (Folketing) and must receive Royal Assent, countersigned by the minister, *see* section 42 in the Constitution.

Concordance between the ministers and the Parliament (*Folketinget*) is secured by practising the parliamentary system. According to this, a minister shall retire when the Parliament has adopted a vote of no confidence in her/him, *see also* above in §1. The Parliament may not decide judicial cases. However, it may adopt statutes on rather concrete matters.

Taxes may be imposed only by statute in accordance with the Constitution section 43. The annual State budget shall be adopted as a statute in accordance with the Constitution section 45.

III. Administrative Law

39. The public administration is composed of the State administration, functioning on the central and the local level, and by the local municipal administration and the five regions.

The State administration is organized in a hierarchical system directed by the government with each minister as a top executive within a certain field. The division of activities between the ministers is established by Resolution of the King according to section 14 of the Constitution. Each ministry is organized in departments, which are divided into subsections.

The local government is executed on the municipal level. The municipal government is in principle autonomous. The extent of self-government is regulated by statute, and the execution of autonomy is submitted to control by the State, according to section 82 of the Constitution. The local government is divided into five State counties (regions) and ninety-eight municipalities. The relationship with the State authorities is regulated by statute.[85] The control of the administration is executed by the State authorities, by the courts and by the Ombudsman of the Parliament.

The right to administrative recourse concerning concrete complaints is regulated by statute. Complaints may be brought before special administrative boards of appeal whose decisions are final on the administrative level. The board of appeal is entitled to consider the legality of the decision in question as well as the elements of discretion. A decision from an administrative court can be brought before the courts. A complaint may be brought before the courts if nothing else has been laid down by statute. In general, legal proceedings may be instituted before the administrative recourse has been exhausted.

According to section 63 of the Constitution, the courts are authorized to decide every question concerning the limits of the administrative authorities. Contrary to administrative recourse, judicial control only concerns the legality of the activities of the authorities, not the decisions left to their discretion.

The courts may examine the concrete circumstances of a case in relation to the correctness of the administrative use of the legal rules in question. However, under the procedure, it might be necessary for the courts also to evaluate elements which are submitted on discretion.

IV. The Ombudsman

40. The Ombudsman is an independent body of control over the executive power which is constituted through the ombudsman, who is appointed by the Parliament. Section 55 of the Constitution provides that the Ombudsman of the Parliament controls the civil and military State administration. By an amendment in the Act on the Ombudsman,[86] this competence has been extended to a very limited control over the municipal authorities: First, the decisions of the municipal boards are excepted from the competence of the Ombudsman. Second, complaints concerning

---

85. Consolidated Act 47/2019 (*Kommunernes styrelse*).
86. Act 473/1996 (*Folketingets Ombudsmand*).

decisions on other levels are subject to decision of the Ombudsman only when the matter in question may be appealed to a State authority. However, the Ombudsman is entitled to consider every matter on his own initiative. A new regulation which allows the Ombudsman to control the municipal authorities is under preparation.

The Ombudsman has to decide issues regarding administrative activities and decisions, not issues regarding the persons who execute the functions. The functions of the ministers are controlled to the extent that they are of an administrative, not legislative, nature. When an administrative matter is brought before the Parliament for reasons of legislation, the Ombudsman has to stop the treatment of a case in question of lack of competence.

In principle, the subject for consideration is the legality, not the discretion of the case. However, the Ombudsman may control not only the legality of a case but also questions of negligence. He is entitled to examine issues if all the relevant objective matters have been considered in the concrete case, not only some of them. Frequently, the administrative treatment of the cases has been submitted to the judgment of the Ombudsman.

Administrative decisions cannot be annulled by the Ombudsman. The Ombudsman may criticize the authorities, eventually combined with an indicative judgment of the legal validity of the decision, and he may give advice for the plaintiff to get a judicial trial free of charge. Furthermore, he may advise the authorities to take disciplinary steps or initiate proceedings against the administrators who have dealt with the case.

Finally, the Ombudsman formulates reports of general critique of the administration and lays down indicative rules on fairness of the administration. In practice, the opinion of the Ombudsman is considered of great importance to the administration.

Part I. Commercial Law

Chapter 1. Concepts and Sources of Commercial Law

§1. Concepts And Sources in General

41. The common legal principle of freedom of contract has been a general principle in Denmark since ancient times.[87] The Danish Code of 1683 Article 5.1.2 provides that 'everyone is obliged to fulfil a promise he has given by mouth, hand or seal'. In 1906, the principle was introduced into the (then common Nordic) Sale of Goods Act (SGA) section 1: 'The provisions of this Act only apply in so far nothing else is expressly agreed, or may be considered included in the agreement or arising by trade usage or custom.'[88] In 1917, the principle was introduced in the Formation of Contract Act[89] section 1, second sentence: 'The provisions in this chapter only apply in so far nothing else is expressly provided by the offer or answer or trade usage or custom.'

Although freedom of contract is an important general legal principle, it should not hide the fact that Danish commerce is relatively strongly regulated by statutes.

In principle, there is no fundamental distinction between civil law and commercial law. The basic regulation of commercial and economic relationships is the same in both disciplines of law. Particular concepts of commercial law are not established in general, but specific definitions and provisions, particularly regarding commercial matters, are found in different statutes, which are important for the economic life. Such specific rules are found, for example, in the SGA, section 4(1), defining 'commercial purchase' *(handelskøb)* as a purchase established between merchants within or for their business. section 4(2) in the Sales and Goods Act defines the term 'merchant' (*handlende*) as 'anybody who operates a business that deals with a range of particularly enumerated activities such as selling goods, making banking or insurance activities, acting as a commissioner, doing trade, manufacturing or industry transport, etc'. The definition is exhaustive. The SGA has laid down special and rather strict provisions for commercial purchases concerning breach of contract, delays, etc. However, the rules are non-mandatory, and the parties may dispense with them by agreement.

---

87. Authors: Christina D. Tvarnø and Sandie Nøhr Nielsen.
88. Consolidated Act 140/ 2014 (*Købeloven*).
89. Consolidated Act 193/ 2016 (*Aftaleloven*).

The consumer-specific perspective arose after the Second World War and has increased as a result of the EU. A range of specific consumer areas has been developed, as well as existing, former less significant areas, for example, the regulation of intellectual property or consumer contract law. Thus, the freedom of contracts in consumer contracts must fulfil the mandatory rules in the consumer law. The concept of consumer purchase (*forbrugerkøb*) has been introduced in the Sales and Goods Act, section 4a, which defines this as a purchase made by a buyer (consumer) from a merchant/businessman who acts in the course of his business when the buyer acts mainly outside his trade. The provisions of consumer purchase are mostly mandatory. Thus, when the consumer engages in business with a businessman, he/she becomes part of the legal system which regulates commercial matters.

Other sources of law establish no distinction between civil and commercial matters, although certain sources of law are more important in commercial than in civil matters.

Traditionally, a distinction is made between the following four types of legal sources: written legislation, precedents from the court judgments, customs and 'the nature of the case'. *See* §§2–4 for details.

§2. Statutes

42. Legislation in the form of statutes lays down general rules within a certain area of law. The text may be exhaustive. When a statute has been amended several times, it is frequently updated and published in a consolidated form in which the amendments are incorporated into the text of the original statute.[90]

The provisions of a statute may as mentioned be mandatory or not. When a provision is mandatory everybody has to comply with it, whereas there may be deviation from provisions that are not mandatory by agreement or by usages. In commercial matters, the traditional legal regulation generally is not mandatory. But for reasons of protection of the weaker party, for example, consumers and employees, mandatory legislation has been established within such sectors submitted to regulation. Furthermore, public law sets up a widespread set of mandatory legislation that regulates industrial and commercial life.

For the interpretation of statutory texts, indications may be found in the preparatory works of the statute in order to clarify the conception of the author, for example, reports from an expert commission, comments to a bill introduced in the Parliament, and the parliamentary debates. Interpretation by analogy can be used when the statutes provide a legal gap. Then the lawyer turns to a provision that regulates another similar area of law and investigates the possibility of applying the provision in the situation not governed by any statute. Where there is a legal gap and the reasons for regulation are the same, an analogous conclusion is permitted. When a provision enumerates specific deviations from a general rule, a conclusion to the contrary can often be made. Furthermore, a provision may be interpreted in a restrictive sense or in a wider sense.

90. Such a consolidated act is designated '*lovbekendtgørelse*' or '*bekendtgørelse af lov*'.

Statutes are published in the official Law Gazette (*Lovtidende)*, section A. This section also includes amendments to the statutes and the updated texts of statutes, i.e., the consolidated acts (*lovbekendtgørelse*) as mentioned above. The Law Gazette, section B contains the Finance Act and similar statutes and the statutes on citizenship. Section C publishes the treaties into which Denmark is engaged with other States. The official Law Gazette is available, in Danish only, at www.lovtidende.dk.[91] An annotated private collection of the entire Danish legislation is issued by the publisher 'Karnov Group', denominated *Karnovs Lovsamling*. This collection constitutes, in general, the latest, complete and updated work.

§3. Administrative Rules

43. Administrative rules form an important part of the Danish legal regulation. Frequently the Parliament, as a legislative power, authorizes the relevant minister to issue general rules in the form of executive orders. The statutes introduce which rules the ministry is allowed to enforce and accordingly which specific provisions that can be issued by the administration. Thus, an order constitutes a general rule, which binds the citizens in the same way as a statute would. Executive orders are also published in the official Law Gazette (*Lovtidende*) section A. Within very limited areas, a regulation may be issued by a royal decree (*kongelig anordning*). The authorization is based on custom and tradition established under absolutism. This type of regulation is no longer an important source of commercial law.

Furthermore, circulars and instructions are issued by the superior authorities to the subordinate authorities, for whom they are binding as official orders. These rules are intended for internal administrative use, and normally they do not bind the citizens. However, the rules may be of informative interest to the enterprises as a means of getting acquainted with the conduct of the public authorities. A number of the internal rules are published at www.retsinformation.dk.

EU-legislation is implemented by parliamentary acts and by executive orders authorized by act. Danish law must be interpreted in conformity with EU law, also called 'consistent interpretation', 'indirect effect', or 'purposive interpretation'.[92] In Danish law,[93] the concept 'the principle of conformity with Directives' is often used.

Danish national courts are obliged to carry out EU conformist interpretation, and the Danish courts have in several cases used EU consistent interpretation and interpreted Danish law in light of a provision of a directive.[94]

---

91. Translations of some of the central acts, etc. can in some cases be found on the homepage of the relevant ministry.
92. *See* for instance Hartley, The Foundations of European Union Law 234–235 (Oxford U. Press 2010), Craig & De Búrca, EU Law – Texts, Cases, and Materials 200 (Oxford U. Press 2011), Drake, Twenty Years after Von Colson: The Impact of 'Indirect Effect' on the Protection of the Individual's Community Rights 30 EL. Rev. 329–348 (2005) and Sawyer, The Principle of interprétation conforme: How Far Can or Should National Courts Go when Interpreting National Legislation Consistently with European Community Law? 28 Stat. L.R. sec. 166, 165–181 (2007).
93. C-334/92, Miret (1993) OJ I-6911, 21.
94. Nielsen & Tvarnø. Danish Supreme Court Infringes the EU Treaties by its Ruling in the Ajos case. Europaraettslig Tidsskrift, no. 2, 2017, pp. 330–326.

§4. Other Sources

44. Danish courts make *ratio decidendi* decisions. Normally court decisions contain no *obiter dicta*. Whether a court decision is considered a good precedent depends on the reasons which support it. When a general principle or solution of dubious legal value is expressed or may be deduced from the court's reasoning, the decision is important and useful even if it is not a Supreme Court decision, but is issued by a lower instance, for example, the Court of Appeal or the Maritime and Commercial Court.

In order to solve a legal conflict, the parties may choose arbitration. Permanent arbitration tribunals or commissions of arbitration are established by business organizations, and private ad hoc arbitration courts may be established as well. Arbitration decisions are unimportant as precedents. They are often known only by the parties, as the parties normally do not want the decision to be published.

The relative importance of administrative practice depends on the authority that has issued the decision, as a subordinate authority has to follow instructions from a superior one. According to section 63 of the Constitution, the courts may review the legality of administrative decisions, but that control is seldom executed. Administrative precedents are applied as indicators in the same way as court precedents. Important precedents are issued within the fields of tax law, environmental law, employment law and social matters.

Court precedents are published in the Weekly Law Report (*Ugeskrift for Retsvæsen, UfR)* which constitutes a collection of the decisions made from the Supreme Court and a selection of decisions from the Courts of Appeal and by the Maritime and Commercial Court. Some administrative precedents are published at www.ret sinformation.dk. Within special fields of administration, in particular, tax law, environmental law and social law, the most important administrative decisions are gathered in published collections.

A legal custom constitutes, in the traditional sense, 'a certain conduct, which has been practised generally, continuously and for a long period in the conviction that one has been legally obliged to do so'. In regard to contract law, a recent theory has pronounced that a long period of conviction is not necessary if it is obvious that a firm persuasion of the legal rule has manifested itself. The courts consider a legal custom as a rule of law, which is recognized when the customary rule fills in a statute (*custom praeter legem*). In general, a custom contrary to the law (*custom contra legem*) is not applicable. A mandatory provision precedes custom. However, it seems that customs may modify commercial matters, and the law of contract is rather flexible. The legal regulation of contracts is mostly non-mandatory. The question of the legal force of the custom may be settled by legislation, as a custom can always be overruled by a later statute contrary to the custom. The question of who is bound by the custom seems limited to those who are affected by it. It is dubious whether a custom binds a subject who ignores it.

The existence of a custom can be difficult to prove. The trade organizations are issuing expert opinions on customs and commercial usages in concrete matters. Information regarding customs can be obtained from the Danish Chamber of Commerce (*Dansk Erhverv*) and the Confederation of Danish Industry (*Dansk Industri*).

Contract practice is important in commercial relations. In a contract law context, a custom has not to be as firm, general and continuous as in other legal areas in order to be considered a binding legal source. Agreed documents are not considered a source of law. However, as contracts adopted by organizations and big entities have developed a certain degree of uniformity, normally within certain trade lines, there is a tendency to apply contract practice as a source of law. This is the case in particular where the contract is based on standard forms issued by agreement between trade organizations or similar entities. Such standard contracts, in which the fundamental clauses are set up in advance, are indicative not only for the members of the organizations, but also for others who may enter into such relationships.

Collective agreements within the field of labour law constitute an alternative to the legislation. The agreements are binding for the employers who apply them or who are members of the organizations which have adopted them. Furthermore, they seem to be indicative of the interpretation of other contracts outside the system of collective agreements.

The nature of the case is not as such a single source of law, but rather constitutes a collection of principles applicable to the interpretation of other sources of law. This legal source consists of types of motives that a judge can use as a wider consideration drawn from the legal reasoning and legal culture. Thus, this source of law can be described as an umbrella term for various reasons and principles, which to some extent include the value of positions. General principles of law can be the principle of legality, the principle of the binding effect of contracts commitment and the principle of procedural negotiating in civil cases.

Chapter 2. The Economic Operators

§1. Personal Status of Merchants

I. Minors and Incompetents

45. Minors and incompetents are subject to the Act on Guardianship.[95,96] Section 1 provides that persons under the age of 18 are minors. Persons who are 18 years or older are competent unless they have been declared incompetent by a court decree. Such a decree should be registered in a public registry at the court in the place where the incompetent person lives. The decree also should be registered in the land registry, if the incompetent person owns real property. A guardian who has to act on behalf of the incompetent person must be appointed. For minors, the parents (the mother of a child born out of wedlock) are the natural guardians. A competent person may apply for a court order of diminished capacity when this is due to physical or mental defects or financial inexperience. In this case, the incompetent person and the guardian have to act jointly concerning the disposition of property and engagement in contracts.

The legal effects of incapacity are laid down in Act on Guardianship, section 44, which provides that an incompetent person cannot dispose of his property or enter into contracts unless otherwise provided. Such a contract is invalid. A party who enters into a contract with an incompetent person may withdraw from the engagement. However, if that party knows or ought to know that the other party is incompetent, he has to wait a reasonable time and see if the contracts shall be deemed valid by approval. Within specific areas, contracts engaged with minors may be valid. Minors who are 15 years old or older may enter into certain contracts, and incompetent persons may enter into all contracts of employment. They can freely dispose of what they have earned by their activities of employment, but they cannot undertake obligations regarding the future. A minor or an incompetent person can never undertake a guarantee, even with the approval of the guardian.

When the contract is and remains invalid, each party has to return what he has received or has to compensate for the value of it. The incompetent person has to pay compensation only to the extent, to which the goods or services, or whatever he has received, have been used for his support or otherwise have been used to his benefit. If the incompetent person has misled the other contracting party concerning his authority, he has to pay an equitable compensation, but as a maximum, the compensation cannot exceed the loss caused by the entering into the contract. If the incompetent person has committed an offence by his act, he always has to compensate for the loss caused by the entering into the contract, the Act, sections 45(3).

46. The Act on Guardianship, section 6, provides for competent persons who are unable to act reasonably because of insanity, mental deficiency or unsoundness of mind. The contracts established by such persons within the period in which they were unable to act are invalid. The regulation of this contractual relationship is the

95. Author: Søren Friis Hansen.
96. Consolidated Act 1015/2007 (*Værgemålsloven*).

same as for incompetent persons. However, if the other contracting party was acting in good faith concerning the validity of the contract, that party may get equitable compensation according to the decision of the court, which may as a maximum correspond to the loss suffered by entering into the contract.

Disposal of the property of persons who have disappeared is regulated in the same way as the property of incompetent persons. An appointed guardian acts on behalf of the missing person.

II. Foreigners

47. Foreigners are subject to the Act on Foreigners.[97] In principle, a distinction is made between citizens from the Nordic countries, i.e., Finland, Iceland, Norway and Sweden (section 1), EU-citizens (section 2), and citizens from other countries (sections 3–5). However, section 2, paragraph 4, authorizes the Minister of Justice (*Justitsministeren*) to lay down provisions for implementing the rules of the European Communities concerning the free movement for persons. Thus, the adaptation of EU-rules to citizens subject to the Agreement on the European Economic Area (EEA), including citizens from Iceland and Norway, is made by executive order or other administrative regulation.

In principle, the Act requires a visa, residence permit and labour permit for foreigners unless they are Nordic or EU-citizens or EEA-citizens, or has a valid visa in a Schengen-State. The visa determines the concrete period of stay for the holder. If a visa is not required, e.g., in case of an agreement between Denmark and the foreigner's home State, the foreigner may stay in Denmark for three months. A reduction is made when the foreigner has stayed in Denmark or in another Nordic country within the last six months before his entry.

A stay beyond those terms requires a residence permit. A residence permit may, under certain conditions, be delivered to refugees (section 7 part. 1) or to other foreigners if they have connections with relatives, marriage or cohabitation in Denmark, or for reasons of professional occupation. In general, foreigners have to get a labour permit for paid work or for exercising independent professional activities or services (section 13). A foreigner who has obtained a labour permit normally gets a residence permit. When a foreigner has resided legally in Denmark for five years, the person may not be expelled unless serious reasons give grounds for it (section 23). When he has resided in the country for nine years, he cannot be expelled except for even more severe reasons (section 22), for example, a serious crime. All persons, nationals as well as foreigners, who take up residence in Denmark, must be registered in the National Register (*Folkeregister*). The only exception is a person staying less than three months in Denmark, or six months if the person comes from a Nordic country.

48. Nordic citizens have, for several years, been entitled to enter and leave all of the Nordic countries without passport or other legitimation of journey, according to

97. Consolidated Act 1117/2017 (*Lovbekendtgørelse om udlændinge*).

the Order on Passport section 1.[98] Working conditions have been laid down in the Nordic Agreement of 1954, according to which no State may require a labour permit with respect to the nationals of any other Contracting State. The Agreement has established equality of treatment by determining that provisions concerning the labour market in each individual State may not place nationals of the other Contracting States in a position inferior to that of nationals of the country concerned, and those nationals of one contracting State employed in another Contracting State are to be accorded the same treatment as nationals of the second State with regard to conditions of pay or employment. Furthermore, Nordic citizens are entitled to settle in the other Nordic countries and to exercise independent professional activities without holding a residence permit or a labour permit, and they benefit from the social services in the State of residence. Currently, the Nordic rules will be applied only to the extent to which citizens from Sweden and Finland cannot invoke the EU-rules and citizens from Norway and Iceland cannot invoke the EEA-rules.

49. EU-citizens and citizens subject to the Agreement on the EEA are submitted to the order on residence in Denmark for foreigners,[99] according to which the nationals from other EU-countries are entitled to stay and to exercise employment or independent professional activities. They are obliged to get a resident permit concerning their stay, for which they must legitimate themselves and produce a declaration of employment from their employer or make evident that they exercise professional activities as self-employed persons.

50. Danish Regulations concerning acquisition of real property are severe. According to the Act on Acquisition of Real Property,[100] a permit of acquisition is required for foreigners who have resided less than five years in Denmark. The requirement may be satisfied by adding up shorter periods, provided that they have not been temporary stays. A permit is not required in case of inheritance or separation of joint estate between married persons. A permit is also required for Nordic citizens. According to the Order concerning certain EC-nationals,[101] which is applied correspondingly to citizens subject to the Agreement on the EEA, EU-citizens are entitled to acquire real property regardless of length of residence in Denmark when they are employed in Denmark or hold a resident permit (*opholdsbevis*), or when they do or have intention to exercise professional activities as independent persons or are doing or intend to exercise services or establish agencies or branches in Denmark. The freedom of acquisition is obtained only for a habitation all the year round or for a necessary habitation for exercising professional activities. Similar rules are applied to EU-citizens who are not workers or independent persons engaged in business. An EU-citizen or a citizen subject to the Agreement

98. Governmental Order 1337/2013 on Passports *(Bekendtgørelse om pas).*
99. Executive Order 474/2011 on Residence in Denmark for Foreigners Submitted to the Rules of the European Communities or submitted to the Agreement on the European Economic Area (*Ophold i Danmark for udlændinge, der er omfattet af de europæiske fællesskabers regler eller aftale om det Europæiske Økonomiske Samarbejdsområde*).
100. Consolidated Act 265/2014 on Acquisition of Real Property (*Erhvervelse af fast ejendom*).
101. Executive Order 764/1995.

on the EEA is not exempted from the requirement of a permit for acquiring a summer habitation. Corporations and companies which are established according to the rules of an EU-Member State, or which establish branches or agencies, are entitled to acquire real property according to the same rules as EU-citizens and citizens subject to the Agreement on the EEA, when they fulfil certain conditions laid down in the Order, section 1, paragraph 2 regarding factual and continuous connection with the economic life in an EU-Member State. The Act authorizes the Minister of Justice to lay down rules according to which certain foreigners and certain foreign companies which have not stayed in Denmark for five years are not required to get a permission to acquire real property for housing all the year round (contrary to summer houses) or for doing business activities or rendering services.

51. Every Danish man is obligated to serve in the military according to the Act on Military Service,[102] section 1, paragraph 1. A Danish man who also holds a foreign citizenship may be exempted from military service by the Minister of the Interior when this is provided by mutual agreement with the State in question, according to section 1, paragraph 2. Denmark has entered into agreements with the States which are represented in the Council of Europe and with a few other States. According to the section 3, paragraph 1, the Military Service Board may exempt a man with double nationality when he has already served the military service in a foreign State.

III. Right to Exercise Trade

52. It is an old and well-established principle that foreigners who are staying legally in Denmark are entitled to equal treatment with nationals on conditions which are laid down in the legal regulation concerning residence and exercise of trade activities. This rule is laid down in the Ordinance of 15 January 1776 on the right of citizenship (*Forordning om indfødsret*). In modern law, the Act on Trade lays down conditions for the exercise of commercial and industrial activities.[103]

IV. Legislation on Equality of Men and Women

53. The legislation on equality of men and women prohibits discrimination on the basis of sex. The statutes in force constitute the implementation of the EU-directives within this field. The Act on Equal Treatment of Men and Women,[104] Article 1, provides that discrimination on the basis of sex is not permitted whether it is made directly or indirectly, e.g., because of pregnancy, the status of marriage or position in the family. Section 5, paragraph 1, first subparagraph, provides that the obligation of equal treatment includes everybody who makes decisions concerning

102. Consolidated Act 225/2006 (*Værnepligtsloven*).
103. Act 595/2011 on Trade (*Næringsloven*).
104. Consolidated Act 645/2011 (*Ligestilling af mænd og kvinder med hensyn til beskæftigelse og barselsorlov*).

the access to, and the execution of, an independent profession. The second subparagraph indicates that the duty also concerns establishment, organization or enlargement of an enterprise and the start or extension of any other sort of non-employed activity including financing of the activity or enterprise. It follows from the Act that limitations because of sex are not permitted, for example, discrimination concerning access to an organization which is important for the execution of a certain profession or the grant of easier terms for men than for women concerning the raising of loans. The EU harmonization of laws on equality also includes wives who collaborate with their husbands, and the national legislation implementing the directives may be applied in order to support the independence of such wives attached to their husband's enterprise as collaborators.

V. Married Persons and Registered Partnership

54. Legislation provides for the legal effects concerning married persons. Since 15 June 2012, the same rules apply to single-sex and same-sex marriage.[105] Prior to that date, persons of the same sex could register their relationship and be submitted to the same legal effects as spouses in a marriage, with certain exceptions.

Persons who are 18 years old or older and who are not incompetent are entitled to marry without consent. Persons submitted to diminished capacity are also entitled to marry without consent.

55. The Act on the Legal Effects of Marriage[106] establishes the principle that the spouses are equal. They have to contribute to the support of each other and of the family life in common through money, work or otherwise, and they have to take decisions in common concerning the community.

§2. Partnerships and Companies

56. Industrial and commercial activities may be exercised within the framework of various types of companies, partnerships, corporations, foundations and other collective entities. The legislation regulates mainly public and private limited companies. The Act on Certain Commercial undertakings[107] regulates the registration of certain types of companies and partnerships. The purpose of the regulation is to provide information and general guidelines on subjects of public interest such as ownership, organization and accounting, as well as to grant representation to employees of the company. The company legislation is subject to the laws within the EU, and the EU-Directives in force are implemented in Danish law. Two types of limited

105. Consolidated Act 87/2019 on Marriage (*Ægteskabs indgåelse og opløsning*).
106. Consolidated Act 1021/2014 on the Legal Effects of Marriage (*Lovbekendtgørelse om ægteskabets retsvirkninger*).
107. Consolidated Act 1295/2013 *(Visse erhvervsdrivende virksomheder).*

companies exist. These are governed by the Danish Act on Public and Private Limited Companies of 2009 (*Selskabsloven*).[108] The public limited company, in Danish called *aktieselskab*, is indicated by 'A/S'. The joint capital of an A/S consists of shares, which with certain exceptions are freely transferable. The second type of company is the private company, called *Anpartsselskab*, indicated by 'ApS'. The joint capital of an ApS is composed of parts, which by provision in the statutes may be made non-transferable. The size of the capital in the public limited company (A/S) has to be at least DKK 500,000. The minimum capital requirement for the private limited company is DKK 50,000. A variant of *Anpartsselskab* is the *iværksætterselskab* (entrepreneurial company), which may be formed with a capital between DKK 1 and DKK 49,999.[109] The public limited companies (A/S) and the private companies (ApS) are registered in the register kept by the Danish Business Authority *(Erhvervsstyrelsen)*. Banks, insurance companies and mortgage societies are subject to special provisions.

I. Partnerships

A. Unlimited Partnerships

57. The most common type of partnership is the *interessentskab*. It is a joint ownership between two or more partners who are personally, jointly and severally liable for the obligations of the partnership. The *interessentskab* is established by written or oral agreement, and normally, the partners have to be competent. Since 1 January 1995, the partnership is subjected to certain provisions laid down in the Act on Certain Commercial Undertakings, according to which the name of the enterprise shall be distinctive and may not be confusing, as well as rules on authorization, which were developed in case law and introduced in the Act. No further special legislation regulates the partnership. Most of the fundamental problems are solved through case law and jurisprudence. Until 1 January 1995, partnerships which were engaged in trade, craftsmanship or manufacturing were registered in the Trade Register of Commerce. After that date, no registration is required, unless all unlimited partners are themselves companies with limited liability.

58. Concerning the relationship between the partners, it may be agreed that the participants have to raise the capital. Normally the contribution of each partner is fixed by contract. Otherwise, it is presupposed that each partner makes equal contributions to the partnership. Decisions on further contributions or augmentation of the capital require unanimity. Each partner is entitled to take part in the activities and the management of the partnership. In principle, the partners have to agree unanimously on all decisions. However, each partner may make transactions of minor significance as well as transactions considered necessary in order to avoid

---

108. Consolidated Act 1089/2015.

109. On 28 Feb. 2019 the Government has proposed to abolish the possibility to form new *iværksætterselskaber* and to reduce the minimum capital requirement for the ApS to DKK 40,000 (draft Amendment Act 2018–19, L 190).

damage or to comply with legal requirements. The partner may agree that some partners conduct most of the partnership's activities and transactions while the other partners' participation in the partnership is limited to financial support. Unanimity is required for all. It is the rule that each partner if nothing else is agreed, has one vote regardless of the size of his contribution, so that the profit will be divided equally between the partners.

The entry of new participants requires the consent of all the present partners. A share in a partnership cannot be transferred to a third party or inherited without the consent of the other partners. Frequently, a new partner is integrated by agreement which includes his contribution, voting rights, part of the profit and his responsibility for the obligations of the partnership. Normally, if nothing else is agreed, the new partner is only liable for the debts incurred after his entry into the partnership while the transferor, who has left the partnership, remains liable for debt incurred before the termination of his participation.

In relation to third parties, a unanimous decision is binding on each partner. One partner may be expressly authorized by the others to sign for the partnership concerning the activities of the enterprise and to bind the enterprise in such engagements. Limitations on this right have no effect on third parties. However, the authority to sell or mortgage real property belonging to the enterprise requires express authority, and that authority may be revoked at any time.

Creditors of the partnership may seek satisfaction from the partnership's capital. Furthermore, creditors can freely claim full payment from every partner until the debt is paid; each of the participants is personally liable. An individual creditor having a claim on an individual partner cannot seek satisfaction from the share of the debtor in the partnership's capital. Satisfaction through a share requires the partnership to be dissolved. A dissolution may be required if the debtor is declared bankrupt, in order to get the net share distributed.

59. A partnership can be dissolved by agreement. Each partner is entitled to terminate his involvement in partnership by reasonable notice if nothing else is agreed; compelling circumstances may entitle a partner to retire from the partnership as well. In case of breach of the agreement, bankruptcy or death of a partner, the others may claim dissolution. Heirs may claim dissolution if not otherwise provided for in the partnership agreement. The partnership may also be dissolved when circumstances have changed, so that the fundamental conditions of the partnership are no longer present, even if no breach of the partners' agreement has occurred, for example, a dissolution because of a partner's serious illness. At the dissolution, the partnership is liquidated. Each partner gets his part according to the agreement on division of profit. If the balance is negative, every partner is personally liable for the whole debt of the former partnership.

B. Limited Partnerships

60. A limited partnership is composed of two types of participants: general partners, who are personally liable and participate in the partnership like partners in an unlimited partnership, and limited partners, who have engaged themselves to make capital contributions to the partnership. The latter have obligations only towards the partnership according to their contractual engagements, which may oblige them to pay supplementary contributions under certain circumstances. The creditors of the partnership cannot assert any claim against the limited partners. The limited partnership is submitted to the same rules of the Act on Certain Commercial Undertakings concerning the name and authorization as the unlimited partnership, and corresponding general rules of case law are applicable.

II. Associations and Cooperative Societies

61. An association is composed of persons who are united in order to realize a common purpose. The purpose of an association may be economic or non-economic. Associations with an economic purpose must be registered with the Business Agency according to the Act on Certain Commercial Undertakings. The general regulation that developed from contract law was established by case law. An agreement is required for the establishment of an association. Normally the agreement is laid down in the association's articles. For associations, it is the general rule that the members are not personally liable for the obligations of the association.

62. Cooperative societies constitute the most important group of the economic associations. When such societies are engaged in trade and business in order to promote the interests of the participants, they are submitted to the Act on Certain Commercial Undertakings. The Act, section 4, defines a cooperative society (*andelsselskab*) or cooperative association (*andelsforening)* as an enterprise whose purpose is to promote the common interests of the participants who are active for the enterprise as purchasers, suppliers or similar activities. It is part of the association concept that the return of the enterprise is divided between the participants in relation to their share of the turnover or remains in the enterprise. The rules on the name of the enterprise and on the authority to sign on behalf of the firm by procuration are laid down in the Act, sections 6 and 7. When the association constitutes a limited enterprise, which is defined in the Act, section 3 as an enterprise where none of the participants are personally, jointly and severally liable, it shall be registered at the Business Authority *(Erhvervsstyrelsen)*. The rule is the same for branches of foreign limited enterprises. Registration is obligatory. According to section 9, registration is a condition for the association (the enterprise) to be entitled to rights and to enter into valid engagements. It follows from the Act, section 18, that associations which constitute limited enterprises submitted to the Act have the duty of giving an annual account according to the rules issued by the Business Authority. However, size requirements apply.

III. Foundations

63. A foundation is an institution without a separate owner; foundations have no members. According to administrative practice, a foundation is established when it has: (1) a capital irrevocably separated from the capital sphere of the founder; (2)

one or more distinct purposes; and (3) a direction which is independent in relation to the founder. It is sufficient for fulfilling the third condition that one member of the board of direction, for example, a lawyer is independent. Foundations, in general, are regulated by the Act on Foundation and Certain Associations.[110] A specialized regulation is laid down in the Act on Business Foundations.[111]

The Consolidated Act on Foundations and Certain Associations applies to all foundations with a capital of DKK 250,000 or more. Foundations with an economic purpose as well as those with a non-economic purpose are subject to the Act. It may be employers' associations, trade unions and other professional associations dealing with the economic interests of the members and associations whose capital is composed of contributions from the associations mentioned. Family foundations and charity foundations are also subject to the Act.

The foundation shall adopt articles which fulfil the requirements of the Act. The purpose of the foundation is to make distributions, normally of money. The board of directors shall be formed by at least three persons. Formerly, the foundations should be entered into a special register, but this requirement has been abolished.

The supervision according to the Act on Foundations is exercised by the Ministry of Justice. The foundation shall present a revised annual account. Amendment of the articles requires a certain procedure and the consent of the foundation authorities. Concerning family foundations, the Act provides for a prohibition of favouring future generations of the family without strict limitations in time, but within these limits such foundations are legal. The influence of the family is limited.

64. The special regulation is laid down in the Act on Business Foundations. A foundation is deemed to do business when it transfers goods, immaterial rights or services in exchange for payment, is dealing with sales or hiring out of real property, or has a certain connection with a public limited company or a private company. A business foundation shall be registered in the Register of Business Foundations (*Registret for erhvervsdrivende Fonde)* kept by the Business Authority *(Erhvervsstyrelsen)*. According to the Act on Business Foundations, the foundation authority is normally exercised by the Minister of Trade and Growth. The capital requirement for business foundations is DKK 300,000 (about USD 50,000). The employees are entitled to representation in the Board of Directors corresponding to the regulation for companies. The annual account is subject to the Act on Annual Accounts like companies. The business foundation is not obliged to distribute the entire annual profit, but rather may consolidate the capital.

IV. Mortgage Institutions

65. Credit associations are to a great extent based on security by mortgage on real estate. Loans are financed by bonds and are secured by a registered mortgage in real estate. The bonds are issued by the mortgage institutions (*realkreditinstitutter*), which hold a central place in business life. Traditionally, they are organized as

---

110. Consolidated Act 938/2012 on Foundations and Certain Associations *(Fonde og visse foreninger)*.
111. Consolidated Act 712/2014 (*Erhvervsdrivende fonde)*.

associations of borrowers, whose members are personally, jointly and severally liable for the obligations of the institutions apart from certain limitations. Currently, the mortgage institutions are subject to the Act on Financial Institutions.[112] The Act lays down rules for the activities of the mortgage institutions, their management and the types of loan which may be awarded in relation to different categories of real estate. Foreign mortgage institutions are admitted to exercise activities in Denmark through a branch office established in Denmark or through cross-border activities when they fulfil certain conditions laid down in the Act.

V. Investment Associations

66. Investment associations are established in order to receive funds from the public or from wider circles of investors for placing investments under observation of the diversification of risk. They are subject to the Consolidated Act on Investment Associations.[113] The institutions shall be organized as associations with members who each own a share of the association assets and who are submitted to the rights and obligations of the association.

VI. European Economic Interest Groupings

67. European Economic Interest Groupings(EEIG) (*Europæiske Økonomiske Firmagrupper* (EØFG), according to the EEC-Council Regulation No. 2137/85 of 25 July 1985 (OJ L 1985 199/1), are subject to the Act on Administration of the EEC-Regulations on Establishment of EEIG.[114] The Act provides that the EEIG is not permitted to exercise activities which may only be exercised by physical persons, and that participation in the EEIG may be excluded or limited for certain categories of juridical or physical persons. Persons who are minors or incompetents, or who are bankrupt, cannot participate in the EEIG. The administration of the Act is placed under the Business Authority (*Erhvervsstyrelsen*). The EEIG shall be registered with the Register of EEIG (*Registeret over Europæiske Økonomiske Firmagrupper*) kept by the Business Authority.

112. Consolidated Act 1140/2017 (*Finansiel virksomhedslov*).
113. Consolidated Act 1154/2018 (*Investeringsforeninger*).
114. Act 217/1989 (*Lov om administration af det europæisk økonomiske Fællesskabs forordninger om indførelse af europæiske firmagrupper*).

Chapter 3. The Economic Institutions

§1. Professional Organizations

68. Danish enterprises and labour forces participate to a considerable extent in organizations, which represent and advise their members on general and specific matters.[115] In this chapter, the organizations considered to be most important for commerce, are discussed.

I. The Danish Chamber of Commerce

69. The Danish Chamber of Commerce (*Dansk Erhverv*) is one of the largest professional business organizations in Denmark with more than 240 employees and offices in the two major Danish cities as well as an EU office in Brussels. The Chamber represents 17,000 Danish companies and 100 trade associations in service sectors such as trade, tourism, business services, IT, welfare services and transport.

The Chamber is a private non-profit organization whose goal is to make running a business easier for its members. By means of political influence and expert advice to its members, the Chamber strives to create conditions that will make it attractive to do business in a globalized world. Furthermore, the Chamber seeks to ensure that development opportunities are maximized for the growth industries by increasing the competitiveness of its members. Finally, the Chamber assumes the functions of secretariat for thirty-five trade organizations. Membership is subject to approval of the Danish Chamber of Commerce. The Chamber also acts as the chief negotiator on behalf of its members on a number of collective agreements with the trade unions. These agreements constitute the basic framework for wages and working conditions for employees in the majority of companies in Denmark. A Chief Executive Officer assisted by two directors manages the Chamber. Its headquarter is situated in Copenhagen at the old Royal Stock Exchange (*Børsen*).

70. The Danish Chamber of Commerce offers information, advice, communication and assistance to its members. It gives commercial advice concerning contact with foreign suppliers and customers, collaboration between enterprises, foreign market conditions and sales promotion, and it assists by market introduction. In connection with import and export, it gives information on customs and business restrictions and keeps the members informed on the latest rules of import and export. The Chamber is authorized to issue ATA-carnets, certificates of origin and other papers used in international commerce. Legal advice is given on the interpretation of statutes and other regulations, establishment of contracts and publication of model form contracts and trade practices. It gives expert opinions and advice and service on employment law. Furthermore, the Chamber offers enterprises involved in Danish and international business the opportunity of settling their disputes through arbitration.

---

115. Author: Peter Møgelvang-Hansen (based on the contribution to the first edition by Peter Arnt Nielsen).

Communication and publication activities constitute an important part of the functions of the Chamber. Periodicals with actual information are issued. Furthermore, the Chamber acts as an intermediary between enterprises looking for contact with others, and it may offer assistance for access to the public service system.

On the international level, the Danish Chamber of Commerce follows the activities of the EU organizations, and as a member of the Economic and Social Committee of the EU, it may influence the decisions of the Community. Furthermore, it promotes the establishment of a North European network in order to develop the connections between the countries around the Baltic Sea. On the worldwide scale, it arranges delegation journeys to foreign countries and maintains contact with the International Chamber of Commerce and with other national committees. It constitutes the National Committee of the International Chamber of Commerce.

II. The Confederation of Danish Industry

71. The organization Confederation of Danish Industry (*Dansk Industri, DI)* DI holds a central position in Danish industrial policy. The organization has been established through a merger in 1992 between the Association of Employers for Industry (*Industriens Arbejdsgivere*) and the Council of Industry (*Industrirådet*).

DI has about 11,000 member enterprises, organized in professional associations. Its purpose is to maintain and promote export as well as to offer services to the members on the national and international level. DI gives advice on export conditions and undertakes export activities. It deals with environmental problems and product standards. Furthermore, it undertakes bargaining and establishment of collective agreements, and it gives advice on commercial law, particularly within the fields of corporate law, competition, patents, contracts, liability and consumer matters, and it also gives advice on risk management and assurance matters. It has a publishing department where documentation, model form contracts and books are issued.

III. The Danish Federation of Small and Medium-Sized Enterprises

72. The Danish Federation of Small and Medium-Sized Enterprises (*SMVdanmark*, prior to 2017: *Håndværksrådet*) was founded in 1879. Today, it is the main trade organization for small and medium-sized enterprises in Denmark, representing more than 20,000 companies within different sectors such as construction, manufacturing, crafts, retail and services. The main objective of *SMVdanmark* is to improve the business conditions of Danish small and medium-sized enterprises. The staff members at the Head Office work as advisors and take part in formulation of political and commercial initiatives, and they are in daily contact with companies, organizations, public administration, political advocacy groups and the media.

Although the members are mainly employers, the organization does not distinguish between employed persons and principals, and it is not engaged in labour market policy. The Council deals with business policy takes up questions of principles with public authorities, and it offers services concerning economic and juridical consultation and assistance in concrete cases. It gives general information through courses and publishing activities.

IV. The Organizations of the Labour Market

73. On the labour market, the main organizations are the Confederation of Danish Employers (*Dansk Arbejdsgiverforening, DA*) and the Danish Trade Union Confederation (*Fagbevægelses Hovedorganisation, FH*), which gathers employees.

DA, founded in 1896, is a non-profit organization funded by subscriptions from member organizations. It represents fourteen employers' organizations with a membership of more than 24,000 Danish private companies in manufacturing, retail, transport, services and construction.

Its main activities are coordination of collective agreements, employment policy and skills, occupational health and safety, labour law, international industrial relations, monitoring in terms of analysis and statistics on wages, absenteeism, conflicts, etc.

DA's objective is to influence national, regional and international policy-makers in order to increase the competitiveness of Danish companies and their access to a skilled labour force.

At the national level, DA represents the interests of its member organizations in relation to the political system. As regards labour market regulation, DA strives to ensure coordination of mutual interests when collective agreements are negotiated. DA is not a direct party in the continuous bargaining but must ensure the necessary and sufficient coordination among its member organizations when concluding new agreements. Any conclusion of a collective agreement is subject to the approval of DA. In keeping with the Danish tradition for regulating the labour market through collective agreement rather than legislation, DA supports and promotes the use of collective bargaining. It considers it vital to ensure that labour markets are regulated through collective agreements as far as possible.

At the European level, DA supports and promotes the use of the Social Dialogue rather than legislative regulation. In the long-term perspective, DA works to ensure that necessary structural reforms are completed in the EU. DA nominates a member to the European Economic and Social Committee and holds a seat on the Social Dialogue Committee. At the international level, DA is a member of the International Organisation of Employers and the OECD's Business and Industry Advisory Committee.

The Danish Trade Union Confederation, FH, is the largest national trade union confederation in Denmark, and it is recognized as the most representative workers' organization in both the private and the public sector. FH is the result of a merger of two former organizations, LO and FTF.

FH's main objective is to handle employee interests towards employers and authorities. FH has seventy-nine member organizations with 1.4 mio. members.

Through its cooperation with associations, cartels and other trade union organizations, FH seeks to influence the government and the political parties when it comes to drafting and implementing legislation, especially in relation to labour market policies.

V. Specialized Organizations

74. There are several specialized organizations in Denmark in various sectors.

In the financial sector, Finance Denmark (*Finans Danmark*) represents the banks, mortgage institutions, asset management, securities trading, and investment funds in Denmark, including Danish branches of foreign institutions. The main task of Finance Denmark is to create good operating conditions for the members. The organization monitors the political process and plays an active role in political decision-making relevant for banks.

The Danish Insurance Association (*Forsikring og Pension)* is the trade organization for the insurance and pension industry in Denmark. Its members are companies, pension funds and general agencies dealing with insurance and pension in Denmark.

75. Danish enterprises are often members of professional organizations such as the Association of Public Accountants in Denmark (*Danske Revisorer, FSR*), the Danish Bar and Law Society (*Advokatsamfundet*), and the Danish Medical Association (*Lægeforeningen*).

The purpose of these organizations/associations is to maintain and promote the reputation and the skills of the members. The organizations lay down standards of ethical behaviour and moral codes and issue opinions on professional practices. In case of non-compliance with the rules, a member risks exclusion from the association.

§2. Administrative Authorities and Advisory Bodies

76. Within the public sector, administrative entities not only assume the authority of legal execution and control but also give advice and offer services to businesses and citizens. Local authorities as well as private organizations might also advise businesses and individuals.

I. The Ministry of Industry, Business and Financial Affairs

77. In particular, the Ministry of Industry, Business and Financial Affairs (*Erhvervsministeriet*) deals with the regulation of commerce and business. The Ministry of Industry, Business and Financial Affairs seeks to improve the conditions for growth in Denmark. The Ministry conducts economic analyses and suggests policy initiatives in areas imperative to economic growth. The Ministry is responsible for a number of policy areas which are important for the general business environment, including business regulation, intellectual property rights, competition policy, the financial sector, the construction sector and shipping. The Ministry is engaged with various international organizations enhancing international framework conditions for growth. In the EU, the Ministry participates in the work of the Councils for Competitiveness and Maritime Transport. The Ministry comprises six authorities and seven agencies, of which the most important will be presented in the following.

78. The Danish Business Authority (*Erhvervsstyrelsen*) deals with a number of subjects, in particular, company law and business organization, IT and telecom, and construction issues.

79. The Danish FSA (*Finanstilsynet*) supervises compliance with financial legislation by financial undertakings and issuers of securities as well as investors on the securities markets. The Authority also contributes to the preparation of financial legislation, and it collects and disseminates knowledge about the financial sector.

80. The Danish Competition and Consumer Authority (*Konkurrence – og forbrugerstyrelsen*) is the secretariat of both the Danish Competition Council (*Konkurrencerådet*) and the Consumer Complaints Board (*Forbrugerklagenævnet*).

The Authority is responsible for the executive administration of the Competition Act and consumer legislation. In respect of competition, the Council rules in major cases, including cases of fundamental importance, and it sets a precedent in other cases. The Danish Competition and Consumer Authority make case presentations and recommendations to the Council. The Competition and Consumer Authority is entitled to make decisions on behalf of the Council.

Decisions made by the Competition Council can be appealed to the Competition Appeal's Board (*Konkurrenceankenævnet*). This independent board consists of a chairman, required to be a Supreme Court Judge and four other members with legal or economic insight.

The Consumer Complaints Board is an independent complaints board that considers consumer complaints related to goods and services purchased from traders. It consists of a chairman and consumer and business representatives. The chairman must be a judge by profession and may not have any particular relations to consumer or business organizations. The Consumer Complaints Board considers complaints from private consumers related to goods, work and services purchased from traders. The Board does not accept complaints from traders or public authorities or institutions. Consumers may complain of traders only if an action concerning the issues at stake can be brought before the Danish courts against the relevant trader under the general rules of Danish law. A number of goods and services are exempted from the Board's scope of authority. Maximum and minimum amounts have been fixed, which means that the price of goods or services must be at least DKK 1,050, but not exceed DKK 100,000. As to complaints of textiles and shoes, however, the minimum purchase price is DKK 680.

The Consumer Ombudsman (*Forbrugerombudsmanden*) is an independent institution regulated by the Marketing Practices Act. The institution, founded in 1975, supervises on compliance with the Marketing Practices Act and other consumer legislation such as the Payment Services, the Legal Counselling Act, the E-commerce

Act, the Act Tobacco Advertising Ban Act as well as a number of civil law provisions in legislation protecting consumers. The Minister of Business and Growth appoints the Ombudsman for a period of six years. The Ombudsman prioritizes the institution's work and activities according to resources and needs. He can on his own initiative or following complaints from consumers examine cases and attempt to persuade businesses to comply with relevant legislation, for instance through dialogue or by setting up guidelines. However, the Ombudsman may also institute court proceedings against businesses.

81. The Danish Patent and Trademark Authority (*Patent og Varemærkestyrelsen)* provides strategic information and protect the rights of both techniques and business marks. The Authority issues patent and design rights and registers trademarks.

82. The Safety Technology Authority (*Sikkerhedsstyrelsen*) focuses on the safety technological aspects relevant to fires, accidents and explosions.

83. The Danish Maritime Authority (*Søfartsstyrelsen*) is responsible for the construction, equipment and operation of Danish ships, port state control of foreign ships calling at Danish ports, ship registration, seafarers' employment, health and conditions of social security, shipping policy, maritime law as well as industrial policy, buoying at sea and navigation marks ashore, navigational information, and the national pilot authority.

84. Denmark's Export Credit Agency (*Danmarks Eksportkredit, EKF*) helps Danish companies to make it possible and attractive for customers abroad to buy Danish products and services. The Agency *insures* Danish exporters against potential financial and political risks of trading with other countries. The EKF is the only organization on the Danish market offering insurance against the risks that are not covered by the private sector. The Agency is operated as a financial institution on commercial terms.

85. The Danish Fund for Growth (*Vækstfonden*) is a State investment fund, which aims at *creating* new growth companies by providing venture capital and competence. Since 1992, the Fund has, in cooperation with private investors, co-financed growth in 3,700 Danish companies with a total commitment of approximately DKK 10 billion. *Vækstfonden* invests equity or provides loans and guarantees in collaboration with private partners and Danish financial institutions.

86. The Financial Stability Company (*Finansiel Stabilitet*) was established in October 2008 as part of *an* agreement between the Danish State and the Danish financial sector on a scheme to secure financial stability in Denmark. This agreement was reached in response to the international crisis and the impact it had on the financial sector. The Company is State-owned, and it ensures financial stability in Denmark, including winding-up of distressed banks.

87. Visit Denmark is an information agency with the goal of developing and marketing Danish tourism. It offers access to databases on products and market data as well as photo service and market analysis. The economic resources of Visit Denmark are procured from enterprises and from government subsidies.

88. Another important institution is the Trade Council (*Eksportrådet*). It is the governmental export and investment promotion organization under the Ministry of Foreign Affairs. The Council comprises all governmental activities designed to promote Danish export and foreign investment in Denmark.

II. Standardization, Technology and Energy Bodies

89. The private, independent organization Danish Standard (*Dansk Standard, DS*) is the national member of the European *standardization* organization Comité européen de normalisation and the international organization International Organization for Standardization. DS deals with the elaboration and implementation of European and international standards and gives information and advice within its field of activity. It is financed by fees from member enterprises and by the sale of standards and other information and services.

90. The Danish Technological Institute (*Teknologisk Institut*) is a self-owned non-profit institution. It develops, applies and disseminates research – and technologically-based knowledge for the Danish and International business sectors. It participates in development projects of use to society in close collaboration with research and educational institutions both in Denmark and abroad. Finally, the Institute carries out consultancy and standardization services.

III. Administrative Recourse

91. Administrative decisions can in most cases be appealed to an appellate administrative authority. Furthermore, according to Article 63 of the Constitution, decisions of the appellate authority may be brought before the courts. However, legislation may provide that the decision of a specified administrative authority is final and thus not subject to court review. Furthermore, administrative decisions may be brought before the Ombudsman of the Parliament (*Folketingets Ombudsmand*), as he has to supervise the civil and military administration according to the Constitution, Article 55. His authority in relation to municipalities is limited, as he may not infringe the right of local authorities to manage their own affairs. He has no right to modify or to nullify administrative decisions. The remedy of the Ombudsman is to pronounce his 'opinion of the case' to the authority involved, which has a far-reaching moral effect.

92. The Danish Commerce Appeal Board of the Ministry of Industry (*Erhvervsankenævnet*) is an independent appeal board under the Ministry of Industry,

Business and Financial Affairs. It deals with administrative decisions made by the Ministry's authorities. Other administrative authorities cannot review its decisions.

IV. Local Bodies

93. Business promotion is carried out at the local level. Most municipalities have an Industrial and Trade Service (*Erhvervskontor*) and a Head of Industrial and Trade Service (*Erhvervschef*). The municipal Industrial and Trade Services give advice on local matters and develop the collaboration between enterprises. In several places, electronic registers of enterprises are established. The municipal libraries may offer a research and documentation service on business matters for payment. Some of the larger municipalities are able to give advice and information on EU-questions. All municipalities have jointly established an information office in Brussels.

The municipalities are gathered in Local Government Denmark (*Kommunernes Landsforening, KL*). It is the interest group and member authority of Danish municipalities. It is voluntary to be a member of the organization, but actually all ninety-eight municipalities are members. The mission of the organization is to safeguard common interests of the municipalities, assist the individual municipality with consultancy services and ensure that the local authorities are provided with up-to-date and relevant information.

§3. Commercial Courts and Arbitration

I. Commercial Courts

94. There are three types of ordinary courts in Denmark; the City Court (*Byretten*), the Court of Appeal (*Landsretten*) and the Supreme Court (*Højesteret*). All courts deal with civil and commercial matters as well as criminal matters.

The Supreme Court has its seat in Copenhagen and is managed by a President. It has sixteen judges, including the President. Normally, at least five judges participate in a case before the court. There are two Appellate Courts; the Eastern (*Østre Landsret*) in Copenhagen with fifty six judges and the Western (*Vestre Landsret*) Court of Appeal in Viborg with thirty-six judges, both headed by a President. In civil and commercial cases, three judges participate in cases before the court. There are twenty-four City Courts, varying in range from between thirty-nine (*Copenhagen*) and one (*Bornholm*) judge. Normally, one judge handles cases before the City Court, but according to Article 12(3) of the Administration of Justice Act, three judges may participate if the pending case concerns a matter of principle; it may be of substantial importance to others than the parties; it is particularly complicated or comprehensive in respect of facts or law, or the special character of the case so requires.

95. In addition to the ordinary courts, there exists a specialized court; the Maritime and Commercial Court (*Sø- og Handelsretten*), seated in Copenhagen. It has a President, two Vice-Presidents, two judges and a number of lay judges specialized in maritime or commercial matters. The Court deals with maritime and commercial cases, in particular, cases concerning EU trademarks, EU designs and other IP Rights and injunctions in such cases; international cases, where knowledge of international commercial relations is of substantial importance; competition law, marketing law, maritime law and insolvency law.

96. According to the Administration of Justice Act, Article 224, all civil and commercial cases shall be instituted before a City Court. However, a City Court may refer the case to an Appeal Court, if the case concerns a matter of principle; *see* Article 226(1) of the Administration of Justice Act. A City Court may also refer a case to the Maritime and Commercial Court, if knowledge of employment law is important, and the case concerns a matter of principle, *see* Article 227(1) of the Administration of Justice Act.

97. A judgment from a City Court can within four weeks from its delivery be appealed to one of the Appellate courts unless it is a default judgment or the value at stake is less than DKK 20,000. However, a judgment from the Appellate Court can only be appealed to the Supreme Court with the approval of the *Appeals* Permission Board (*Procesbevillingsnævnet*). A first instance judgment of an Appellate Court can be appealed to the Supreme Court within eight weeks from its delivery. A judgment in a civil and commercial matter from the Maritime and Commercial Court can be appealed to the Supreme Court within eight weeks from its delivery.

II. Arbitration

A. Regulatory Framework

98. Arbitration is very attractive for Danish businesses, in particular, because proceedings are held in private. In international cases, Danish businesses prefer arbitration for the same reason and because of the efficiency and widespread global acceptance of the New York Convention of 10 June 1958 on the Recognition and Enforcement of Arbitral Awards, to which Denmark is a Contracting State.

Denmark, with its new Arbitration Act of 24 June 2005 (*Voldgiftsloven*), is a Model Law Country, as the new Act is based on UNCITRAL's Model Law of 11 December 1985 on International Commercial Arbitration. In the Danish Act, no distinction is made between domestic and international arbitration, so the Act applies to both types of arbitration. The Danish Act is in complete compliance with the Model Law of 1985, except for the Model Law's provisions in Articles 1–3 that have not been copied. The amendments adopted in 2006 to the Model Law are not part of the Danish Arbitration Act. Finally, according to Article 38, an arbitral award from any State in the world will be recognized and enforced in Denmark in compliance with the New York Convention even if the award originates from a State that is not a Contracting State to the New York Convention.

B. Arbitration Institutions

99. Both ad hoc and institutional arbitration are accepted in Denmark. There are two major arbitration institutions: the Danish Institute of Arbitration (*Voldgiftsinstituttet*) dealing with all types of arbitrable disputes and the Arbitration Institute for Construction (*Voldgiftsnævnet for Bygge- og anlægsvirksomhed*), dealing with mainly construction disputes. Their rules of arbitration are by and large in accordance with the Danish Arbitration Act.

Chapter 4. General Obligations on Economic Operators

100. Enterprises engaged in trade and industry must comply with the regulation on registration, on the use of names and on bookkeeping, as well as environment protection requirements.[116]

§1. The Act on Business Enterprises

101. The Act on Certain Business Enterprises[117] lays down rules on registration for certain types of enterprises. According to section 1, the Act is applicable to sole proprietorships, associations, cooperatives, partnerships, limited partnerships and societies with limited liability, which are not subject to the legislation on public limited companies (A/S), private companies (ApS), or the Act on foundations. Branches of the corresponding foreign enterprises are also subject to the Act. An enterprise is an enterprise subject to the Act, if it transfers goods or immaterial rights, or provides services against remuneration. Furthermore, such an enterprise will be deemed to carry out a business for profit if it conducts activities involving selling or renting real property if it is considered a parent enterprise in relation to a limited public or private company or similar enterprise (section 1(3) of the Act).

§2. The Registration System

I. Registration in General

102. Registration of companies which is mandated by Danish company law legislation is carried out by the national company registration authority called 'The Danish Business Authority'.[118] Specific registration requirements are laid down in the Ministerial Order on Registration of companies.[119] Registration, which is mandated by Danish tax legislation, e.g., registration prescribed by the Act on VAT, is also carried out by the Business Authority. However, the legal effect of a registration based on the tax legislation differs considerably from the registration mandated by company law.

103. All real property, irrespective of ownership, shall be recorded in accordance with the land registration system. Registration which is based entirely on digital documents[120] is kept by the national digital Land Registration *Authority.*

---

116. Author: Søren Friis Hansen.
117. Consolidated Act 1295/2013 on Certain Commercial Undertakings (*Visse erhvervsdrivende virksomheder*).
118. *Erhvervsstyrelsen*; www.erhvervsstyrelsen.dk.
119. Executive Order 1466/2015 (*Anmeldelsesbekendtgørelsen*).
120. Act 539/2006.

II. Registration of Enterprises and Companies

104. Public limited companies (*aktieselskaber*, A/S) private limited companies (*anpartsselskaber*, abbreviated, ApS) and limited partnership companies (*kommanditaktieselskaber*, P/S) are subject to the Danish Companies Act of 2009.[121] All public and private limited companies must be registered with the Danish Business Authority (*Erhvervsstyrelsen*) in order to obtain legal personality.

Partnerships and limited partnerships are in general not required to register with the Danish Business Authority but may be subject to registration requirements for tax purposes.

Partnerships and limited partnerships, in which all partners or general partners are limited liability companies or similar types of companies must, however, register with the Danish Business Authority (*Erhvervsstyrelsen*).[122]

A special Danish company type is the limited liability undertaking *(selskab med begrænset ansvar)*. This type of company must be registered according to the Act on Certain Business Enterprises (section 3). Through registration, the company obtains legal personality. This provision applies to cooperatives with limited liability as well *(andelsselskaber med begrænset ansvar)* as defined in section 4 of the Act.

105. Foundations doing business have to enter into a special register (*Register for Erhvervsdrivende fonde*) kept by the Danish Business Authority (*Erhvervsstyrelsen*), and are subject to the Act on Enterprise foundations.[123]

106. EEIG (*Europæiske økonomiske Firmagrupper, EØFG*) are, *registered* in a special register *(Registeret over europæiske økonomiske firmagrupper)* kept by the Danish Business Authority (*Erhvervsstyrelsen*).[124] Banks and similar financial institutions must be authorized by the Supervisory Authority of Financial Affairs (*Finanstilsynet*) to conduct activities in Denmark and to be registered with the Business Agency.[125] This applies to insurance companies as well.

107. For tax purposes, registration is required when an enterprise is obliged to collect Value added tax (VAT), withholding tax based on salaries of employees, and import or export duties. Registration for tax purposes is carried out through the Central Company Register (*CVR-registeret*).[126]

---

121. Consolidated Act 1089/2015 (*Aktie- og anpartsselskaber (Selskabsloven)*).
122. Act on Certain Commercial Undertakings s. 2(3).
123. Consolidated Act 712/2014.
124. Act 217/1989 on the Administration of EEC-Regulation on European Economic Interest Groupings *(Lov om administration af det Europæiske Økonomiske-Fællesskabs forordninger om indførelse af europæiske økonomiske firmagrupper)*, s. 5.
125. Consolidated Act 1140/2017 on Financial Enterprises (*Lovbekendtgørelse om finansiel virksomhed*).
126. Consolidated Act 653/2006 as amended by Act 516/2009. The Danish term is *CVR-registeret.* The English term *Central Company Register* is officially used for this register, although this term is somehow misleading. The CVR-register thus registers all types of enterprises, associations, self-employed persons, Danish companies and branches of foreign companies, which are required to register with the Danish authorities for tax purposes.

§3. Name and Procuration of the Enterprise

108. The provisions laid down in the Act on Certain Business Enterprises, section 6, concerning names of the enterprises correspond to the corresponding legislation applicable to public and private limited companies (section 2 of the Companies Act). Names of companies and other enterprises shall be distinctive. Family names or other names which the enterprise is not entitled to use may not be part of the name of the enterprise. The name of a partner who has left the enterprise may not be used unless he or his heirs permit it. The name may not be misleading or indicate activities which have no connection with the enterprise in question. The indication concerning the legal structure and liability of the enterprise must be correct. Cooperative societies with limited liability may only indicate the limitation or liability by the designation 'A.M.B.A.'. A branch of a foreign enterprise or company shall include in its name the word *filial* (branch) and clearly indicate the nationality of the enterprise. The power of procuration is regulated by the Act on Business enterprises, section 7, which provides that a person who is granted power of procuration is authorized to act on behalf of the enterprise in business activities and to engage the enterprise regarding these matters. The authorization does not include the sale or mortgage of the real property of the enterprise. The procuration cannot be limited or transferred to anyone else, but the authorization may be revoked. More persons may be authorized to sign jointly for the firm, which is called a 'collective procuration'.

§4. The Duty to Keep Books

109. The duty to keep books is generally regulated by the Act on Bookkeeping (*Bogføringsloven*).[127] Section 1 of this Act provides that the duty is laid on public and private limited companies, associations and other entities doing business, as well as persons and partnerships entitled to do business. The duty includes persons and partnerships in commerce dealing with a widespread range of services.

Also, agricultural and similar enterprises of a certain size shall keep books of accounts. The Act, section 2, lays down the principle that books shall be kept in an orderly and careful way and shall give such complete information as is considered reasonable for creditors and public authorities. Books must be safeguarded for five years after the last entry.

110. Limited liability enterprises and cooperative societies with limited liability, which are subject to registration requirement under section 3 of the Act on Business Enterprises, have to send their annual accounts to the Danish Business Authority, prepared in accordance with the rules on Annual Accounts.[128] Special regulations apply to certain companies and institutions. Public limited companies and private limited companies must always send in their Annual Accounts to the Business

127. Consolidated Act 468/2006 on Book-keeping (*Lovbekendtgørelse om bogføring*).
128. Section 3(1) 4 of Consolidated Act 1580/2015 on Commercial Enterprises' Presentation on Financial Statements (*Årsregnskabsloven)*.

Authority (*Erhvervsstyrelsen*) within five months of the end of the financial year. This also applies to partnerships and limited partnerships, in which all partners or general partners are limited liability companies or similar types of companies (section 2 of the Act on certain Business Enterprises). Annual accounts are in general subject to audit by an approved auditor, regulated by the Act on Approved Auditors and Audit Firms.[129] However, companies which fulfil two of the following three requirements, may elect not to carry out statutory audit (section 135 of the Act on Commercial Enterprises' Presentation on Financial Statements): a balance amount of at least DKK 4 million, a turnover of at least DKK 8 million, and more than 120 employees on average).

§5. Requirements Concerning Bank Accounts

111. No specific legislative requirements are established for opening a bank account. Thus, anyone may open a bank account. In cases where a cash credit has to be opened, the bank requires, according to its internal instructions and local agreements between the banks, a budget elaborated by an auditor and information on the income, the private budget, any life insurance and on engagements elsewhere, for example on credit cards. Furthermore, the bank checks the solvency of the client before the grant of a cash credit account. No distinction is made between accounts kept by enterprises and by private customers concerning the payment of fees.

§6. Requirements Concerning the Local Situation

112. The plant of an enterprise is subject to a differentiated regulation concerning purchase, ownership and application of real property, and concerning production. The Act on Planning provides for a planning covering the whole country and safeguards the public interests in application of the ground area.[130] The Act contributes to set up a protection regulation for nature and environment, as it provides for the global, regional and local planning. A regulation concerning buildings is established by the Act on Preservation of Buildings.[131]

Regulations concerning the environment are established by the Act on Protection of the Environment.[132] Regulation of waste is laid down in Chapter 6 of the Act. According to section 43, everybody dealing with waste shall prevent pollution. The local authorities shall take care of the removal of the waste, section 45. In order to prevent damages to the working environment, the Minister of Labour keeps a register of chemical agents, materials and products (*Produktregisteret*), which is not open to the public.

---

129. Act 1287/2018.
130. Consolidated Act 287/2018.
131. Consolidated Act 219/2018.
132. Consolidated Act 1121/2018.

Chapter 5. Business Assets, Goodwill and Commercial Property Rights

§1. Business Assets

113. Business assets are a broad concept, used in different disciplines.[133] This chapter deals primarily with intangible assets as business assets. Some of the company's intangible assets, notably goodwill and know-how, are important but difficult to define. Whereas goodwill is normally defined as encompassing reputation or non-identifiable assets, know-how includes knowledge and skills needed to complete a business task. Other intangible assets, such as trade names and trademarks, are also widely considered as business assets. In contrast to intellectual property rights, which are subject to separate laws, intangible business assets are normally protected by laws against unfair competition.

The discussion here will focus on the protection of intangible business assets which do not fall under traditional intellectual property rights.

I. Trade Names

A. *Legislation*

114. Trade names serve as means of distinguishing a company from other companies and are used as a link between the company and its customers. The rules governing the use of trade names are spread over various acts, each covering a separate and well-defined area. The overall aim of the rules is to ensure a clearly defined, general system for identifying companies. Most notable, in this sense, are the provisions of the Marketing Practices Act,[134] the Companies Act,[135] and the Business Enterprises Act.[136] The Trade Mark Act[137] only protects real trademarks but has some interactions with the other acts. Less important is the Act on Names[138] and the Act on Funds Engaged in Business.[139]

115. The following section concentrates on the regulation of trade names of the two most common *types* of companies, i.e., the public limited company (*aktieselskab*) indicated by 'A/S' and the private limited company (*anpartsselskab*) indicated by 'ApS'.[140] Companies formed as either A/S or ApS must carry, and have

---

133. Author: Andrej Savin on the basis of the 1995 version text written by Henrik Engmark.
134. Act 426/2017 as most recently amended by Act 309/2018 (*Markedsføringsloven*).
135. Consolidated Act 1089/2015 (*Selskabsloven*).
136. Consolidated Act 1295/2013 (*Visse erhvervsdrivende virksomheder*).
137. Consolidated Act 88/2019 (*Varemærkeloven*).
138. Consolidated Act 1816/2015 (*Navnelov*).
139. Consolidated Act 1712/2014 (*Erhvervsdrivende* fonde).
140. *See* Ch. 2, §2. Partnerships and Corporations.

the sole right to use, the designations A/S and ApS, respectively in their names. The provisions regulating trade names for these companies are found in the Companies Act, section 2.

B. Registration

116. The company name must be registered with the Danish Business Authority (*Erhvervsstyrelsen*). After registration, the Business Authority performs a simple investigation to establish whether the same name has already been registered. A thorough investigation of the trade name in relation to other registers, intellectual property rights and unregistered names, must be carried out by the applicant itself. An application for registration of a name will be turned down if the Business Authority finds that the name is identical – phonetically or visually – with a name registered with the Authority. If the application for registration is turned down, the decision may be appealed to the Danish Commerce Appeal Board of the Ministry of Industry (*Erhvervsankenævnet*).[141]

If a third person believes that a registration interferes with his rights, the question can be referred to courts. The case must be brought within six months after publication in the Business Authority's online information system. Before registration is made, it is possible to check the name with the online information system.

C. Scope of Protection

117. Protection of a trade name is offered if the name meets the criteria set out in the Companies Act, section 2. The key element of the system is that names of such companies must be of distinctive character. The name must clearly individualize the company in such a manner that makes it possible to distinguish this particular company from others.

A company cannot, in a trade name, refer to family names, trademarks, business signs, etc. which the company does not have a lawful title to or use them in a manner which causes confusion. A company name may not refer to types of business which are not within the range of the business(es) in which the company deals. If a company changes business, it cannot continue to use the same name if the change is of a substantial character, i.e., a completely new line of activity.

118. Numbers, letters, family names, geographic names and purely descriptive names need to be individualized with other words before being able to be used. Names which are not distinctive enough may be offered protection if they cannot be confused with other names and if they are, at the same time, generally well established. Names which are distinctive are normally combinations of public names from different groups of words such as geographic names, family names, industries,

141. The Ministry of Industry, Business and Financial Affairs (*Erhvervsministeriet*) means the same as the Ministry of Industry.

numbers, etc. or original made-up names. Unoriginal made-up names, i.e., those in the public domain, may be individualized like other public names.

119. Denmark adheres to the Paris Convention[142] which, in Article 8, gives all foreign trade names protection without prior registration. The Convention is not implemented directly in Denmark, but the laws mentioned above produce the same effect. It is assumed that Article 8 in the Paris Convention offers protection to foreign names per se, but tests of how known the name is and how well the trade name is established are more likely to be used.

120. The foundation for the general protection of different trade names is contained in paragraph 22 of the Marketing Practices Act. The provision prevents other companies from using business characteristics or names which are not lawfully in their possession or using signs or names that would create confusion with other companies' assets including trade names. The wording 'signs' is interpreted broadly to cover assets established according to law and may include patents. Although exhaustive criteria cannot be given, courts have dealt with the problem extensively. Various factors must be taken into account, such as whether the use of a similar name is within the same industry. Violations of paragraph 22 of the Marketing Practices Act are sanctioned by fines.

II. Goodwill

A. Legislation

Goodwill denotes the value of an asset which is intangible but can be quantified for accounting purposes. No precise definition of goodwill exists in Danish law. Regulation of goodwill is found in the different areas and in particular in tax law, law on accounts and marketing law. Each area operates with a specific concept.

With regard to the legal protection, a company's goodwill is usually defined as its customer base. Goodwill is a result of the company's position in the market expressed by several components, including the company's geographic situation, the management in charge, major investment in advertising, etc. Although goodwill is rarely if ever explicitly mentioned directly, a variety of laws including trademark, marketing, tax, and competition law are assumed to apply nevertheless.

B. Scope of Protection

121. In case of a sale of a company in which remuneration for goodwill is included, a clause regarding future competition to protect the newly bought goodwill is often included.

---

142. The Paris Convention on the Protection of Industrial Property of 20 Mar. 1883 with later amendments.

122. It is established in case law that goodwill can be used as a collateral.[143] The Danish Supreme Court overturned prior case law, establishing that goodwill in business is used as the basis for credit and therefore potentially an object for collateral. It was established that goodwill may be used as collateral and be registered as such with the courts.

III. Know-How and Trade Secrets

123. The Danish legal system has no institutionalized protection of know-how, which is generally defined as the sum of a company's practical experiences and skills with regard to the production of specific products, provision of services or general *operation* of the company. The knowledge must be particular to that company and must have a secret or confidential character. Skills and experiences a person possesses merely due to its profession are not considered to be know-how.

124. Case law has defined two areas of protection with regard to know-how. First, the owner of the know-how enjoys protection against unauthorized exploitation by former employees.[144] Second, it has been established that know-how may be transferred and that a breach of contract may result in a ban on further use by the licensee.[145] Patent licences often include a clause on reciprocal exchange of know-how in connection with the patent and methods used to implement the invention. In case such a combined patent and know-how licence is terminated or the patent expires, the licensor is nevertheless entitled to royalty for continued use of the know-how.

125. The Law on Trade Secrets, implementing the 2016 EU Directive,[146] protects know-how used as a trade secret and has been in force since June 2018.[147] The law consolidated the rules from different sources which have hitherto been applicable to the matter. After the consolidation, the majority of the rules are located in the new Act, with the exception of rules on industrial espionage (criminal law) and good marketing practices (marketing law).

126. The text of the Act follows the directive closely, with very few exceptions. Like the Directive, the Act regulates acquisition, the use and disclosure, procedures, remedies and sanctions.

127. The Act defines trade secrets as secret information, with a trade value, which has been subjected to reasonable protective acts. Since this has hitherto been the working definition in Danish law,[148] the Act brings no changes.

143. *See* UfR 1993 p. 392/2 (Supreme Court).
144. *See* UfR 1963 p. 582 (Supreme Court) and UfR 1980 p. 717 (Supreme Court).
145. *See* UfR 1955 p. 765 (Supreme Court).
146. Directive 943/2016.
147. Act 309/2018 on Trade Secrets (*forretningshemmeligheder*)
148. *See* UfR 1960 p. 236.

128. The Danish implementation of the Directive follows its source rather closely, including the uncertainties which the main text contains. Thus, it would seem from Article 4, which covers unauthorized access, appropriation or copying of information but also 'any other conduct', that appropriation of trade secrets expressed orally may also be covered although this is not expressly mentioned. It is equally uncertain to which extent technical drawings, recipes, models, etc. might be protected.

129. A novelty in the Danish law is a six-month time limit for applying for provisional and precautionary measures. The limit runs from the moment the company learns of the violation. The rules on whether a provisional or precautionary measure could be issued are no longer to be found in the civil procedure rules but are located in the new Act. Contrary to the old rules, it is no longer necessary to demonstrate that irreparable damage would follow from continued violation, thus making the process of obtaining the measure somewhat easier. The extent of the possible measures in provisional and precautionary measures has also been somewhat extended. Finally, when demanding compensation, it is no longer necessary to demonstrate the extent of one's loss (as long as that loss exists) but it is sufficient to rely on the gain that the violator obtained. The new law modifies Danish Criminal law, which contains criminal sanctions for violations including fines and prison.

130. The general clause in the Marketing Practices Act requiring companies to conduct marketing in a good manner (section 3 of the Act) also provides a basic level of protection. This protection affects copying in particular and is less detailed and specific than similar rules in the laws regulating the intellectual property rights. As opposed to the intellectual property rights, the courts require that the person who copies is aware of his violation. The Marketing Practices Act only offers protection from misuse conducted by people from 'inside' the company. 'Outsiders' who unlawfully get access to the company's trade secrets may be stopped via a criminal law procedure.

131. The EU's competition law contains a group exemption of know-how licences from the general prohibition of competition distortion.[149] The provisions of this regulation also apply to Danish know-how licences.[150]

§2. Intellectual Property Rights

132. Intellectual property rights provide protection based on a legal monopoly granted to the holder against all the others. The protection varies depending on the type of intellectual property right and the special considerations relevant to each

149. Commission Regulation (EU) No 316/2014 of 21 Mar. 2014 on the application of Art. 101(3) of the Treaty on the Functioning of the European Union to categories of technology transfer agreements, *OJ L 93/17, 28.3.2014.*
150. Cf. Executive Order 622/2004 as most recently amended by 486/2005, issued under the Consolidated Competition Act 155/2018 s. 10.

type. The intellectual property rights are territorial, but international treaties have facilitated applications and registrations for adhering countries in different areas.

133. The EU operates the exhaustion principle with regard to all the intellectual property rights, compare Articles 34–36 TFEU and Case 78/70 *Deutsche Grammophon v. Metro*.[151] The owner of an intellectual property right cannot uphold the protection for patented, branded, or other types of goods which the owner or others with the owner's approval have lawfully marketed within the EU.

I. Trademarks

A. Legislation

134. The Danish law regulates trademarks in the Trade Marks Act and the Executive Order on Trademarks, which implements the EC Trademark Directive.[152] The executive order regulates in detail the procedures for application and registration.[153] Denmark has adhered to the Paris Convention[154] and the Nice Arrangement.[155] Denmark was not a member to the 1981 Madrid Arrangement until 1996 but has since acceded.[156] The Act also takes into account the EU trademark. Collective marks are owned by an association of undertakings whose members apply the marks to goods or services. A guaranty mark is a mark owned by a legal person who controls or regulates goods or services. The regulation of common marks is to a large extent the same as for trademarks. Only individual trademarks will be discussed hereinafter.

B. Registration

135. A trademark may be established by registration with the Patent and Trademark Authority (*Patent – og Varemærkestyrelsen*). Trademarks consist of all types of signs which serve the purpose of distinguishing the company's goods or services and which can be reproduced graphically; words, slogans, letters and numbers, figures, product's form, equipment or packages. Trademarks that only consist of signs or information designed to describe the product, for example, geographical origin, time production or value, do not constitute the required distinctive character. Trademarks may also legally be established simply by being used for goods or services.

151. *See* Directive 2001/29 (Copyright Directive) Art. 4, and Case 78/70 *Deutsche Grammophon v. Metro* (1971) ECR 487.
152. The Consolidated Trade Marks Act 88/2019 (*Varemærkeloven*) is based on the EU Directive 2015/2436 and Regulation (EU) 2017/1001.
153. Executive Order 1685/2018 on Application and Registration, etc. of Trade Marks and Collective Marks (*Ansøgning om registrering af varemærker og fælles mærker*).
154. The Paris Convention on the Protection of Industrial Property of 20 Mar. 1883 with later amendments.
155. Convention on International Classification of Goods and Services of 1957.
156. Executive Order 131/1996.

In case a trademark does not meet the required distinctive character by the time it is taken into use, it may later become a legally protected trademark if the distinctive character is developed simply by virtue of the mark becoming well established. Trademarks are normally registered because registration offers a number of advantages. Most important is probably the Patent and Trademark Authority examination of possible violations of the existing trademarks, which is performed in connection with the trademark registration. Registration also means protection against violations through future registrations. Part 2 of the Trade Mark Act concerns the registration of trademarks. A trademark is registered via an application that includes a reproduction of the trademark and information on the applicant. The application must also include an indication of which goods or services the trademark is sought for.

136. The registration of a trademark must be published. After the publication, anyone may send objections to the Patent and Trademark Authority in writing within two months from the date of publication. It is not a requirement for registration that the trademark is in use, but the registration will be terminated if the trademark is not in use within five years unless the non-use can be justified. The Patent and Trademark Authority decisions may be brought to the Appeal Board for Patents and Trademarks (*Ankenævnet for Patenter og Varemærker*) by the applicant. The complaint must be submitted within two months after the Patent and Trademark Authority's decision. Decisions of the Appeal Board may be challenged in courts.

137. The principle of priority, i.e., the 'first to file principle', is found in section 7 in the Trade Mark Act. This is *modified* by section 8, which states that a later registered trademark may exist regardless of an earlier trademark if the applicant applied in good faith and the owner of the earlier trademark knew and accepted the use in Denmark of the later trademark for five consecutive years.

138. A number of reasons for denying registration of a trademark are listed in section 13. For example, trademarks *cannot* be registered if they are contrary to other laws, regulations on product descriptions, etc. Trademarks contrary to the public order and decency will also be denied registration as will be trademarks intended to mislead, for example with regard to the product's nature, quality or geographic origin. Trademarks will also not be registered if they contain a part of, the name of a person or a company which another person is entitled to.

139. It is a matter for the courts to decide whether the use of a trademark is contrary to any regulation; with regard to registered trademarks, anyone with a legal interest may have the Patent and Trademark Authority examine whether the conditions for a valid trademark exists. In cases of a deliberate violation of a trademark, section 42 of the Trade Mark Act offers fines as a sanction and, in certain severe cases of trademark violation, prison terms of up to one year and six months.

C. Scope of Protection

140. Section 1 of the Trade Mark Act states that the protection is a right which prevents others from using signs which are identical or mistakable with the trademark in their business. The rule is supported by section 22 in the Marketing Practices Act,[157] which also prevents any company from using business signs, etc. which are not legally in their possession. Private use of trademarks owned by others is allowed. The content of the protection offered to a trademark is found in section 4 of the Trade Mark Act. It states that the owner of a trademark may prevent others from using signs which are either identical to or which appear similar to the trademark in the owner's business if:

(1) the sign is identical with the trademark, and the goods or services for which the sign has been put to use are identical with the goods or services for which the trademark is protected; or
(2) the sign is identical with or similar to the trademark, and the goods or services are identical or similar if there exists a likelihood of confusion including a likelihood of association with the trademark.

In deciding whether a trademark violates an existing trademark both criteria must be examined, i.e., is there resemblance between the trademarks and the resemblance between the type of goods. The first involves a judgment of the graphical appearance of the trademarks and the second involves the market analysis for the goods, for example, to what degree the products are similar or substitutable. It is important to note that the judgment is a general impression of the two criteria with equal weight. Case law shows a connection between the two criteria; if, for example, the goods are the same then the requirements for constituting trademark resemblance are less stringent and vice versa. Section 4, paragraph 2 of the Act introduces an exception to the main rule with regard to well-known trademarks. This is known as the 'Kodak doctrine' and offers a trademark owner the possibility of preventing the use of a trademark regardless of the lack of goods similarity, if the trademark is generally well-known (e.g. Coca Cola).

141. Section 5 in the Trade Mark Act lists limitations in the rights of the owner of a trademark. In accordance with good marketing practice, others may use:

(1) their own name and address;
(2) indications concerning the kind, quality, quantity, intended purpose, value or geographical origin of the goods or services, the time of production of the goods or of rendering the services or other characteristics of the goods or services; or
(3) the trademark when it is necessary to indicate the purpose of goods or service especially fittings or spare parts.

---

157. Act 426/2017 on Marketing Practices as most recently amended by Act 309/2018 (*Markedsføringsloven*).

142. If a trademark becomes a common designation or description for something, the trademark may be declared invalid. This kind of development must be controlled carefully since the examples of cases regarding old trademarks which have become general descriptions of goods are numerous, for example, Gramophone, compare section 28 paragraph 2, subparagraph 2 in the Trade Mark Act.

D. *Transfer*

143. Trademarks may be transferred and licences may also be granted. As opposed to other intellectual property rights, compulsory licences are not possible. As with patents, trademarks are subject to litigation by creditors. Trademarks may be inherited in accordance with Danish laws of succession.

E. *Duration*

144. There is no limitation on how long a trademark can exist. The registration needs formal renewal every ten years. A non-registered trademark is valid as long as the trademark is used.

F. *Employee Rights*

145. No statutory provisions exist with regard to employees' rights to trademarks. Thus, problems that occur with inventions do not exist. A trademark remains the company's property.

II. Copyrights

A. *Legislation*

146. In 1961, a Nordic cooperation in the field of copyright resulted in a number of similar acts in the Nordic countries. The Danish Copyright Act is still based on the principles resulting from that cooperation, although it has been altered several times, most recently in 2014.[158]

In February 1994, the Danish Minister of Culture had put forward a new Draft Act on Copyright. The proposal was again a result of negotiations between the Nordic countries and its main purpose was to carry out a thorough revision of copyright regulation. It rested on a major reform of the copyright area based on eight reports

158. Consolidated Act 1144/2014 on Copyright (*Ophavsretsloven* as most recently amended by Act 719/2018.

from the period of 1981 to 1990. The central elements were the following: the Photograph Act was incorporated in the Copyright Act; the right to produce private copies was made more precise, emphasizing that it only covered physical persons and not legal persons; the right to freely use recordings of radio and television broadcasts in hospitals, prisons, etc.; an improvement in the licence system for photocopying in companies, etc. Extensive discussions took place and a final new Copyright Act went into effect in 1995. Most of the provisions of the present Act stem from the 1995 one.

Denmark has ratified the Rome Convention,[159] the Bern Convention,[160] and the Universal Copyright Convention.[161] These Conventions are administered by the World Intellectual Property Organization. Besides the acts mentioned, extensive case law exists. Danish law has also been markedly influenced by copyright harmonization within the EU, for example, the Copyright Directive, the Software Directive and the Rental and Lending Rights Directive.

In the future, it is expected that the Commission of the European Union will put forward new proposals that adequately address the changes that the information society brings. Also, The Agreement on Trade Related Aspects of Intellectual Property Rights, effective from 1996, includes copyright and has had a significant effect on the future regulation of international trade and intellectual property rights.

B. Registration

147. The creation of a copyright does not require public registration or other action. The copyright is granted immediately when the work is created.

C. Scope of Protection

148. Copyright was originally intended to offer protection from plagiarism of works of art but has shown to offer valuable means of protection within the area of technological innovation. Chapter 1 of the Copyright Act deals with the regular copyright which grants protection to literature and works of art regardless of the means of expression. Maps, drawings and computer software fall within the definition of literature. Chapter 5 deals with the so-called neighbouring rights, which are regulated in the above-mentioned Rome Convention and Phonogram Convention.[162] These rules concern protection of performing artists, phonogram producers, radio and television broadcasts, catalogues and press releases. They will not be dealt with further.

159. Rome Convention on Protection on Performing Artists, Phonogram Manufactors and Radio companies of 1961 adhered to in 1965.
160. Bern Convention on the Protection of Literary and Artistic works of 1886 with amendments of 1903.
161. Universal Copyright Convention of 1952 with amendments in 1971 ratified in 1979.
162. Phonogram Convention of 1971 ratified by Denmark in 1977.

149. The content of the copyright more is laid down in section 2 in the Copyright Act, which states that a copyright is a sole right to control the creation by producing copies and by making it available to the public in the creation's original form or in an altered form.

150. The Copyright Act offers no specific criteria which a certain creation must meet to obtain protection. There is the requirement of originality, i.e., the creation must originate from the creator himself by means of an independent intellectual process. As opposed to patent law, there is no requirement regarding the creation's novelty. A copyright is obtained even in cases of unoriginal or works of mediocre quality, as long as no direct copying takes place. No quality requirements exist apart from the fact that the creation must be the product of a certain independent intellectual process, enhancing the creation with a certain distinctive character. Copyright does not protect ideas but only their 'expression', i.e., their concrete embodiment. Creations within the technical world must seek protection in patent law.

151. Translations, revisions and other modifications of main works are offered copyright protection in their own right. A new and independent creation based on the main work is, therefore, protected independently.

152. Exceptions to copyright are laid down in Chapter 2 of the Copyright Act. These are a result of the classical contrast between a monopoly right and the societal interest in spreading innovation. Section 11 allows transient and temporary copies in the technical process of transferring works in a network (e.g., computer caching). Section 12 states that copies of an otherwise protected creation may be made for private use. The provision does not allow other exploitation of protected creations and does not apply to the copying of software programmes. Other exceptions include reproduction for educational purposes (section 13), reproduction by business enterprises (section 14), reproduction by hospitals (section 15), archives, libraries and museums (section 16) and disabled persons (section 17).

153. Quotation from a copyright-protected work is allowed in accordance with good practices and in a scope determined by the quotation's purpose. Good practices are open to court interpretation. Exact criteria cannot be given for the application of the exception but a wide right to quotation is granted when the quotation is part of a scientific analysis. However, the right to quote cannot be used to circumvent the right holder's exclusive right. The sanctions for violation of copyright are interim measures, fines, damages and confiscation or destruction (Chapter 7, Copyright Act).

D. Transfer

154. Rights in literary and artistic works can be transferred partially or completely, to one licensee or several, in respect of one territory or several. The possibility of creditor litigation in copyright is limited. The creator's right to control his creation cannot be the object of creditor litigation if the right rests with the right holder or anyone who has acquired it by means of succession. Creditor litigation is limited to individual copies of copyright-protected works. An exception to this covers scripts, certain preparations for works of art and copies that are not exhibited or in any other way intended for publication. Rights to literary and artistic works can be subject to succession laws.

155. After having transferred the copyright, the author is still entitled to be identified by name as such. This right is referred to as the creator's 'droit morale'.

E. Duration

156. The old Copyright Act provided that protection was granted for a period of fifty years after the death of the author or if the work was published anonymously, fifty years after the year of publication. The protection period for foreign works is based on the Bern Convention. Works which enjoy a longer period of protection in foreign countries will not be automatically granted longer protection in Denmark. When the period of protection expires in a foreign country, the work is not entitled to protection in Denmark. The period of protection has been extended to seventy years in the new Copyright Act.

F. Employee Rights

157. Employees' creations are not covered in the Copyright Act and unless the matter is otherwise subject to agreement, the copyright will belong to the employee. An exception exists when general exploitation of the creation is a major part of the company's business, for example, with newspapers.

III. Protection of Photographs

A. Legislation

158. Until 1995, photographs were not covered in the Copyright Act but were subject to a separately regulated right of short duration. Today, section 70 protects authors of photographic works for the duration of fifty years from the date when the picture was taken. Other sections of the Copyright Act apply correspondingly to photographic works.

IV. Patents

A. Legislation

159. Danish patent law has undergone various changes in the past years, the most recent taking place in 2012. Of the modern treaties on international cooperation in the field of patents, Denmark has ratified and implemented the Patent Cooperation Treaty (PCT),[163] the Budapest Treaty,[164] the European Patent Convention (EPC)[165] and the EU Patent Agreement (ECPA).[166] These are all incorporated in the Patent Act,[167] which is built on the major Nordic revision of patent law in 1967. By joining the EPC system in 1989, the case law of the European Patent Organization is now a guide for the Danish administration. Furthermore, Denmark has acceded to the Paris Convention[168] and the Convention of 1961 on establishment of the World Intellectual Property Rights Organization, as well as other conventions.[169]

The main source of patent law is the Patent Act and a number of executive orders which have been issued to lay down detailed regulations concerning secret patents, patents on drugs, yearly fees, the Patent and Trademark Authority (*Patent og Varemærkestyrelsen*), the Appeal Board for Patents and Trademarks (*Ankenævnet for Patenter og Varemærker*) and patent applications. Other orders of minor importance have also been enacted. The case law is, in spite of the importance of the area, relatively scarce. Disputes, however, are often settled through mediation and arbitration.

In 2014 Denmark proceeded with the ratification of the Agreement on a Unified Patent Court,[170] which constitutes the legal basis for the establishment of a Unified Patent Court (UPC) in the EU. UPC will become a common EU patent court open for participation of all EU Member States once the agreement is ratified. Additionally, Denmark participates in the European patent with unitary effect.[171] Patent with unitary effect can be requested from the date UPC enters into force.

B. Registration

160. The administration of the Danish patent system is handled by the Patent and Trademark Authority (*Patent- og Varemærkestyrelsen*) which is organized under the Ministry of Industry. Without giving a positive definition, section 1 of the Patent

163. Patent Cooperation Treaty signed in Washington 1970.
164. Budapest Treaty on International Recognition of Deposit of Microorganisms of 1977.
165. European Patent Convention signed in Münich 1973.
166. EC Patent Agreement agreed in Luxembourg in 1989.
167. Consolidated Act 90/2019 (*Patentlov*).
168. The Paris Convention on the Protection of Industrial Property of 20 Mar. 1883 with later amendments.
169. Convention on International Classification of Patents on Inventions of 1971 and The European Council Convention signed in Strasbourg in 1963 on Co-ordination of Certain Parts of the Material Patent Law.
170. Agreement on a Unified Patent Court, OJ C 175/1, 20.6.2013., (not yet in force).
171. Regulation (EU) 1275/2012.

Act provides that inventions which may have industrial application can be patented. Sections 2, 3 and 4 enumerate what cannot be regarded as invention, including discoveries, scientific theories, mathematical methods, artworks, computer software, surgical methods and animals. In 1983, medical patents were included as patentable, but therapeutical methods are still excluded. The term 'invention' in the Patent Act equals the generally accepted international understanding of the concept, which limits patents to technical matters.

It is a prerequisite that inventions have an industrial application. This must be understood in the widest sense and includes any kind of industry. The interpretation of the term in practice is in accordance with the Paris Convention, Article 1, paragraph 3, and EPC Article 57. The invention must also be reproducible, which may influence the possibility of the granting patents on biological matters.

161. Patents are granted on the basis of an application for registration. When filing a patent application, it is necessary to decide whether the application shall cover only Denmark, be an international application according to the PCT (Chapter 3 in the Patent Act), or be an application for a European Patent according to the European Patent Office Regulations (Chapter 10a of the Patent Act). All three types of applications may be filed with the Patent and Trademark Authority. If filing is for an international patent, the countries which the application covers must be specified. The procedures differ but for all three types of applications the Patent and Trademark Authority will perform a preliminary examination and publication of the invention.

The patent application must be in a written form and must contain a description of the invention including any necessary drawings. The application must precisely indicate what is sought, i.e., the patent claim. The invention must be described in such a way that a skilled person in the art will be able to carry out the investigation.

An applicant is granted priority from the day of application, i.e., the 'first to file principle'. Section 6 of the Patent Act gives a patent applicant one year from the application day to file in other countries adhering to the Paris Convention without loss of priority.

162. The price for a patent effective in Denmark varies, with the application fee being DKK 3,000 and yearly fee DKK 500 for the first year but rising afterwards. The Patent and Trademark Authority offers several kinds of services against fees including investigations of patents and novelty. A representative in Denmark is required in case the applicant does not have a permanent address.

163. The invention to be patented must be new and must distinguish itself substantially from what is known at the day of the application, i.e., the invention is required to have a certain qualitative level. These concepts are in conformity with European case law and patent practice. The requirement for the invention to be new has been interpreted quite strictly so that the invention in terms of novelty must be both global and objective. A qualitative level of an invention is difficult to assess. The Patent and Trademark Authority will check the invention against the state-of-the-art within the field, which must be improved so that the invention is not obvious to a person skilled in the art.

C. Scope of Protection

164. The Patent Act defines the scope of the sole right obtained by the applicant in accordance with ECPA.[172] Section 3 paragraph 1 of the Patent Act includes production, supply, trade or use of the invention as patent holder's sole rights. The basis for the scope of patent claim is the application including the descriptions and drawings. This is equivalent to EPK Article 69 with the protocol.

165. In addition to private use, other limitations on the patentee's rights are introduced. Section 4 of the Patent Act allows others to use the invention if it was already in use before the date of the application or if substantial amounts were invested in preparation for its use. This implies that the use must have been secret; otherwise, the invention would not have met the novelty requirement in the first place. A formal application to establish this right of pre-utilization is not needed. The right cannot subsequently be extended in a qualitative manner.

166. The patentee may bring complaints about the decisions regarding a patent's validity to the Patent and Trademark Authority or applications for extension to the Patent and Trademark Appeal Board. The complaint must be submitted within two months after the Authority's decision. Decisions from the Patent and Trademark Appeal Board may be challenged in court.

167. The sanctions a patent owner has at its disposal in case of violation fall into four categories. First, it is possible to invoke interim measures. Interim measures require a collateral, which is usually a substantial amount of money.[173] Danish case law gives examples of several million DKK. Second, the Patent Act operates with fines and imprisonment for up to one year (section 57, Patent Act). It is a prerequisite that the violation is conducted intentionally. Cases of imprisonment for patent violation are rare and require aggravating circumstances. Third, the patent owner is entitled to payment for unauthorized use of the invention and compensation for any losses caused by a violation. In practice, negligence about the existence of the patent is enough to establish a violation but may result in a reduction in compensation. The compensation is usually small and the causal link difficult to prove. The patent holder may claim lost profits from sales, reduction of goodwill or the expenses to establish a violation. Payment for unauthorized use will always be levied regardless of whether an actual loss is proved. Finally, section 59 in the Patent Act gives the possibility of destruction of the violating items if the court finds it reasonable.

D. Transfer

168. The patent may be transferred by several means. Licensing an invention for commercial purposes is covered in section 43 of the Patent Act, which also states that a licence of a patent cannot be transferred to others without the consent of the

172. ECPA Arts 29, 29a, 29b, 29c, 30, 3 1, 3 la, 3 lb and 3 lc.
173. Consolidated Administration of Justice Act 1284/2018 *(Retsplejeloven)* Ch. 40.

licensor. The EU competition law operates with a group exemption of the patent licences[174] from the general prohibition against distortion of competition. This regulation applies to Danish patent licences if they affect community trade.

169. The Patent Act lays down the procedures for compulsory licensing. Compulsory licensing is relatively rare and requires several conditions to be present, as well as a court decision. In addition to copyright regulations, creditor litigation is applicable. Patents may also be inherited according to Danish laws on succession.

E. Duration

170. Patents expire twenty years from the day of application. The patent also expires if the yearly fee had not been paid. Danish patent law operates with the principle of exhaustion of patent rights. Section 3, paragraph 3, subparagraph 2, states that the patentee must tolerate acts regarding products which have been marketed lawfully in Denmark. Due to Denmark's obligations within the EU, exhaustion of rights covers the entire EU.

F. Employee Rights

171. Employee inventions are regulated in the Act on Employee Inventions,[175] which states in section 3 that employees who make a patentable invention acquire the right to the invention. If the invention falls within the business of the employer's company or it is the result of a specific assignment given to the employee, the employer acquires the right to the invention. The employee shall immediately notify the employer about any inventions, and the employer has four months to decide whether the invention shall be patented. The employee has the right to a fair compensation for the invention if the value of the invention exceeds what the employee reasonably is supposed to perform, compare section 8 in the Act. The relationship may – with exemption of the right to compensation – be subject to an agreement between the parties.

V. Utility Models

A. Legislation

172. In 1992, the Act on Utility Models was introduced.[176] Before 1992, Denmark had no form of protection for small inventions and other technical innovations

174. Regulation 316/2014 on technology transfer agreements (Technology Transfer Block Exemption).
175. Consolidated Act 104/2012 on Employees' Inventions (*Arbejdstageres opfindelser*).
176. Act 91/2019 on Utility Models (*Brugsmodeller m.v.*).

like tools, etc. Innovations of this kind were often in the grey area between the protection of a patent and the protection of a registered design. Usually, such innovations lacked the quality level required by patent law and were disqualified for protection by industrial design laws, which only cover the visual aspects of a design or a pattern. The Utility Model Act is, with some simplifications, based on the same principles as the Patent Act. It has been of paramount importance in creating a system which is perceived by companies as an easy, fast and cheap way of acquiring protection.

B. Registration

173. Section I of the Utility Model Act states that any innovation which may be used industrially and which implies a solution to a technical problem may be registered as a utility model. Plants and animals, raw materials and other examples listed in section 1 paragraphs 2, 3 and 4 of the Utility Models Act cannot be granted status as a utility model.

The innovation must be new in relation to what was known before the date of the application, but the requirements are less strict than those in the Patent Act. An innovation must include some technological progress so that it is not obvious to a person skilled in the art. Contrary to the Patent Act, procedures cannot be registered as utility models. Case law and practices from administration of the patent law are assumed to be applicable. The Patent and Trademark Authority is responsible for administration of the Utility Model Act. Complaints against Authority decisions may be brought to the Patent and Trademark Appeal Board[177] and eventually before the courts.

C. Scope of Protection

174. To develop adequate protection for inventors, section 11 of the Utility Model Act allows the applicant to rely on a patent application completely or partly as the basis for an application for registration of a utility model. The procedure is especially valuable in cases where a patent is not granted, for example, because of the level of the invention. However, an application for a utility model cannot be the basis for a patent application.

175. Contrary to the registration procedure for patents, the Patent and Trademark Authority will only confirm that certain formal conditions are met, such as whether the innovation can be used industrially, and that it does not fall into a category of excluded innovations, etc. To hasten the application period, the Patent and Trademark Authority is not obliged to investigate the level of the innovation and its novelty. It is the applicant's option to require the Authority to examine the utility

177. Executive Order 892/2009 *(Ankenævnet for patenter og varemærker)*.

model's novelty and its level of invention against a fee. Moreover, any person may pay a fee and request the Authority to start the above-mentioned investigations for a certain utility model.

176. Finally, Part 3 of the Utility Model Act deals with international utility models. These follow the PCT[178] application procedures, which offer the opportunity for applying for a patent and a utility model in the same international application. The formal requirements for the application and the registration are laid down in an executive order.[179] A registration of a utility model may be invalidated by others in procedures similar to those in the patent system.

D. Duration

177. The period of protection is ten years. The period consists of two consecutive periods of three years and one period of four years. The application fee covers the first period of three years. Thereafter new fees must be paid.

E. Employee Rights

178. These are the same as for patents, compare above.

VI. Design Protection

A. Legislation

179. Since the introduction of the common Nordic Act on Design in 1970[180] very little case law in this area has been reported. The EU introduced Community Design in 2002.[181] This is a unitary EU-wide right with both a registered and unregistered form.

180. Design protection lies in the grey area between copyright and patents. The Copyright Act states that design copyright does not exclude protection by copyright. Design protects the two-dimensional visual look of a product and therefore does not prevent the granting of a patent with regard to the product's technical functions.

178. Patent Cooperation Treaty signed in Washington 1970.
179. Executive Order 1605/2006 on the Treatment of Utility Model Applications and Registered Utility Models. (*Bekendtgørelse om brugsmodelansøgningers og registrerede brugsmodellers behandling*).
180. Consolidated Act 219/2017 on Design (*Designlov*).
181. Regulation 6/2002 on Community Design, amended in Regulations 876/2007 and 877/2007.

B. Registration

181. Section 1 of the Design Act defines a design as the image of a product's visual look or an ornamental image. Protection may not be obtained for a mere idea of the product but rather only for the visual look which the design represents. As with patents, designs must meet the criteria of novelty. Section 2 of the Act states that a design must distinguish itself from what is known before the date of the application. In case the protection of a design is granted in another country, the registration may be given priority in Denmark if the foreign registration is not more than six months old. Danish law does not contain mandatory provisions with regard to creations made by employees.

182. The application procedures are largely similar as for patents. A written application must be submitted to the Patent and Trademark Authority and must be in conformity with the specified requirements.[182] The application needs to have a picture enclosed which adequately represents the design. The Authority examines the application to ensure that the terms of registration are met. This type of examination is not the same as patent examination. The Authority only examines whether the design can be registered and whether it is violating an already registered design.

C. Scope of Protection

183. The protection brings a sole right to commercial exploitation of the design. It is worth noting that commercial exploitation does not cover private use of the design. The protection is also only offered to commercial production and marketing of products. Thus, there is no protection against the image of the design copyright in printing.

184. The Design Act includes a provision covering design exhaustion in section 12. The exhaustion principle applies to design in the same manner as with the patent law. In the Design Act, the protection is limited only to products of the same or similar kind as those for which the design is registered. The impact of this is that protection is not offered for commercial exploitation of the design when the exploitation is within a completely different industry or product line. This principle is known from trademark law but is not internationally widespread in design protection.

185. Any applicant has the right to bring the Patent and Trademark Authority decision before the Patent and Trademark Appeal Board.[183] A decision of the Appeal Board may be appealed in court.

---

182. Executive Order 1099/2008 (*Ansøgning og registrering af design*).
183. Executive Order 892/2009 (*Ankenævnet for patenter og varemærker*).

D. Duration

186. The maximum period of protection is fifteen years. A registration of a design copyright is valid for five years from the day of the application and may be further renewed for two periods of five years.

VII. Computer Chips

A. Legislation

187. The protection of computer chips or semiconductors was established by law in 1987 with the Semiconductor Act.[184] The Act is an implementation of an EU Directive[185] intended to establish a system equivalent to that already in existence in the USA and Japan for the protection of circuit layout designs also referred to as 'mask works'. The Semiconductor Act defines semiconductors technically and in a manner consistent with the knowledge available in 1987. In Article 1, paragraph 2 of the Directive, it is stated that the Council of Ministers may change the definition of semiconductors if technical development so requires. A semiconductor's topography is defined in the act as a number of connected pictures which, regardless of their fixing or coding, represent the three-dimensional pattern of those layers of which the semiconductor is made.

B. Registration

188. Registration of the topography is necessary to obtain protection. The application must be submitted to the Patent and Trademark Authority no more than two years from the day that the topography was used in business for the first time. It is not significant where in the world the first use took place. If the topography is a result of the inventor's own intellectual efforts and not common knowledge within the semiconductor industry, a sole right to the topography can be granted. If the topography consists of elements which are common knowledge within the semiconductor industry, protection will only be granted if the combination of these elements meets the requirements stated above.

---

184. Consolidated Act 92/2019 on Protection of the Topografy of Semiconductors (*Beskyttelse af halvleder produkters udformning (topografi)). See also* Executive Order 482/2003 on Application of Protection of Semiconductor's Topography (*Ansøgning om beskyttelse af halvlederprodukters udformning (topografi*)).
185. EC Directive (87/154) on the Legal Protection of Semiconductors' Topography of 16 Dec. 1986.

C. Scope of Protection

189. To obtain protection, the acquirer of the sole right must have allegiance to the EU. Protection can be given to a person who has citizenship or lives in a country of the UU, or to a company conducting business in the EU when the topography is invented by a person employed in the company. The Minister of Industry may extend the scope of the act to physical and legal persons who do not have the said allegiance to a EU country. The WTO countries are subject to this exception.[186]

190. The protection does not cover others' use of the topography or semiconductor when it is marketed by the inventor himself in a EU country, i.e., European Union exhaustion. In addition, the original inventor cannot prevent reverse engineering that leads to new topographies. Protection is offered against pure copying, and the burden of proof is with the alleged infringer. The measures under protection stretch from fair compensation and damages to destruction, fining and, under severe circumstances, imprisonment.

Complaints over decisions made by the Patents and Trademarks Authority may be brought to the Patent and Trademark Appeal Board within two months after the Authority's decision.

D. Duration

191. The period of protection runs from ten years from the year of registration. The protection runs from the day the application for protection is submitted to the Patents and Trademarks Authority.

E. Employee Rights

192. In accordance with the Act on Employee Inventions, a company will acquire the sole right to a semiconductor topography invented by an employee, unless otherwise agreed, if such an invention falls within the scope of the employee's contract.

VIII. Biotechnical Inventions

193. The protection of biotechnology is one of the hotly debated topics within the area of intellectual property rights. The debate arises partly because of the importance of innovations in genetic engineering and partly because of the ethical questions arising from technological advances.

186. Executive Order 1274/1996 on Extension of the Legal Protection of Semiconductor's Topography to Encompass Persons from Certain Countries and Territories (*Udvidelse af den retlige beskyttelse af halvlederprodukters topografi til også at omfatte personer fra visse lande og territorier*).

194. In general, there is no protection offered for new varieties of animals or any biological processes essential for the production of animals or plants, section 1, paragraph 4 of the Patent Act. This is in accordance with other European countries and EPC Article 53(b). It is modified by the fact that a patent may be granted for microbiological processes and their products. The distinction between micro – and macro-biology is traditional and cannot be relied on for future technology advances. For example, patents in brewing technology and pharmacology have long been based on yeasts and ferments, which are living organisms.

195. The general requirement of description in the Patent Act may cause complications with regard to microbiological processes. It is often practically impossible to describe the microorganism, and usually, when it is possible it may be difficult for any third party to develop it. In these cases, the Budapest Treaty,[187] which Denmark adheres to, requires a deposit of samples of new or inaccessible microorganisms in recognized culture collections. This gives other persons the possibility of having a sample delivered in Denmark. Many inventors do not approve of this provision, which gives others the possibility to grow large quantities of the same microorganism. This, and the fact that the legal regulations do not follow the technological advances has led to a situation where many inventors treat biotechnology inventions as trade secrets. This is particularly the case for companies that produce synthetic penicillin. The cultures which are the bases for these inventions are regarded as trade secrets. This is a consequence of the implicit principle in the Patent Act that an invention must be reproducible. The result of the existing provisions is that only genetically engineered microorganisms may be patented.

196. The EU Commission has recognized that protection of biotechnological inventions is crucial to strengthening the competitiveness of the European bioindustry. The EU passed a Directive on the Protection of 'biotechnological inventions',[188] which led to a debate on the ethical issues involved. The Directive is implemented in Danish legislation. Patents on the human body and its elements including genes or gene sequences cannot be granted (Article 5(1)). However, an element which is isolated from the body or produced with the aid of a technical process, including the sequence of a gene, may constitute a patentable invention. The Directive states that a patent cannot be rejected because its subject is a living organism. Microorganisms, plants and animals will be patentable as long as they do not establish a sort or a race.

The EPO approved a much disputed patent application in 1992. The application covered the so-called Oncomouse. The 'Oncomouse' is a genetically produced mouse that quickly develops cancer. The mouse was initially developed and patented in the US. Since Denmark adheres to the EPC, a patent issued outside Denmark can technically also be granted in Denmark. As mentioned above, there is no conflict of rules between the Patent Act and the EPC, which both state that patents cannot be granted on animals. In the argumentation for granting the patent, EPO has

187. Budapest Treaty on International Recognition of Deposit of Micro-organisms of 1977.
188. European Parliament and Council Directive 98/44/EC of 6 Jul. 1998 on the legal protection of biotechnological inventions.

considered the Oncomouse to be a product of microbiological processes and thus not an animal. The decision was and remains controversial. After an unsuccessful challenge that ended in 2004, the patent expired in 2006.

IX. Plant Breeders' Rights

197. Contrary to animal breeders', plant breeders' innovations are protected by law. The Act on New Plants[189] is the Danish implementation of the 1978-version of the 'Union Internationale pour la Protection des Obtensions Vegetables'. The protection offered to plant breeders is similar to the protection known from the Patent Act in the sense that the right may be used to prevent third parties from commercially offering propagating material without a licence. To obtain protection of a particular variety of a plant life, the variety must be registered with the Board of New Plants (*Plantenyhedsnævnet*). The Board of New Plants conducts an examination to control if the variety is registerable; if so, it will be registered in the Register of New Plants (*Plantenyhedsregisteret*). The right only covers the particular plant which has been registered. Anyone is free to use a registered variety for further breeding.

198. If the owner of a variety does not live in the EU, the application for registration must be submitted by a representative with full powers who lives in Denmark. The Register of New Plants is open for public access, but information on hybrid varieties, genealogical components and descriptions may be kept secret on request. Violations of plant breeder's right are punishable with fines. The registration requires the payment of a fee.

199. The Board of New Plants issues a letter of protection valid for one year which may be prolonged every year for twenty-five years starting from the issuing date of the letter of protection.

189. Consolidated Act 10/2017 on New Plants (*Plantenyheder*).

Chapter 6. Bankruptcy and Related Institutions

§1. General Survey

200. In Denmark, the legal provisions for proceedings in bankruptcy and similar proceedings can be found in the Bankruptcy Act of 1977 (hereinafter 'BA').[190,191] Besides bankruptcy, the Act contains legal provisions for reconstruction. Reconstruction may be compositions with creditors or a transfer of the business activity. Reconstruction gives a period in which a reconstructor shall try to implement a composition or a transfer of the business activity in order to continue the company. If the business activity is transferred, the debtor (a natural person or a company) will probably be adjudged bankrupt. In order to achieve a legal framework in the period of reconstruction, the reconstruction has to be adjudged by a Bankruptcy Court.

201. The Danish system has been built up in such a way that an insolvent debtor – whether a company or person – may file a petition of reconstruction to the Bankruptcy Court. The petition is voluntary but is used by the majority of those who have become insolvent to such an extent that the activities cannot continue without establishment of an arrangement with the creditors. However, a creditor does also have the opportunity to file a petition of reconstruction. The rules about reconstruction are dealt with in §2.

202. Under the BA, an arrangement with the creditors can take place as a composition scheme which implies a partial renunciation of the claim. This can only take place if a majority of creditors is not against it. As these rules are very oriented towards bankruptcy, they will be dealt with in paragraph 4 following the rules about bankruptcy. An arrangement, with the creditors, can, of course, take place as a voluntary arrangement which means that an arrangement, is made – without the interference of the Bankruptcy Court – with the creditors who agree to enter into an agreement.

203. Furthermore, the BA contains a special set of rules called 'rescheduling of debts' (*gældssanering*), which implies that natural persons who are not – or no longer – engaged in commerce or industry and who are hopelessly in debt according to the decision of the Bankruptcy Court, could have the debt reduced to an amount to be paid by the debtor during a shorter number of years – it could even be decided that the debt should be completely annulled.

204. If an arrangement with the creditors cannot be established, the debtor will generally be adjudged bankrupt and often on account of his own petition. If the debtor is under construction and if a composition with creditors or a transfer of the business activity cannot be established, the debtor is adjudged bankrupt. In this connection, it should be added that an insolvent company cannot be liquidated. If an

190. Author: Hans Viggo Godsk Pedersen.
191. Consolidated Act 11/2014 on Bankruptcy (*Konkursloven*).

insolvent company is going to be wound up, it is subject to bankruptcy proceedings. Therefore, the rules of bankruptcy are applicable to companies as well as enterprises run as personal enterprises.

§2. RECONSTRUCTION

205. A debtor who finds himself unable to fulfil his obligations may file a petition of reconstruction, BA, section 7 and section 11. The petition of reconstruction should be presented to the Bankruptcy Court proposing a person to be appointed as reconstructor and a person to be appointed as so-called mandatory who has knowledge of accountancy (accounting expert), compare further details about reconstruction below under Part I, Chapter 6, §2.I. A petition of reconstruction may also be filed by a creditor. When a petition of reconstruction has been given, the so-called date of notice sets in, which, among other things, is of importance when fixing the deadlines of voidance. During the reconstruction, special rules apply as to the debtor's disposal of his property, and the creditors will be restricted in their access to seek satisfaction of their claims in the debtor's assets. In return, the creditors get a certain knowledge of the debtor's financial circumstances during the reconstruction. In order to avoid that, one creditor should prevent the establishment of a mutual agreement with all the creditors. The BA section 24 states that the Bankruptcy Court is to postpone the treatment of a petition in bankruptcy during reconstruction, so the reconstruction can be continued.

I. Reconstructor and Mandatory Person

206. As already mentioned, the Bankruptcy Court appoints a reconstructor and an accounting expert when petition of reconstruction has been given. The Bankruptcy Court is not bound by the proposal in the petition but is free to appoint another reconstructor, BA, section 11 a. In most cases, the persons proposed in the petition of reconstruction will be appointed. In the majority of cases, the reconstructor will be a lawyer, but this is not mandatory. Normally a registered accountant or a State-authorized public accountant will be appointed, as the accounting expert.

207. Not later than one week after the appointment, the reconstructor must inform all known creditors about the reconstruction, BA, section 11 b. The latest available accounts must be attached to the notification as well as: (1) information about the debtor's most important assets and liabilities; (2) information about the debtor's keeping of accounts; (3) a statement of the reasons for, and the purpose of, the reconstruction; and (4) information about the date for a meeting which should be held with the creditors within four weeks from the judgment of the reconstruction, BA, section 11 a, paragraph 2.

208. The reconstructor has to give a proposal for the plan for the reconstruction to the creditors not later than one week before the meeting with the creditors, BA, section 11 c. The proposal for a plan must contain a reasoned explanation of the type of reconstruction to be made (composition with the creditors or a transfer of the business activity) and an evaluation of significant issues, which might prevent a reconstruction. The proposal must also as far as possible inform about the balance per day for the start of reconstruction due to subsequent changes occurred. Furthermore, the proposal must contain information on whether in the accounting experts, conviction is lacking at the debtor's most recent annual report. Finally, the proposal must indicate the planned major steps. The proposal for the plan for the reconstruction must be accepted by the debtor. The proposal shall be accompanied by an asset valuation from the accounting expert, and a statement from the reconstructor and the accounting expert about the plan in their view is feasible.

209. At a meeting with the creditors, which should be held within four weeks from the start of the reconstruction, the proposal is considered. The proposal may be amended at the meeting, BA, section 11 e paragraph 1. The proposal is adopted unless a majority of the creditors votes against it, and that majority represents at least 25% of the total amount of the known creditors who would have the right to vote.

The Bankruptcy Court may if there are special reasons postpone the consideration of the proposal to a later meeting which is to be held within four weeks, BA, section 11 e, paragraph 5. However, postponement cannot be granted if a majority of the creditors vote against it, and that majority represents at least 25% of the total amount of the known creditors who would have the right to vote.

Within three months, the reconstructor must send a statement to all known creditors and to the Bankruptcy Court about all significant aspects of reconstructive treatment including the outcome of continued operation of the debtor's business activity, BA, section 11 f.

If preconditions for reconstruction treatment are changed significantly, the reconstructor must without undue delay give notice to all known creditors and to the Bankruptcy Court. In that case, the Bankruptcy Court convene a meeting for considering if the reconstruction treatment should cease or if the plan for reconstruction should be amended, BA, section 11 f, paragraph 2.

At the latest six months after the (first) meeting with the creditors, a meeting is to be held in the Bankruptcy Court for the purpose for voting on the proposal for reconstruction, BA, section 13. Under special circumstances, the Bankruptcy Court may extend the period with two months at a time, but not more than four months, BA, section 13 a.

If the reconstruction treatment ceases before a reconstruction is completed, the debtor's estate is taken into bankruptcy, BA, section 15, paragraph 3.

II. Dispositions During the Reconstruction

210. After the reconstruction has been initiated, the debtor is not allowed to make substantial dispositions without the consent of the reconstructor, BA, section 12. Debts are only to be paid in accordance with the order of priority of creditors or if payment is necessary in order to prevent losses. Furthermore, the debtor must present his accounts to the reconstructor according to the latter's further instructions. If attempts have been made to arrive at an agreement with the creditors, which means continuation of the activities, naturally, the reconstructor will give permission for continuing ordinary business.

211. These rules are supplemented by a special rule in BA, section 72. If the debtor has made dispositions exceeding the ones mentioned above, these are voidable, unless the other contracting party acted in good faith. If the reconstructor has given his acceptance, the dispositions may be voided only if the reconstructor has obviously exceeded his powers.

III. Relations with the Creditors

212. As already mentioned, the creditors should be informed about the reconstruction and should be called in for a meeting, which should be held within three weeks from the date of notice. At this meeting, the creditors will have the opportunity to express their opinion on the proposed plan for reconstruction. Furthermore, at the meeting the Bankruptcy Court may appoint more reconstructors or another accounting expert so the creditors may have the opportunity to put forward proposals thereon.

213. The reconstructor or at least 25% of the creditors of the total amount of the known creditors who would have the right to vote may submit a request that the reconstructor takes over the management, BA, section 12 a. However, this does not apply if the debtor is a natural person. To deal with the application, the Bankruptcy Court shall convene a meeting with the debtor, the creditors and the reconstructor. The request is adopted if a majority of the creditors represented in the meeting does not vote against it, BA, section 12 a, paragraphs 2 and 3.

214. During reconstruction, the individual creditor cannot make proceedings. According to the BA, section 12 c, arrest of property or execution cannot be made during the reconstruction. Furthermore, the mortgagee cannot enjoy the possession of the debtor's property and dispossession based on execution cannot be made. Without the consent of the debtor and the reconstructor, enforcement cannot take place. This does not apply for attachment of debts. However, the privileges of pledge with regard to movables and company charges in debts may be executed during reconstruction. Upon request, the debtor should pay the current expenses on the mortgage debts as they fall due.

§3. Bankruptcy

215. If an insolvent debtor does not succeed in establishing an agreement with the creditors, the debtor will normally be adjudged bankrupt. By that means, an equitable satisfaction of the creditors' claims has been aimed at, although special rights of secured creditors must be enforced. The equality of creditors is not only safeguarded by the distribution of the assets but allowance is also made for by the fact that the BA contains rules about voidance of preferential treatment of individual creditors.

The Bankruptcy Court plays an important part in the bankruptcy proceedings. It is the Bankruptcy Court that issues the bankruptcy notice as well as supervises the administration of the estate and settles disputes about the estate.

I. Petition in Bankruptcy: Terms of Bankruptcy

216. A petition in bankruptcy can be presented to the Bankruptcy Court by the debtor himself or by a creditor, (BA, section 17). The prerequisite for the debtor to be adjudged bankrupt is that he is insolvent. According to the Act, the reference to 'insolvency' is, to be more specific, 'illiquidity', (BA, section 17 paragraph 2), which runs as follows: 'A debtor is insolvent if he cannot fulfil his obligations as they fall due, unless his inability to pay must be considered temporary.'

In principle, freedom to consider evidence exists with regard to the debtor's insolvency, but BA, section 18 contains some rules of presumption. If the debtor admits his insolvency, if the debtor is under reconstruction, or if it has not been possible to levy an execution on the debtor's property within three months from the filing of the petition in bankruptcy to obtain a settlement, insolvency is normally found. These rules, however, are only rules of presumption, which may be proved wrong.

217. However, a creditor, who has sufficient security for his claims on the debtor's assets cannot file a petition in bankruptcy. However, the security for claims on a third party's property does not prevent the creditor from filing a petition in bankruptcy, unless it is a condition for the security or if the claim has not fallen due, BA, section 20.

II. The Disposal of Property

218. Immediately after the notice of bankruptcy, the Bankruptcy Court appoints a trustee, BA, section 107. More trustees may be appointed or elected by the creditors, BA, section 108, but this is not common.

219. The trustee takes charge of the debtor's business books and commercial papers and makes the necessary arrangements in order to prevent undue disposal of the property of the estate, BA, section 110. Consequently, the debtor loses his right to dispose of the property which forms part of his estate and he loses his right of disposal on behalf of the estate, BA, section 29. If the debtor has held the right of disposal of his property within the expiry of the first twenty-four hours after the bankruptcy has been announced in the Danish Official Gazette (*Statstidende)*, this will only affect the person who knew or ought to have known about the bankruptcy, BA, section 30.

220. The Bankruptcy Court will immediately publish the notice of bankruptcy in the Danish Official Gazette. The Bankruptcy Court may determine that it will call in for a meeting of creditors to elect more trustees. In that case, the meeting is to be held not later than three weeks after the notice. Such a meeting may also be requested by the trustee or by a creditor within three weeks after the notice, and the meeting must be held within three weeks after the request. If demanded a committee of creditors not exceeding the members should be appointed, BA, section 115.

221. The trustee is in charge of the settlement of the estate and works out statements of the estate. Therefore, it is the trustee who acts on behalf of the estate.

III. The Assets of the Bankruptcy Estate

222. The bankruptcy includes the property of the debtor on the date of the bankruptcy notice and whatever devolves upon him during the bankruptcy, BA, section 32. This does not apply to assets that cannot be seized unless special provisions exist, BA, section 36. To illustrate the assets which have been exempted from seizure, one could mention assets included in the 'beneficium of need' (*trangsbeneficium*) of the Administration of Justice Act, section 509, such as furniture in a plain home and the cash value of a life insurance policy, compare the Consolidated Act 999/2006 on Insurance Contracts, section 116. Special provisions for seizure of assets which are exempted from execution exist as regards amounts which, according to special legislation, have been placed in specialized accounts for fiscal reasons, as these are normally exempted from seizure; this applies for instance to investment funds accounts.

223. The debtor's income derived from his own activities during the bankruptcy and whatever might replace it is not part of the estate, BA, section 33. This applies whether it is a matter of earned income or (rarely) an income resulting from other business activities.

224. Inheritance which goes to the debtor during the bankruptcy is part of the estate unless the testator has otherwise indicated by a valid testamentary disposition, BA, section 34. If the testator, by a valid will, has made decisions about tying up the inheritance, this must be enforced by the estate. The estate cannot object to a will which restricts the right of inheritance of the debtor.

225. Normally, the estate can enter into the rights of the debtor according to a reciprocally burdening agreement. By doing so, the estate is not only entitled to but also bound by, the terms of the agreement, BA, sections 55 and 56. This implies that the estate has to make the payment in full as a so-called preferential claim; a claim which shall be paid prior to other debts, compare *see* further details below nos. 223–231. If the estate does not enter into the agreement, the other contracting party can only claim damages for the loss resulting from the agreement not being fulfilled. This claim will be an unsecured claim which is ranking with the claims of the ordinary creditors, BA, section 59. The claim for damages can even be reduced, as the BA, section 61, contains provisions to the effect that long-term notices could be adjusted to usual or reasonable notices.

226. These rules give the trustee the possibility to 'sort out' the debtor's agreements so that the estate enters into the favourable agreements but not the unfavourable ones. Provided that the estate gives notice immediately of its entry in accordance with the BA, section 55, and conditional on payment or security in accordance with the BA, section 57, the estate has this right. An arrangement to the effect that the estate cannot enter into the agreement will not be valid. However, the BA, section 53 makes reservations to the effect that entry may be impossible due to special legal provisions as to matters of law or the special nature of the same. Legal provisions which prevent entry do exist, for instance, as far as authority and commission are concerned. The fact that entry is impossible as a consequence of the nature of the matters of law applies when the estate cannot meet the liabilities which the debtor should have paid, for instance, because the debtor plays a decisive part as regards the fulfilment, or because it is a question of a long-term service obligation.

227. As far as lease agreements and employment agreements are concerned, special rules are included in the BA, sections 10 a, 6l–63 and 98.

IV. Voidance

228. In order to secure the equality of the creditors and protect against a possible abuse by the debtor, the BA, section 8, contains a number of voiding rules, and some other acts also have voiding rules; to put it more simply, the rules of voidance aim at neutralizing some dispositions which have been made before the bankruptcy.

The rules of voidance can be divided into various groups, partly conditional upon the terms of voidance, partly in opposition to the terms – depending on the type of disposition in question. Traditionally, the rules are divided into three groups. One group concerns preferential treatments of creditors. These are dispositions where a creditor who should have ranked as an ordinary creditor has had his claim paid in full or has obtained security for his claim. In other words, one could say that the dispositions disturb the order of the creditors. The second group concerns legal proceedings. The third group concerns dispositions, which have reduced the property of the debtor, for instance, gifts.

A. *Terms of Voidance*

229. The most comprehensive rule of voidance is that of the BA, section 74, as it affects all undue preferences of the creditors and all dispositions which might have reduced the estate. The voidance according to the rule is subject to the estate being able to prove that the debtor was or became insolvent when the disposition was made and that the creditor knew or ought to have known about the debtor's insolvency and the circumstances which made the disposition undue. This is often expressed in the terms that the rule demands insolvency and bad faith.

The rule of the BA, section 72, which only affects dispositions made under reconstruction, also demands bad faith, although in a somewhat different form.

230. As it can be difficult for the estate to prove insolvency and especially the creditor's bad faith, some rules apply which strengthen the position of the estate. The rules apply to certain dispositions which objectively seem suspicious because for some of these dispositions the rules of voidance have been made purely objective. However, these rules are restricted by fixed time limits; normally three or six months. The crucial point according to these rules is that a certain disposition has been made within a fixed time limit. For instance, a security for a previously incurred debt is voidable if it has been given later than three months before the 'date of notice', compare *see* further below nos. 232–238.

231. Most of the objective rules are, in a special form, applicable as far as the debtor's close relations are concerned. Within the category described as 'close relations', the objective rules are applicable to dispositions which have been made later than two years before the 'date of notice', but the creditor may prevent having the disposition voided if he can prove that the debtor neither was nor became insolvent by the disposition. Of course, this burden of proof can be difficult to demonstrate when the debtor has been adjudged bankrupt.

The term 'close relations' is defined more precisely in the BA, section 2. The provision enumerates a certain category of persons who should be regarded as 'close relations'. These are not only spouses, ascendant or descendant relatives, brothers and sisters, and the spouses of the persons mentioned but also other persons who have been closely connected to the debtor are included. A person or a company can be considered to be a 'close relation' if the person or someone closely connected to him directly or indirectly owns a considerable part of the capital of the company. Furthermore, two companies are considered 'close relations' if one of the companies or a company closely connected to it directly or indirectly owns a considerable part of the other company's capital, or if the same person or company directly or indirectly owns a considerable part of the capital of both companies. Finally, similar joint interests may result in subjects being considered 'close relations'.

B. Voidance of Preferential Treatment of Creditors

232. Preferential treatment of creditors concerns, as already mentioned, dispositions which disturb the order of the creditors. This sort of preferences may normally appear by payment of unsecured debt or by giving security for the debt at a time when the debtor was insolvent. As far as some objective suspicious dispositions are concerned, BA, section 67, which deals with payments, and BA, section 70, which concerns security, give objective rules of voidance.

233. BA, section 67 concerns payments which have been made later than three months before the 'date of notice', if payment has been made before the normal time of payment, if payment has been made by unusual means, or if the debtor has made a payment which has seriously reduced the solvency of the debtor. This does not apply to payments which seemed normal. Normally, a payment will be considered effected before normal time of payment if it has been made before the debtor was liable to pay. Special conditions may, however, lead to another conclusion, for instance, if the claim returned high interest. Fulfilment of a claim for money by other means of payment should only be considered normal if the creditor needed the payment in question either for his private use or because he is dealing in these particular items. However, it will always be an unusual means of payment if goods which the creditor has sold, without having made retention of ownership until payment is made, are being returned to him. Payments that seriously reduce the solvency of the debtor exist, such as large sums which, on the whole, have demanded the last part of the debtor's liquidity.

234. According to BA, section 70, security rights which the creditor has not been promised when the debt was incurred, or which have not been secured against proceedings without unnecessary delay after the debt was incurred, may be claimed void, if the 'perfection of the security rights' *(sikringsakten)* has been made later than three months before the 'date of notice'. However, the rule does not include rights which have been secured when the debt was incurred or secured rights which will not be established until later. Nor is the rule applicable to the replacement of a security by another security, unless the disposition results in a real extension of the security. By the expression 'not secured against proceedings without unnecessary delay after the debt was incurred', it is possible to maintain the security rights, even if the perfection of the security rights has not been made later than the date of incurring the debt. This part, however, should be understood in a narrow sense. If, without special reasons, a couple of days have passed from the date debt was incurred until the perfection of security rights has been made, it is not a question of unnecessary delay.

235. The BA, section 67 paragraph 2, and section 70 paragraph 2, give special rules which apply as far as 'close relations' are concerned. According to these rules, the above dispositions are voidable if they are made to the advantage of the debtor's 'close relations' and not later than two years before the 'date of notice', unless it can be proved that the debtor neither was nor became insolvent due to the disposition.

236. In principle, BA, section 74, includes all undue preferences of creditors, but, as mentioned above in Part I, Chapter 6, §3.IV, A. voidance is, according to the rule, subject to the estate being able to prove that the debtor was insolvent, and that the creditor knew or ought to have known about the insolvency of the debtor as well as the circumstances which made the disposition undue. The fact that the rule demands voidance of impropriety implies reservations to the effect that certain dispositions which give the creditor a preference might be due. This, for instance, could be the case if payment is necessary in order to prevent a loss which might affect all creditors.

237. The BA, section 74, does not give any time limit. Therefore, according to the circumstances, it is applicable to all dispositions of the nature mentioned in sections 67 and 70 of the Act, but which have not been made within the time limit of these rules. As voidance is subject to the bankruptcy being due to the debtor's situation of insolvency when the disposition was made, and as the estate has to prove the creditor's bad faith, it will hardly be possible to use the rule as regards dispositions which have been made more than six months before the 'date of notice' as regards dispositions which are voidable, both according to the objective rules and according to section 74, the estate might have an interest in invoking section 74, as the effects may not always lead to the same economic result.

238. Also the rule of the BA, section 72, contains preferences of creditors. Paragraph 1 of the rule comprises all payments, which are not made in accordance with the order of priority of creditors or which are not necessary. The rule, however, is of very little importance, as paragraph 3 states that a disposition which has been accepted by the appointed reconstructor is only voidable if the reconstructor has obviously exceeded his powers.

C. Legal Proceedings

239. According to the BA, section 71, seizure which has been made later than three months before the 'date of notice' has no legal effect on the estate. In case of seizure, where perfection of security rights shall be made in order to obtain protection against third party, the time limit should be effective from the date of the perfection of security rights, for instance, registration of seizure in real property, (BA, section 73).

If seizure has been made upon request of the debtor's close relations, it has no legal effect on the estate if it had been made later than two years before the 'date of notice', unless it can be proved that the debtor neither was nor became insolvent when seizure was made, (BA, section 71 paragraph 2).

D. Reducing Dispositions

240. According to the BA, section 64, gifts which have been given later than six months before the date of notice are voidable. If the gift has been given more than six months, but later than one year, before the 'date of notice', it is voidable, unless it can be proved that the debtor neither was nor became insolvent by granting the gift. The same applies as far as the debtor's close relations are concerned if the gift has been given later than two years before the 'date of notice'.

241. If the debtor more than six months before the date of notice has renounced an inheritance, such renunciation is voidable, BA, section 65. Similarly, renunciation given later than two years before the 'date of notice' is voidable unless it is proved that the debtor neither was nor became insolvent due to the renunciation. This rule only applies to 'fallen' inheritance. The debtor can, irrespective of the creditors, renounce the inheritance which he still has not received, but which he would receive upon the testator's death.

242. Furthermore, some special rules apply as to voidance of unreasonable payments of wages to 'close relations', section 66, payments of bills and cheques, section 68, and voidance of counterclaims, section 69.

243. This general rule of the BA, section 74, is, of course, also applicable to reducing dispositions, if the estate can prove insolvency and the creditor's bad faith. Similarly, section 72 is applicable to dispositions, which have been made after the 'date of notice', but, as previously mentioned, it is not applicable to dispositions which have been approved by the reconstructor, unless the reconstructor has obviously exceeded his powers.

244. Also some other rules of voidance exist which are not included in the BA. The consolidated Companies Act 1089/2015 (*Selskabsloven*), section 138 paragraph 2, contains rule according to which members of the board of directors and managing directors in case of bankruptcy of the company, and irrespective of good faith, should repay the amount they might have received as commission on profit during the last five years before the 'date of notice', subject to the company being insolvent when the commission on profit was laid down.

E. The Effects of Voidance

245. The effects of voidance are to some extent invariably dependent on which rule applies to the voidance. If voidance is made according to section 72 or section 74 of BA, which both demand bad faith, the creditor shall pay damages according to ordinary rules, BA, section 76. This implies that the estate, as far as economy is concerned, should be situated as if the disposition had not been made.

246. If voidance is made according to the objective rules (sections 64–71), the creditor has to disclaim the enrichment he has gained, not exceeding, however, the loss of the estate, BA, section 75. The difference between the two principles appears, for instance, if a third party has provided security for a debt which has been discharged by a voidable payment. By voidance according to section 74, the creditor shall pay back the amount. By voidance according to section 67, only the enrichment should be paid. If the security provided by the third party is sufficient to cover the claim, the creditor has not obtained any enrichment and nothing has to be paid.

However, the BA, section 80, makes it possible to put forward a claim of voidance on a third party who has not been claimed as a result of the debtor's payment.

V. Claims on the Estate

247. The debtor's property will be used to pay the creditors, who had a claim on the debtor when the notice of bankruptcy was made, as well as claims for income tax according to the acts dealing with company tax and fund taxation concerning income year which expire when notice of bankruptcy is made, BA, section 38.

The administration of the estate can, of course, only take place if payment is being made for the work done. Furthermore, certain claims have priority over other claims for social or fiscal reasons. However, certain claims are secondary to ordinary claims for practical reasons and/or for the sake of reasonableness.

Further rules on this subject can be found in the BA, Chapter 10, regarding order of priority of creditors.

A. The Order of Priority of Creditors

248. In the BA, Chapter 10 has been adjusted in such a way that claims, to which the individual rules apply, will be paid equally, and only if creditors having been paid in full will a possible surplus be divided among the secondary group. This, however, does not apply to the secondary claims included in the Act, section 98, which should be paid according to the order of priority stated in the rule.

1. Preferential Claims

249. According to the BA, section 93, the following should be paid in equal proportions prior to other debts:

(1) *Costs occurring when entering into bankruptcy.* These are costs in connection with the petition in bankruptcy and modest court fees on same.
(2) *Costs in connection with the administration of the estate.* These are mainly fees for the trustee, valuers and possible assistance pertaining to accounts as well as costs in connection with the realization of the property of the estate.
(3) *Debts which the estate might incur during the administration of the estate.* This includes special claims due to agreements which the trustee enters into on behalf of the estate, and claims due to agreements entered into by the debtor before the bankruptcy, if the estate enters into the agreement, compare further details nos. 201–203. Claims for income tax according to the acts dealing with company tax and fund taxation have been individually exempted from the status as preferential claims in the Act, section 93 No. 3. This implies that payment of such claims is ranking with ordinary creditors.

2. Secondary Preferential Claims

250. According to BA, section 94, a preferential position has been given to a number of different claims which have turned up as a result of attempts to avoid bankruptcy, on a par with these claims court fees on the estate will also be paid.

251. The claims to which the rule applies are reasonable costs resulting from attempts to establish a total settlement of the debtor's financial circumstances by reconstructing, winding up, making composition scheme in bankruptcy, or by some other means and other debts which, after the date of notice, the debtor has incurred with the consent of the appointed reconstructor.

Furthermore, the rule also applies to reasonable costs due to initiated liquidation of a limited company or a private company. This is due to the fact that such a company, as mentioned in the first section, shall be administered in bankruptcy if, during the liquidation, it appears that the company is insolvent.

3. The Wage Privilege

252. In addition to the secondary preferential claims, some wage claims are covered according to the BA, section 95. This applies to wage claims which have fallen due later than six months before the 'date of notice' and before the bankruptcy notice was given, as well as claims for discontinuation of the working conditions and claims for compensation. The rule also applies to claims for holiday allowances.

The wage claims are not only secured by the wage privilege but also within certain limits the claims secured by the 'Wage Earners' Guarantee Fund (*Lønmodtagernes Garantifond*), from which payment of wages under certain conditions can be claimed. If the 'Guarantee Fund' has paid the wages, it will enter into the wage earners' privilege.

4. Claims for Purchase Taxes

253. Some purchase taxes which are being collected in the wholesale trades have been granted a privilege according to BA, section 96 as far as wholesalers are concerned. However, the privilege only applies to taxes stated in the rule and which should be paid by the wholesaler. This is a result of the fact that no possibility of repayment applies to these taxes if the wholesaler does not have his claims covered. However, the rule does not grant a privilege as far as the VAT is concerned, but the wholesaler has the possibility to reduce his liability to pay tax by the non-payment.

5. Ordinary Claims

254. Not until fulfilment of the above-described claims has taken place shall the ordinary creditors have their claims paid. These creditors will normally receive a very modest dividend if, in the end, there is anything left for them.

It should be added that depending on the circumstances, a special bankruptcy tax shall be paid pursuant to the Consolidated Bankruptcy Tax Act 1242/2010 (*Konkursskatteloven*). Payment of such a claim should, however, rank with the ordinary claims.

6. Secondary Claims

255. When all other claims have been met, payments of claims for interest accrued after the date of the bankruptcy notice will be made in the following order, compare the BA, section 98. This, however, does not apply to interest on the claims mentioned in section 94, which will be fulfilled on the same level as the actual claim. Nor does the rule apply to interest on claims for which security has been given, as the interest can be covered by the security, even prior to the actual claim.

Thereafter, certain claims for fines and agreed penalties and, finally, claims according to promises of a gift will be covered. Fulfilment of secondary claims is, however, very exceptional.

B. Joint and Several Debts

256. In BA, sections 47–52 lay down a detailed set of rules about the amounts of which dividend should be paid in matters of joint and several debts. Roughly stated, the rules imply that the creditor is entitled to dividends as far as the total claim on the bankrupt estate is concerned, even if part of the claim has been paid by a joint debtor who has the right of recourse, or if the payment has been made by a joint debtor later than three months from the 'date of notice'.

C. Set-Off

257. Normally, a creditor who owes an amount to the debtor could plead a set-off for the total amount of the claim. In BA, sections 42–44 lay down, however, a rather detailed set of rules which should prevent that a set-off is being used as part of a preferential treatment of a creditor or will have the effect of such preferential treatment. Furthermore, BA, section 69, lays down a rule, which makes voidance possible if the rules of set-off have been used to give the creditor a preferential treatment before the bankruptcy.

D. Fulfilment of Secured Rights

258. As was already mentioned, the estate must enforce third party's valid rights to the assets of the estate, BA, section 82. This, however, does not imply that the third party can seek satisfaction independently of the bankruptcy. On the contrary, the composition scheme enforced by a majority of the creditors with regard to real property and movables in possession of the estate can only take place at the request of the trustee or with his consent, BA, section 85.

259. The privileges of pledge with regard to movables and debts can, however, be realized without consent, but a request for payment must be sent to the estate which by that means will get the opportunity to safeguard its interests.

E. Winding-Up of the Estate

260. If it appears during the administration of the estate that no means are available in excess of what is necessary to cover the expenses, the estate will be wound up at the first meeting of the creditors or at a special meeting to which the creditors have been called, BA, section 143.

When the assets have been realized and possible disputes have been settled, the trustee prepares a draft of the accounts. Thereafter, the Bankruptcy Court calls the creditors for a meeting at which the creditors and the debtor get the opportunity to comment on the draft. Possible disputes are dealt with by the Bankruptcy Court and, furthermore, the Bankruptcy Court affirms the draft unless it is found to be defective, in which case it must be rewritten. After the affirmation and after the expiration of the time limit for an appeal, dividends can be distributed (BA, Chapter 18).

Especially as far as natural persons are concerned, the rule applies that they are still liable for the unsettled part of the debt until the creditors might lose their rights through limitation.

§4. Composition Scheme Under Reconstruction

261. Under reconstruction, a compulsory composition scheme has to be made or the business activity has to be transferred. If the debtor does not succeed in this, the debtor will be adjudged bankrupt.

I. The Progress of a Compulsory Composition Scheme

262. The reconstructor and the accounting expert who must be independent of the debtor, will have to make a statement of the debtor's assets and liabilities, stating which debts are 'secured debts' (BA, section 13 b). They also have to make a statement containing information about possible voidable dispositions. Furthermore, they must comment on the proposal for a compulsory composition scheme to whether, in their opinion, the proposal is reasonable and offers sufficient security for the fulfilment of the composition scheme and which kind of settlement is supposed to take place in case of bankruptcy, BA, section 13 b paragraph, No. 3, litra h. This material has to be presented to the creditors within a meeting with the creditors. The Bankruptcy Court calls a meeting for the treatment of, and voting on, the proposal for the composition scheme, (BA, section 13). Only the creditors whose claims are affected by the composition scheme without being annulled have a right to vote. The proposal for a compulsory composition scheme is adopted if not a majority of the creditors who are participating in the voting vote against the proposal.

If the proposal is adopted, it will be affirmed by the Bankruptcy Court unless quite special reasons should exist. After the expiration of the time limit for appeal, the composition scheme is said to be final. It can, however, under very special circumstances, be annulled at a later date, if the debtor has committed fraud or seriously neglects his duties according to the composition scheme (BA, section 14 e).

II. The Contents of the Composition Scheme

263. In principle, a compulsory composition scheme aims at three different forms (BA, section 10 a):

(1) A reduction in percentages of the claims (ordinary compulsory composition scheme).
(2) It may be a condition that the debtor's estate is distributed between its creditors.
(3) Respite (moratorium).

264. These forms can be combined. The most common combination is that of an ordinary composition scheme and a moratorium in such a way that a certain percentage of the claims will be paid by instalments over a period of one to two years.

265. In case of a compulsory composition scheme it is the claims (which are unsecured claims in case of bankruptcy) that will be affected by the result of the composition scheme. The fact is that the rights of secured creditors will be enforced, and claims which have a priority over ordinary claims in bankruptcy should be paid in full by a forced composition scheme. Most of the claims, which are secondary claims in bankruptcy, will be annulled in case of a forced composition scheme. However, claims for fines will be ranked with ordinary claims (BA, section 10 a).

266. The rules about rights to dividends in matters of joint and several obligations and set-off in case of bankruptcy will similarly apply as far as a forced composition scheme is concerned. As regards joint and several obligations, it should particularly be mentioned that the part of the recourse claim, which cannot be held within the dividend being estimated for the claim will be annulled. A deviation from these rules can only take place with the consent of the creditors to whom the deviation is detrimental, BA, section 10 c.

III. The Effects of the Composition Scheme

267. A compulsory composition scheme is affirmed under reconstruction. Therefore the rules of voidance of the BA are being used if a compulsory composition scheme is affirmed for the debtor. Hereby the principle of equal rights will have the same effects as in case of bankruptcy. The compulsory composition scheme will, in principle, affect all claims which have been incurred before entering into reconstruction. This applies even if the claims were not known at the time in question; for instance, a claim for damages will, as a result of a defective performance, only get a dividend of a composition scheme, even if the defect does not show up until later.

Chapter 7. Negotiable Instruments

§1. Promissory Notes

I. Promissory Notes in General

268. The Act on Promissory Notes provides for promissory notes in general and lays down special provisions regarding negotiable promissory bonds. [192,193,194] For dematerialized financial instruments, including shares and bonds, the rules are found in the Act on Capital Markets[195] and for digital mortgage deeds on real property in the Land Registration Act.[196]

269. A promissory note (*gældsbrev*) is a unilateral, unconditional admission of debt concerning the payment of a definite amount of money. The Act on Promissory Notes distinguishes between an ordinary promissory note or claim (*simpelt gældsbrev*) and a negotiable bond (*omsætningsgældsbrev*). Section 11 of the Act establishes the following four types of negotiable bonds: a promissory note according to which the payment shall be made to the bearer or which leaves blank to whom the payment shall be made; a promissory note according to which payment shall be made to an individual person or his order; a mortgage deed on registered ship or aeroplane, unless the words 'not to order' or a similar reservation has been inserted in the note; a promissory note according to which payment shall be made to an individual person, when the note explicitly indicates that it is negotiable.

II. Debtor's Claims Against the Creditor

270. Within the relationship between the debtor and the original creditor, the distinction between ordinary and negotiable promissory notes has no importance. It is the general rule for every kind of promissory note, negotiable or not, that the debtor may invoke every objection he may have against the creditor. The debtor is, for example, entitled to object that he has not received the goods for which the promissory note constitutes the payment.

271. When the promissory note is transferred, the main rule applies on ordinary promissory notes. The assignee requires no right other than those that the creditor had. For negotiable bonds, special rules are provided in order to maintain the bonds' reliability. On certain conditions, the assignee who has now become the creditor of the debtor obtains a particular right which is more comprehensive than the one the

192. Author: Camilla Hørby Jensen.
193. Consolidated Act 333/2014 on Promissory Notes (*Gældsbrevsloven*).
194. *See* B. Iversen & L.L. Petersen, *Danish Business Law*, 6th edition, pp 449–458 (DJØF Publishing 2015).
195. Consolidated Act 12/2018 on Capital Markets. (*Kapitalmarkedsloven*) as most recently amended by Act 1520/2018.
196. Consolidated Act 1075/2014 on Land Registration (*Tinglysningsloven*) as most recently amended by Act 1722/2018.

original creditor had. For that to happen it is required that the assignee must have acquired the negotiable bond in the course of a transaction such as sale, mortgage or as a gift, but not by way of inheritance, bankruptcy or execution. Second, the transaction from the assignor to the assignee must be valid and incontestable. Furthermore the assignee must have the note or bond in his possession, and he must have acted in good faith concerning the objections to be invoked by the debtor. On these conditions, the debtor is prevented from invoking objections concerning his relationship to the original creditor, for example the validity of a sales contract being the reason for the issue of the negotiable bond, or objections relating to the performance incumbent on the creditor, or fraud concerning the emission of the negotiable bond after due signature by the debtor. However, the debtor keeps the right to invoke certain serious objections, for example, that the promissory note is false, or that he has paid the instalments and interest which were falling due before the transfer to the assignee. These rules are found in sections 15–17 of the Act on Promissory Notes.

Similar rights are granted the assignee of dematerialized shares and bonds and digital mortgage deed under the Act on Capital Markets and the Land Registration Act respectively, provided that the assignee's right is registered, as possession of the document is not possible.

III. Rules of Transfer

272. As mentioned, the general rules on transfer of negotiable bonds are found in the Act on Promissory Notes.[197] Almost similar rules for dematerialized shares and bonds and digital mortgage deeds are found in the Act on Capital Markets and the Land Registration Act respectively but requiring registration and not possession of the document as a basis for the rights of the assignee.

A. The Relation Between the Assignor and the Assignee

273. In the relationship between the assignor and a later assignee, it is required that the assignor as well as the assignee endorse the document. When the endorsement is complete, it constitutes a proof of good faith in favour of the holder of the document. For transfer of bearer securities, the endorsement is not required. In the case where the negotiable bond has been stolen from the assignor and transferred by the thief with due endorsement, even if false, to an assignee without knowledge or suspicion about the theft, the assignor-victim of the theft has lost his right to claim the negotiable bond back from the assignee in good faith, cf. Act on Promissory Notes, section 14. The same is true when the transferor is minor with no authority to transfer the document.

197. In the following text, only the regulation of negotiable bonds is dealt with. For ordinary promissory notes, it is the rule according to the Act, section 31 that the transaction is valid against other assignees and against the assignor's creditors when the debtor has been informed on the transfer.

B. The Relation Between the Assignor's Creditors and the Assignee

274. In the relationship between the assignors, creditors and the assignee, the conclusion of the transfer agreement is decisive. When ownership is transferred to the assignee through the agreement, the assignee is protected against claims from the creditors and the bankruptcy succession of the assignor. However, if the negotiable bond is transferred to the assignee as a mortgage, the assignee obtains protection only when he has the bond in his possession, cf. Act on Promissory Notes, section 22.

C. Transfer to Different Assignees

275. When different parties claim that the assignor has agreed with them on transfer of the negotiable bond, i.e., a double transfer, the right goes to the assignee, provided that he has the negotiable bond in his possession. When the assignor retains the negotiable bond, the assignee who first made the agreement acquires the right. *See* the Act on Promissory Notes, section 14.

IV. Release of the Debt

276. The debtor is released from his debt when he has in good faith paid the holder of the negotiable bond even if it is proven that the holder is a thief or a minor without right to the document, cf. Act on Promissory Notes, section 19.[198] However, the debtor has to require that the receipt for an extraordinary instalment is signed directly on the promissory note. A separate receipt is not sufficient. When the promissory note is paid off, the debtor must have the document handed over into his possession, cf. Act on Promissory Notes, section 21.

V. Dematerialized Instruments

277. The two most important groups of dematerialized (non-physical) instruments are negotiable dematerialized shares and bonds and negotiable digital mortgage deeds on real property.[199]

Negotiable dematerialized shares and bonds often but not necessarily listed on a regulated market are subject to registration in a central securities depository, cf. Act on Capital Markets, section 3, no. 34. This registration replaces the physical appearance of these instruments. At the issuance, the dematerialized shares and bonds are

---

198. The debtor of an ordinary promissory note may pay the assignor, when he does not know and ought not to know about the transfer. When he has been informed of the transfer, he is released when he pays the assignee indicated by the transfer information in good faith, cf. Act on Promissory Notes, section 29–30.

199. *See* B. Iversen & L.L. Petersen, *Danish Business Law*, 6th edition, pp 458–460 (DJØF publishing 2015).

registered on an account. When the shares or bonds are sold, the sale has to be registered at the central securities depository and the shares or bonds sold are transferred to the accounts of the acquirers. The registration is carried out by an account-holding institution, typically a bank. The registration is considered completed at the moment of notification of the central securities depository.

For negotiable digital mortgage deeds on real property registration in accordance with the rules in the Land Registration Act is required and substitutes possession of the document.

§2. Bills of Exchange and Cheques

278. The regulation is laid down in the Act on Bills of Exchange and in the Act on Cheques,[200,201] which are based on international conventions issued on Geneva conferences in 1930 and 1931. As the Danish legislation is in conformity with the international rules, only the main principles shall be described below.

279. A bill of exchange may be issued in the form of a promissory note. More frequently, it is issued as an agreement according to which the creditor requests the debtor to pay the amount of the bill at a certain time. The debtor complies with the request by accepting the bill. The acceptance is performed when the debtor writes his signature across the front of the bill.

280. According to the Act on Bills of Exchange, section 1, a bill of exchange must include the word *veksel* (bill of exchange) in the text, the amount of the bill, the name of the drawee, the name of the payee, the signature of the drawer, the time of payment, the place of payment, and the date and place of the issue of the bill. The designation *veksel* must be written in the language in which the bill of exchange is drawn up. The amount may be written in numbers as well as in letters. The latter has priority in case of non-conformity between the number and the letters, cf. section 6. The time of payment may be a definite date or a definite time after the issue. The bill may be indicated as payable at sight or after sight. When the place of payment is not indicated, the bill is payable on the residence of the drawee, cf. section 2. Normally a bill bears no interest. However, according to section 5, the drawer may decide on the payment of an interest which shall then be indicated on the bill.

281. According to the Act on Administration of Justice,[202] section 478, a bill of exchange can form the basis for legal enforcement. According to the Act on Administration of Justice, section 501 paragraph 3, objections from the debtor can be made only if they concern immaturity, incapacity, falsification or non-conformity with the formal requirements in the Act on Bills of Exchange.

---

200. Consolidated Act 1661/2018 on Bills of Exchange (*Veksselloven*) and Consolidated Act 558/1986 on Cheques (*Checkloven*).
201. *See* B. Iversen & L.L. Petersen, *Danish Business Law*, 6th edition, pp 460–468 (DJØF Publishing 2015).
202. Consolidated Act 1284/2018 on the Administration of Justice (*Retsplejeloven*) as most recently amended by Act 1711/2018.

282. When the bill has been transferred to a third party, no compensation claim can be asserted against the holder of the bill when he is in good faith concerning the claim.

283. The original creditor according to the bill of exchange, the payee, may transfer the bill by endorsement, which may be complete or in blank. According to the Act on Bills of Exchange, every endorser guarantees the acceptance and the payment of the bill in relation to the acquirer and to the subsequent endorsers. The liability is joint and several.

284. The title-holder of the bill may have recourse against the endorsers and the drawer. Certain formal requirements must be observed. The bill must be presented. When it is not paid at the date of maturity, it must be formally submitted to protest in order to furnish sufficient proof of non-payment. Protest must be made within two working days after the date of maturity. The holder of the bill has to notify the last endorser and the drawer on the protest within four working days after the day of protest. The endorser-receiver of the notification has to transfer the message to his nearest endorser within two working days, and so on, until everybody who is liable has received notification, cf. section 43–45 in the Act on Bills of Exchange.

285. The rules for cheques are similar to those for bills of exchange. Differences follow from the fact that the cheque may not be used as a means of credit. Payment may always be claimed on presentation, even if the date of issue is a later date than the date of presentation. A cheque may be issued only as a money order. The payee may be a third party or the issuer. Cheques may only be drawn on banks and savings banks and certain similar institutions. The issuer is the drawer, the financial institute is the drawee. The cheque is submitted to the same rules on endorsement as the bill of exchange. However, the endorsement to the drawee bank constitutes a receipt. Cheques may be crossed. The drawee bank may assume a duty of payment through certification.

Chapter 8. Stock and Commodity Exchanges

§1. The Primary Trading Venues

What is generally understood as a stock exchange is known in EU law as a regulated market.[203] The predominant regulated market in Denmark is operated by NASDAQ Copenhagen A/S and is operated under that name. The regulated market is subdivided into different lists, which besides equity also includes a very large bond market and a smaller list of UCITS. Nasdaq Copenhagen also runs a multilateral trading facility (MTF) called First North, which could be seen as a second-tier stock exchange for SME's.[204] NASDAQ Copenhagen is part of the NASDAQ Nordic Exchanges, which includes exchanges in Sweden, Finland, Iceland and the Baltic Countries. The exchanges, including the MTFs, that are operated by Nasdaq Nordic are based on the same systems and have joint trading rules which provide the impression of a single trading platform, although the national exchanges are formally subject to domestic legislation. NASDAQ Copenhagen is a public limited company acting as an operator of these trading venues and as so is licensed by and under the supervision of the Danish Financial Supervisory Authority, abbreviated DFSA (*Finanstilsynet*).

286. As an EU Member State, EU directives are implemented into Danish legislation, whereas EU regulations are directly applicable and thus supplement national legislation. The regulation of trading venues is found in the 2018 Danish Capital Markets Act (DCMA),[205] which implements the relevant EU directives, notably the amended Directive on Markets in Financial Instruments (MiFID2),[206] and the Transparency Directive,[207] and is supplemented by EU regulations, notably the Regulation on Markets in Financial Instruments (MiFIR),[208] the Regulation on

203. Author: Professor, Dr. Jesper Lau Hansen, University of Copenhagen, Faculty of Law.
204. *See* generally on stock exchanges and the law in Denmark, P.K. Andersen, N.J. Clausen & J.L. Hansen, *Børsretten*, 6th ed., DJØF Publishing, København 2019.
205. Consolidated Act 12/2018.
206. Directive 2014/65/EU of the European Parliament and of the Council of 15 May 2014 on markets in financial instruments and amending Directive 2002/92/EC and Directive 2011/61/EU.
207. Directive 2004/109/EC of the European Parliament and of the Council of 15 Dec. 2004 on the harmonisation of transparency requirements in relation to information about issuers whose securities are admitted to trading on a regulated market and amending Directive 2001/34/EC, as amended by Directive 2013/50/EU of the European Parliament and of the Council of 22 Oct. 2013 amending Directive 2004/109/EC of the European Parliament and of the Council on the harmonisation of transparency requirements in relation to information about issuers whose securities are admitted to trading on a regulated market, Directive 2003/71/EC of the European Parliament and of the Council on the prospectus to be published when securities are offered to the public or admitted to trading and Commission Directive 2007/14/EC laying down detailed rules for the implementation of certain provisions of Directive 2004/109/EC.
208. Regulation (EU) No 600/2014 of the European Parliament and of the Council of 15 May 2014 on markets in financial instruments and amending Regulation (EU) No 648/2012.

Derivative Markets (EMIR),[209] and the Regulation on Central Securities Depositories (CSDR).[210] Directives and regulations adopted by the Council and the European Parliament are considered as EU legislation, often referred to as level 1 texts. Both directives and regulations on level 1 may be supplemented on level 2 by orders issued according to enabling provisions in these level 1 texts according to the procedure laid down in Articles 290–291 Treaty on the Functioning of the EU and these level 2 orders are almost always issued as directly applicable regulations. Thus, MiFID2 is supplemented by a host of level 2 regulations with direct effect. Also, the DCMA may have its own level 2 texts issued according to enabling provisions in the Act. Consequently, there are directly applicable level 1 legislation such as the DCMA and the EU MiFIR, EMIR, and CSDR, and there are directly applicable level 2 orders stemming from the DCMA or EU legislation on level 1. The DFSA provides a very useful overview of the applicable regulation with links to the original texts at its homepage arranged by subject.

287. The regulation of regulated markets and MTF's is found in Parts V–VI DCMA, respectively. These rules reflect a high degree the implementation of MiFID2. Trading on a trading venue must be carried out in an honest, proper and effective manner. This means, for example, that NASDAQ Copenhagen must apply objective criteria for matching orders, ensure efficient and timely execution of orders in its trading system, and establish a stock watch system.

288. Further, NASDAQ Copenhagen must establish its own trading rules for the *members* of its trading venues[211] and rules for *issuers* on the conditions for admission and listing of securities at the market.[212] These private rules issued by the operator of a trading venue used to be narrowly regulated by statute, but as part of the increased harmonization by MiFID2/MiFIR and the increased competition among operators of trading venues, the Danish legislator has refrained from adopting special requirements and to a large extent leave the content of these private rules to the operators.

§2. Admission to Trading

289. Shares and other financial instruments can be admitted and listed on the regulated market operated by NASDAQ Copenhagen provided that the regulated market's conditions for admission are met and a prospectus has been drawn up,

209. Regulation (EU) No 648/2012 of the European Parliament and of the Council of 4 Jul. 2012 on OTC derivatives, central counterparties and trade repositories.
210. Regulation (EU) No 909/2014 of the European Parliament and of the Council of 23 Jul. 2014 on improving securities settlement in the European Union and on central securities depositories and amending Directives 98/26/EC and 2014/65/EU and Regulation (EU) No 236/2012.
211. *See* Nasdaq Nordic Member Rules version 3.6, dated 24 Sep. 2018. The Member Rules are harmonised for all Nasdaq Nordic exchanges.
212. Rules for issuers of shares (Copenhagen) dated 3 Jan. 2018. These rules for issuers may carry minor differences among the different jurisdictions of the Nasdaq Nordic exchanges. There are also rules for issuers in respect of UCITS, bonds and ETF's.

approved and made public. On admission NASDAQ Copenhagen must ensure that the conditions for admission are fulfilled and that a prospectus has been published, cf. section 75 DCMA.

290. Traditionally, the authority to admit an issuer's securities for trading was decided by the stock exchange itself and since most exchanges were natural monopolies, they often had a quasi-public character. The decision to admit a security was known as *listing*, which basically refers to the fact that the security was now listed among the admitted securities. As the regulation of exchanges grew, the concept of listing became connected with legal requirements and when exchanges became private enterprises in the late 1990s, the authority to decide on listing was referred to public authorities. This, in turn, led to a distinction between listing (*notering*), which was decided by a public authority, and admission (*optagelse*), which was decided by the operator of the exchange. This distinction is found in Danish law in section 75 DMCA on admission decided by the operator and section 83 on public listing decided by the DFSA. The distinction is practically moot, which is evidenced by the fact that section 83 is dependent on the prior decision to admit the security according to section 75. Although the decision to list a security requires observation of the Listing Order,[213] the requirements in this order which implements Consolidated Directive 2001/34[214] are also contained in the private rules issued by Nasdaq Copenhagen that often go beyond these requirements. Thus, the main decision is the one made on admission by Nasdaq Copenhagen, although all issuers also opt to have their securities listed mostly by tradition.[215] The DFSA has accepted this and delegated its authority to decide on listing to Nasdaq Copenhagen, who can then made a decision on admission and listing simultaneously.

291. Admission to a regulated market requires the publication of a prospectus. Chapter 3 DCMA implements the Prospectus Directive,[216] which will be replaced by the directly applicable Prospectus Regulation[217] in July 2019. The DFAS is the national competent authority and has the exclusive regulatory power with respect to prospectuses.

213. Executive Order 1170/2017.
214. Directive 2001/34/EC of the European Parliament and of the Council of 28 May 2001 on the admission of securities to official stock exchange listing and on information to be published on those securities.
215. For example, publicly traded companies are often referred to as 'listed companies' and in layman's term the concepts of listing and admission are often conflated.
216. Directive 2003/71/EC of the European Parliament and of the Council of 4 Nov. 2003 on the prospectus to be published when securities are offered to the public or admitted to trading and amending Directive 2001/34/EC, as amended by Directive 2010/73/EU of the European Parliament and of the Council of 24 Nov. 2010 amending Directives 2003/71/EC on the prospectus to be published when securities are offered to the public or admitted to trading and 2004/109/EC on the harmonisation of transparency requirements in relation to information about issuers whose securities are admitted to trading on a regulated market.
217. Regulation (EU) 2017/1129 of the European Parliament and of the Council of 14 Jun. 2017 on the prospectus to be published when securities are offered to the public or admitted to trading on a regulated market, and repealing Directive 2003/71/EC.

292. The prospectus must be made available to the public and the issuer may not make an offer of securities to the public until the approved prospectus is made public, cf. section 10 DCMA. Generally, it is required that the prospectus includes all information deemed necessary for investors and their investment advisors to form a well-founded estimate of the assets and liabilities, financial position, results and future prospects, and of any guarantor, and of the rights attaching to the securities offered to the public or admitted to trading. Further, the prospectus must be drawn up in conformity with the regulations laid down by the DFSA and shall be presented in such a manner that it is possible to understand the contents and to assess the importance of the information given.[218] The detailed requirements on prospectuses are found in the DFSA's Executive Order on Prospectuses.[219]

NASDAQ Copenhagen may suspend or remove a security from trading on the market, if the security no longer meets the regulations of the market, cf. section 78 DCMA. However, suspension or removal may not take place if it is likely that this will be of significant detriment to the interests of the investors or the proper functioning of the market.

§3. Rules on Stockbroking

293. EU law use the term *investment firm* for stockbrokers and securities traders. Whereas Danish law generally applies EU legal terms, for historical reasons the EU law term is not applied and is not exactly covered by an equivalent term. Instead, the term *securities trader* (værdipapirhandler) is used to cover all with a permission to trade and only as a subdivision within this term is found the notion of *securities firms*. This is explained by the fact that historically most securities trading in Denmark has been undertaken by banks that have securities trading as one of their many authorized activities (universal banking), while securities trading as a main activity by an independent firm is less important. This is reflected in the Danish Financial Enterprises Act (DFEA),[220] which regulates financial enterprises of all sorts, including banks and other securities traders. Section 9 DFEA defines the overall term of *securities trader* (værdipapirhandler), which in subsection 1 covers all with a permission to trade securities for the public. This mostly includes banks. Only in subsection 2 is mentioned *stockbrokers* (fondsmæglerselskaber) as those who do not have an authorization to trade securities due to another permission under the Act such as a banking license. Consequently, stockbrokers in Danish law are considered a subdivision of the overall term securities trader. When implementing EU law, the EU term of *investment firm* is mostly translated as *stockbroker*, except where the EU provision seeks to regulate securities trading in general, in which case the term *securities trader* will be used.

294. Stockbrokers must be public limited companies, they must observe the general requirements laid down in the DFEA concerning fit & prober requirements for

218. Section 23 paras 3 and 6 of the Securities Trading Act.
219. Executive Order 1176/2017.
220. Consolidated Act 1140/2017.

members of the board of directors and major shareholders and rules related to the internal organization and to the carrying of business activities. As other authorized financial enterprises, they must observe the specific requirements for stockbroking in section 72 DFEA. Thus, they must: (1) have appropriate rules and procedures for transactions with the financial instruments which cover the management and employees of the undertaking; (2) be able to identify conflicts of interest which could damage the interests of clients; (3) secure the property rights of clients in their funds and the instruments; (4) protect the rights of clients and shall not, without express consent, act with their funds and instruments; and (5) keep and store complete lists of all services and transactions carried out for no less than five years after the service was performed or the transaction was completed.

295. Stockbroking companies must carry out their business in conformity with the general principle of good practice for financial undertakings, cf. section 43 DFEA. More specific requirements in that respect are found on level 2 in the Executive Orders on investor protection,[221] and on execution of orders.[222] A stockbroking company must act honestly, loyally towards its customers and act in the best interest of its clients. This includes trying to avoid conflict of interest between the company and its clients or mutually between more customers and if that is not possible disclose the conflict of interest to the customer. Further, stockbrokers must observe the rules regarding the principles of know your customer and know your securities, and they are imposed substantial disclosure requirements in relation to their clients. Most of this regulation is laid down in the level 1 instrument MiFID and the level 2 texts that supplement it and the Danish implementation is often very close to the EU law provisions.

§4. Obligations on Issuers and Parties Related to the Issuer

296. From the time of applying for listing at a regulated market the issuer must observe a continuous disclosure obligation to the public requiring the issuer to publicly disclose all new price-relevant information, known in EU law as *inside information* as defined in Article 7 MAR. The general disclosure obligation is found in Article 17 MAR. An issuer of shares admitted to trading must, as soon as possible, disclose publicly all inside information that pertains directly to its activities. The issuer is required to disclose the information as and when it arises. Where the new information is developing in stages, the duty to disclose it arises when there is a realistic prospect that the development will reach a stage or outcome where the information could affect the pricing of the security.

297. The issuer shall ensure that public disclosure of inside information is effected in such a manner that provides the public with rapid access to said information and that the disclosed information is sufficient for complete, correct and timely assessment of the inside information to be carried out. Without undue delay

221. Executive Order 1580/2018.
222. Executive Order 917/2017.

and for an appropriate period after publication of inside information, the issuer must display all disclosed information on its website.

298. The issuer may postpone disclosure according to Article 17, subsection 4, MAR if disclosure would hurt its legitimate interests and the postponement would not confuse the market, which would be the case if the new information contradicts earlier announcements by the issuer. It is also a condition that the issuer can keep the information confidential during the postponement and if confidentiality is compromised, the issuer must immediately disclose it. If the issuer has postponed disclosure, it must notify the DFSA, which may require a report to satisfy that the conditions for postponement were met.

299. Issuers with securities admitted to a regulated market must publicly publish their financial accounts, which includes the annual accounts and the half-yearly accounts, cf. sections 26–27 DMCA. Quarterly reporting used to be mandatory but is now voluntary. It is, however, recommended by the Danish Corporate Governance Committee. The recommendations of the Committee apply on a comply-or-explain basis, and issuers admitted to the regulated market operated by Nasdaq Copenhagen are obliged to observe this requirement as part of the conditions for admission.

300. In Denmark, an issuer may acquire and dispose of its own shares, and issuers whose securities are admitted to trading on a regulated market must disclose transactions that cross thresholds of 5% and 10% of its share capital, cf. section 31 DMCA.

301. Persons occupying a managerial role with the issuer, also known as *insiders*, and related parties such as spouses, must disclose to the issuer any transactions made in the shares of the issuer above a threshold of 20,000 EUR during a calendar year, who will then report them to the DFSA, cf. Article 19, subsection 1–10, MAR. These reports are made public by the DFSA. Also, insiders are forbidden to trade in the shares of the issuer within thirty calendar days of the issuer's publication of major financial reports, cf. Article 19, subsection 11, MAR, unless the issuer may dispense from the obligation due to special circumstances according to Article 19, subsection 12, MAR.

302. Major shareholders must publicly disclose their holdings if these exceed 5% of an issuer, whose shares are admitted to trading on a regulated market, and any subsequent increase or decrease based on thresholds of 5% or a multiple thereof, cf. Chapter 7 DMCA. These provisions require disclosure of transactions that give the shareholder control of shares directly or indirectly and the reporting obligation is divided in respect of shares, cf. section 38, and share derivatives, cf. section 39, and a combined reporting obligation covering both categories, cf. section 40. This arrangement is to ensure that the shareholder does not circumvent the report obligation by using or combining shares, equity instruments and derivatives.

§5. TAKEOVERS

303. Bids that are made publicly to obtain control over an issuer, whose shares are admitted to trading on a regulated market, are subject to special regulation by Chapter 8, DMCA, which implements the Directive on Takeover Bids.[223] These rules are supplemented on level 2 by the Executive Order on Takeover Bids.[224]

304. If the shareholder has obtained *control* of the issuer, by individual acquisitions of shares, by way of a public bid, or by acting in concert with other shareholders in connection with the acquisition of shares, the shareholder is obliged to make a public bid to all remaining shareholders to acquire their shares at a price determined by law, known as *a mandatory bid*, cf. sections 44–45 DMCA. The obligation to make a bid does not arise if the control was acquired by inheritance or due to payment of debt or within a group of companies; or if control arose by way of a public bid if that bid was accepted by shareholders representing more than half of the votes of the issuer, cf. section 46, subsection 1, no 1–2. Equally, where control is duc to acquisition subjcct to an cmission guarantcc, thc obligation may be averted by unloading the shares within five working days, cf. no 3 of said provision. Finally, the obligation may be set aside by decision of the DFSA if it is deemed necessary, for example, to ensure the recapitalization of a company in financial distress, cf. section 46, subsection 3, DCMA.

305. The purpose of the mandatory bid rule is to provide the minority of shareholders with an exit in case they do not approve of the new controlling shareholder. The rule is controversial because it makes takeover bids more costly and thereby prevents restructuring and protects incumbent management. As the minority is not normally protected against changes of control, where this is determined by management, the rule with its origin in English company law may be seen as a covert protection of management. Especially the fact that a costly mandatory bid is required where shareholders act in concert to challenge present management would seem to go against the intent to support shareholder engagement that is otherwise promoted in EU law and also in Danish company law.

306. Irrespectively of whether the bid is voluntary or mandatory, a detailed offer document must be drawn up that discloses the facts of the offer, notably the price offered for the shares[225] and stating the offer period which must be at least four weeks and cannot extend beyond ten weeks.[226] The offer document must be approved by the Danish FSA and made public.[227] The offer must treat all shareholders equally to the extent that they are in an equal position and is obliged to extend

223. Directive 2004/25/EC of the European Parliament and of the Council of 21 Apr. 2004 on takeover bids.
224. Executive Order 1171/2017.
225. Section 10 of the Executive Order on Takeover Bids.
226. Section 9 of the Executive Order on Takeover Bids.
227. Section 3–4 and 20 of the Executive Order on Takeover Bids.

any special treatment to all shareholders if offered to any one shareholder.[228] This obligation to offer equal treatment also extends six months after the bid has been concluded.[229]

307. If the offer is voluntary, the bidder may set the price and decide on any conditions for the bid, however, conditions may not be subject to the discretion of the bidder.[230] If the offer is mandatory, the price must at least correspond to the highest price paid in the preceding six months, and if issuer has different classes of shares trading at different prices and the bidder has not acquired shares in that class, the price must proportionally reflect the best price paid within the last six months.[231] If a class of shares is not admitted to trading and it is thus not possible to determine a market price, the difference in price between the price paid for admitted shares and the price for these shares cannot exceed 50%.[232] If the price that emerges according to these rules appears unfair, the DFSA may set another price taking into account certain objective criteria, for example, the best price paid within the last twelve months.[233]

308. The bidder may change its bid, but only to the benefit of the shareholders in the target company, and any change must give at least two weeks for the shareholders to assess the change, which means that a change cannot be made if the bid extends beyond the ten weeks maximum.[234]

309. If another bid is made, while the first bid is still pending, this bid is regarded as a competing bid. A competing bid must comply with the usual provisions mentioned here, including setting an offer period of four to ten weeks. The offer period of the first bid is automatically extended so that it now expires at the same time as the competing bid irrespectively of the ten weeks maximum unless the offeror withdraws its bid.[235] The same applies should more competing bids be made.

310. The central management body of the offeree company shall draw up a report setting out its opinion of the bid and the reasons on which such opinion is based, including its views on the effects of implementation of the bid on all the company's interests, in particular, employment, and on the bidder's strategic plans for the offeree company and their likely repercussions on employment and places of business as set out in the offer document.[236]

---

228. Section 5–6 of the Executive Order on Takeover Bids.
229. Section 7 of the Executive Order on Takeover Bids.
230. Section 18 of the Executive Order on Takeover Bids.
231. Section 13 and 14, subsections 1–2, of the Executive Order on Takeover Bids.
232. Section 14, subsection 3, of the Executive Order on Takeover Bids.
233. Section 15 of the Executive Order on Takeover Bids.
234. Section 24 of the Executive Order on Takeover Bids.
235. Section 25 of the Executive Order on Takeover Bids.
236. Section 22 of the Executive Order on Takeover Bids.

§6. Market Abuse

311. Market abuse covers insider dealing and market manipulation and is regulated by the directly applicable MAR. MAR also covers the issuer's continuous disclosure obligation and certain rules on insider's obligation to disclose their transactions in the shares of the issuer, *see* § 4 above.

312. Insider dealing as defined in Article 8 MAR arises when a person is in possession of inside information about a security that is traded on a regulated market, *see* § 4 on inside information as defined by Article 7 MAR above. The essential characteristic of insider dealing consists in an unfair advantage being obtained from inside information to the detriment of third parties who are unaware of such information, cf. recital 23 MAR. Consequently, there is a causal requirement that the insider applied the inside information to the detriment of others affected by the transaction. Where a person in possession of inside information enters into a transaction to which that information relates, it should be implied that that person has abused the information and thereby committed insider dealing, however, that presumption is without prejudice to the rights of the defence and may be rebutted cf. recital 24 MAR. The understanding of what constitutes insider dealing in Article 8 MAR is supplemented by Article 9 MAR, which describes certain scenarios where the presumption of abuse where trading is done in possession of inside information is inapplicable and where the abuse must be proven, for example where certain employees of a company are in possession of inside information but trading was done by other employees and the company apply informational barriers to keep them separated and does not otherwise encourage the intercommunication of inside information. Furthermore, the offence of insider dealing is secured by making it a separate offence to selectively disclose inside information to other persons, unless it was a necessary part of one's task, cf. Article 10 MAR. In order to facilitate investigations of suspected insider dealing, issuers are obliged to keep lists of persons in possession of inside information, known as insider lists, and these lists must be continuously updated, cf. Article 18 MAR. The lists are confidential but must be provided to authorities upon request.

313. Market manipulation is defined in Article 12 MAR and its definition are supplemented by an annex to MAR and further indications in a level 2 instrument. There is no general definition, but rather a range of examples of what would constitute manipulation. The gist of the prohibition appears to be any act that would interfere with the informational process that constitutes the pricing mechanism of the market in such a way as to disturb the pricing signals transmitted by ordinary market activity to the market participants and the general public.

314. When an issuer engages in buy-back programmes or when support is arranged in connection with public emissions such as IPOs, there is a special risk of insider dealing and market manipulation. In order to provide a safe harbour, Article 5 MAR outlines how issuers and others may behave to ensure that their actions are guaranteed not to violate the regulation on market abuse.

315. The EU respects human rights, including the freedom of speech and press freedom. Consequently, special considerations are shown to editors and editing employees who, in their professional capacity, disseminate information, cf. recital 77 and Article 21 MAR. However, this does not apply if the relevant editor or editing employee derives, directly or indirectly, an advantage or profits from the dissemination of the information in question.

316. Securities dealers and the employees of these undertakings carrying out transactions with securities, shall, without undue delay, inform the DFSA if it is reasonable to assume that a transaction constitutes a violation of the prohibition on insider dealing or market manipulation, cf. Article 16 MAR. It should be noted that the presumption of abuse where trading is done in possession of inside information does not apply where a market-maker or a securities dealer simply perform their services in a normal way, cf. Article 9, subsection 2, MAR. In respect of securities traders, it is thus reasonable to assume that they are not liable for carrying out a transaction even if that transaction constitutes insider dealing if they have not in any way encouraged or initiated the transaction, even if they suspected it and reported their suspicion to the DFSA. The same probably applies to transactions that constitute manipulation.

317. Insider dealing is prohibited, cf. Article 14 MAR, as is market manipulation, cf. Article 15 MAR. MAR is accompanied by a Directive on Criminal Sanctions, which prescribes criminal sanctions in case of intentional insider dealing and market manipulation.[237] Denmark is not subject to EU law in respect of criminal law and is therefore not subject to the Directive, however, insider dealing and market manipulation are considered criminal offences, which cover both intentional and negligent activities, and are subject to imprisonment up to six years.[238] The Danish Supreme Court has decided that breach of the prohibition on insider dealing and on market manipulation normally results in unsuspended imprisonment unless special mitigating circumstances prevail.

237. Directive 2014/57/EU of the European Parliament and of the Council of 16 Apr. 2014 on criminal sanctions for market abuse (market abuse directive).

238. Section 249 DMCA sanctions violations of MAR, including insider dealing and market manipulation, with fines or imprisonment up to 18 months, whereas gross violations of insider dealing and market manipulation are punishable with up to six years imprisonment according to section 299d, subsection 1, no 1, of the Criminal Code.

Chapter 9. Commercial Contracts

§1. General Principles of Contract Law

318. The regulation of contracts is laid down in the Contracts Act (*Aftaleloven*), originally enacted in 1917.[239] The Act corresponds to similar acts in the other Nordic countries. The Consolidated Contracts Act[240] contains the provisions in force. The Contracts Act regulates agreements on both commercial and non-commercial transactions. It is not applicable to testamentary wills and matters of family law, but contracts between spouses concerning property and business matters are subject to it. Denmark is party to the United Nations Convention on Contracts for the International Sale of Goods (CISG).

I. Formation of Contracts

A. General Rules

319. The Contract Act has adopted the offer and acceptance model. A contract is comprised of two declarations of will: the offer and the acceptance. An offer is binding on the party who has made it. In bilateral contracts, the acceptance includes a communication addressed to the promisor as well as a promise of fulfilling the acceptant's own duties. The contract is formed when the promise is duly accepted.

320. The Contracts Act, Chapter 1, regulates the formation of contracts. The rules of the chapter are not mandatory. They are applicable only when nothing else follows from the offer or acceptance or from customs of trade or other usages. An offer is a promise which is limited in time depending on the agreed or legal time limit of the acceptance. An offer binds the offeror from the moment where it has come to the knowledge of the addressee. Consequently, the offer may be revoked until this moment, compare section 7. A revocation constitutes a command, as it places a deprivation of rights on the addressee. A command binds the addressee from the moment that it reaches it. It is not required that it has come to the attention of the addressee. But if the offer is not revoked, or the revocation arrives too late, the offeror is bound until the expiry of the delay of acceptance, unless the offer is rejected. Danish contract law is based on the 'theory of promise' (*løfteprincippet*). According to this theory the binding force of the two declarations of will, which form the contract, are not dependent on each other. This is therefore contrary to the 'agreement theory', under which the binding force follows the consent of the contract parties.[241] A unilateral promise may constitute a contract. Such is the case when the offeror promises a gift by a written declaration and the addressee is the beneficiary without obligations towards the offeror. Here, the contract has come to

239. Author: Marie-Louise Holle.
240. Consolidated Act 193/2016.
241. Peter Møgelvang-Hansen, *Danish Law in a European Perspective* 238 (Børge Dahl, Torben Melchior & Ditlev Tamm eds., 2d ed., Thomson 2002) (hereafter: *Danish Law*).

existence without the acceptance of the addressee. The fact that a gift tax may be imposed on the addressee has no importance for the establishment of the contract. In cases where the gift promise is oral, it must be accepted immediately.

321. General provisions on the delay of acceptance are laid down in section 3, according to which the delay may be determined by the offer or it may be calculated according to certain rules. The regulation on late or inconsistent acceptance is close to the German rules.[242]

322. According to section 9, a declaration constituting an offer may state that it has no binding force. In that case, the communication is only to be regarded as an invitation to make an offer with the contents of the communication.

323. As for the acceptance by silence, there is no general rule. According to court practice, it should be considered if under the specific circumstances of the case, the offeror could reasonably expect the other party to declare that it will not accept the offer, so that silence constitutes acceptance. It depends on commercial practice or other customs between the parties, for example, previous contractual engagements. Generally, it is more likely for a party to be bound by silence in business relationships than in consumer contracts and between private parties. If, after negotiations, a letter of confirmation containing unusual or onerous terms is sent from one of the parties to the other one, the addressee will probably not be bound by the terms unless the sender proves that the other party has accepted them.[243]

324. Contract parties may establish a document outlining an agreement between two or more parties before the agreement is finalized, a letter of intent. Letters of intent generally being communications stating specific negotiation points or negotiation framework, the main question is to decide if the letter of intent in question constitutes a binding agreement with legal effects. General principles of contract law apply to the interpretation of letters of intent.[244]

B. Standard Terms

325. Both offeror and offeree may make reference to standard terms when concluding a contract. Standard terms are not submitted to general regulation. If reference is made to terms which are not enclosed, the courts take into consideration the extent to which these terms are accessible. As a general rule, the more the terms are onerous or unusual, the more it is required that they are pointed out and easily within range.[245] In cases where the terms may be characterized as 'agreed documents', they might be considered as part of the contract even when there is only a

242. Consolidated Act on Contracts, ss 4, 5 and 6, cf. the German Bürgerliches Gesetzbuch, ss 149 and 150.
243. *Danish Law,* p. 245 f.
244. *Danish Law,* p. 241 f.
245. *Danish Law,* p. 245 f.

faint reference to them if the parties are expected to be quite familiar with the terms. In cases where both parties use their own standard terms, the offer and the reply may not be compatible. The so-called *battle of forms* is a rather controversial question. Where both parties refer to their own standard terms and have a reached agreement except on those terms, the courts will most likely hold that there is a binding contract if the parties in one way or another show that they consider the contract to be concluded. It is doubtful which terms the courts will apply to the contract, and doctrine is not unanimous.

C. Electronic Transmission

326. The Contracts Act only mentions letters and telegrams as means of transmission. However, the provisions of the Act may be applied to transmission by telex, fax, e-mails and other form of electronic data interchange, etc. As the time of receipt by the addressee is exactly known in case of expedition by these means, it is not complicated to determine the point in time in which the declarations of the contract have become binding on the parties. In Danish contract law, the commands which are declarations imposing burdens on the addressee are sent on the risk of the sender. This sender has to prove that the command has reached its destination. In cases where an offeror sends a revocation of his offer to the other party by telex, fax or e-mail, the offeror is not bound by his offer when the time of arrival of the declarations indicates that the revocation has come to the addressee before the offer itself has come to the addressee's knowledge.[246]

II. The Form of the Contract

327. In general, the form of the contract has no relevance to its validity. As a general principle, Danish law does not require that contracts be made in writing. However, certain contracts must be made in writing, for example, consumer credit contracts.[247] Commercial agency contracts must be in writing if requested by one of the parties.[248] The parties may agree to have the contract laid down in writing. A contracting party may have an interest in setting up a written contract, as the party who claims its rights according to the contract has to prove its existence.

III. Interpretation of Contracts

328. Rules on interpretation of contracts follow from case law. The important elements are the determination of the intention of the promisor, the general meaning of the wording and terms as well as more pragmatic considerations of equity

246. *Danish Law,* p. 243 f.
247. Cf. s. 8 of the Consolidated Act 1336/2015 on Credit Contracts (*Kreditaftalelov*).
248. Act 272/1990 on Commercial Agents and Commercial Travellers (*Lov om handelsagenter og handelsrejsende*), s. 3, which is mandatory.

and reasonableness. In cases where the general meaning of a contract term differs from the parties' understanding of the term, the intention of the parties prevails. Generally, the courts seek to interpret the contract (or the contract term In question) in a manner giving it some effect instead of being meaningless. Courts seem to prefer a solution corresponding with the purpose of the contract and to give a word or a term the same meaning everywhere it appears in the contract. When it seems impossible to discern a common intention, the courts might use a more objective method by interpreting the contract in accordance with the literal meaning of the words and the text as a whole. However, if a literal interpretation is not in accordance with principles of fairness and reasonableness, the courts may apply more pragmatic considerations in interpreting the contract terms in order to obtain a result complying with the principle of equity. The principle of *in dubio contra stipulatorem* (meaning that where a contract clause is ambiguous, the preferred meaning should be the one that works against the interests of the drafting party) is particularly applied to standard contracts and contracts drawn up solely by one of the parties.

329. As contract parties normally do not expressly agree on every single point, the courts fill in the gaps in the actual agreement of the parties with implied contract terms taken from usages of trade or practice in order to achieve a reasonable and fair comprehension of the agreement.

IV. Validity of Contracts

A. *General Rules*

330. The contract itself may be contested in relation to the circumstances of conclusion as well as to the content of the terms. A contract may be void because one of the parties is incapable. As Danish law adheres to the theory of promise, the validity of the contract relates to the declarations of will made by each of the parties. When only one of the declarations, the promise or the acceptance, is affected by the invalidity, the other declaration is considered void, and the whole contract is deemed invalid.

B. *Incapacity*

331. Capacity to contract requires the age of 18 years.[249] If a person is under guardianship, the guardian acts on the incapable person's behalf, except in case of diminished capacity where the incapable person and the guardian act jointly. The Act on Legal Guardianship regulates the question of termination of contracts established between a capable and an incapable party. However, according to the

249. Consolidated Act 1015/2007 on Legal Guardianship (*Værgemålsloven*).

so-called money rule,[250] a contract is normally valid when an incapable person has paid the full amount in cash for goods or services, and the capable person had reason to believe that the incapable party might have the sufficient authority or capacity to bind itself. Furthermore, an incapable person may be authorized by its guardian to carry on trade, however subject to approval from the Minister of Justice. Consequently, contracts concluded by such a person concerning the activities of the enterprise are valid.

C. Declarations of Will

332. The Contracts Act, Chapter 3, regulates the validity of declarations of will. A declaration of intention that has been wrongfully obtained by actual or threatened imminent violence is not binding on the person coerced, compare section 28. This rule is applicable to, for example, usury (lending money at unreasonably high rates of interest). This provision constitutes a so-called strong ground for a declaration of invalidity; the ground for voidability being 'strong' (as opposed to 'weak' grounds) means that it is a remedy against even an innocent contract party. When the declaration of will has been obtained by any other form of duress than the above mentioned, this constitutes a 'weak' ground of voidability as the rule is a remedy only against a contracting party acting in bad faith (because that party knew or ought to have known about the duress), compare section 29. Fraud (section 30),[251] usury and undue influence (section 31), mistake (section 32, paragraph 1) and unfair use of a favourable position (section 33) all constitute weak reasons for a declaration of invalidity. These remedies are remedies only against a contracting party acting in bad faith. The provision is applicable not only on errors following from the declaration, but also errors of motivation (*error in motivis*) such as miscalculation. Section 32, paragraph 2, provides that in cases where a declaration of will is distorted through the transmission by telegraph or through the verbal transfer by a messenger,[252] a contracting party is not bound by this declaration, not even towards an innocent party (who did not know about the mistake), if the person having made the declaration notifies the addressee without an unreasonable delay from the time where he was informed about the mistake. Section 32, paragraph 2 constitutes a 'strong' ground for a declaration of invalidity. Under certain conditions, it is applicable to electronic transmission. The reason is that the security is high and that to a wide extent it is possible for the receiver to control the correctness of the message. The Contracts Act, section 34, concerns *pro forma* contracts where the contracting parties have agreed on pretending to establish a contract, however, with no intention of giving effect to it. When a right deriving from such a contract is conferred to a bona fide third person, the contract is considered valid in relation to the third person.

---

250. *Aftaler og mellemmænd*, p. 141 f.
251. Cf. for an example of fraudulent suppression of essential facts (silence concerning a third person's financial conditions), UfR 1990.390 H.
252. A messenger is understood in a broad sense, for example a lawyer who transmits a message to his client.

D. Implied Terms

333. As well as the terms expressly laid down in the contract by the parties, further terms may in some circumstances be read into contracts by the courts, aiming at completing the contract terms.[253] An implied term constitutes an assumption which has not been manifested as an express or implied contract term. In practice, it is rarely possible to make an exhaustive contract in which every relevant term is laid down expressly. By claiming an implied term, a contract party may be released from performing its contract duties when circumstances arise changing the relationship in such a way that the assumptions which have been decisive for the party's engagement no longer hold true; in other words, the party would not have entered into the contract if it had known of the supervening circumstances. Moreover, it is a condition for the release from a contractual obligation that the other party realized or should have realized the assumptions of the first party and their importance for it. It should also be reasonable and equitable to put the risk on the other party. The assumptions may have existed before the establishment of the contract, or they might have appeared later. The doctrine constitutes a supplement to the above-mentioned rules of Chapter 3 of the Contracts Act, which in fact provide for important traditional implied conditions without being exhaustive. The doctrine has been rather frequently applied in case law. For illustration *see* Supreme Court judgment UfR 1985.334 2/H, where a textile manufacturer purchased an IT system (hardware and various computer programs); at the conclusion of the contract the seller estimated the price for the system. The actual price to be paid by the purchaser turned out to be ten times more than the originally estimated price, because the purchaser wanted to his usual procedures to be applied in the new IT system. The Supreme Court stated that at the establishment of the contract, none of the parties had been aware of how important an enlargement the usual procedures caused to the IT system. Therefore, the Court ruled that it was reasonable, owing to the circumstances, to put the risk for the termination of the contract on the seller, who was supposed to know about the IT system, and who had not found it necessary to take further information on the requirements of the purchaser.

E. Unfair Contract Terms

334. It is a well-established principle that a contract may be set aside in whole or in part when contract terms are considered to be so unfair to one of the contract parties that the legislature or the courts intervene to prevent an injustice. It follows from the Danish Code from 1683, that contracts that are not contrary to law and decency must be performed in accordance with their terms.[254] A general clause concerning the content of the contract is laid down in the Contracts Act, section 36. Paragraph 1 of section 36 provides that a contract may be amended or disregarded if it would be unreasonable or contrary to principles of fair conduct to maintain its

---

253. *Danish Law*, p. 254 f.

254. Danish Code (*Danske lov*) 5–1-2.

validity. A contract may thus be modified or set aside, in whole or in part. This provision allows the courts to replace an unreasonable clause by construing a new clause, for example, reducing and to a certain extent augmenting a price. The courts can also both reduce and prolong a time limit within certain limits. Paragraph 2 provides that several elements can be considered when applying section 36: circumstances present at the establishment of the contract, the content of the contract as well as subsequent circumstances. Although it has been presumed that section 36 should be applied mainly to consumer contracts, it is also applicable to business agreements and every other sort of contract, both individual and standard agreements. In practice, section 36 has been useful, for instance in modifying irrevocable distributor contracts in order to permit the distributor to terminate its engagement within a reasonable time limit.[255] The general clause cannot eliminate every risk of entering contracts; the parties have to take a normal business risk of loss or chance of benefit.

335. Special rules on consumer contracts are introduced in section 38 a through d.

336. When the parties' attempts to conclude a contract do not succeed, the costs of the negotiations must be covered by the parties themselves. Danish law does not contain provisions holding a party liable if it has broken off negotiations, and the other party has relied on a future contract. Even if the party has been negligent, it will generally not have to pay for the other party's transaction costs or loss of profit. However, compensation for costs may be awarded in exceptional circumstances; a contract party in good faith may claim damages for *culpa in contrahendo*.[256]

V. Authority

337. The Contracts Act, Chapter 2, regulates the authorization of an agent, meaning an individual who makes a contract on behalf of someone else, the principal. The Act distinguishes between two types of authorization. The first type in which the power of the agent is manifest to the surroundings due to exterior measures. The second type is based exclusively on a declaration from the principal to the agent, the so-called verbal authorization, which might derive from a written internal paper (section 18). The manifest type may be communicated to the surroundings through the professional occupation of the agent (section 10, paragraph 2), through a particular declaration to a third person (section 13), by a published announcement (section 14), or by a written authorization which is kept by the agent for the purpose to show it to a third person (section 16). The legal consequence following from the manifest authorization is that the principal is directly bound by the declaration of the agent and is the direct beneficiary of the contracts and legal acts established by the agent on behalf of the principal within the limit of the agent's power (section 10, paragraph 1). In cases where the agent has received an order

255. *See* for example, the Supreme Court decision reported in UfR 1988.1042.
256. Cf. for illustration the Supreme Court decision reported in UfR 1996.1625.

from the principal to follow certain instruction, section 11, paragraph 1, provides that the legal act established by the agent contrary to the instruction does not bind the principal when the third party knew or ought to have known about the order. Consequently, a bona fide third party may claim performance of the contract according to its terms despite opposite instructions from the principal to the agent. Nevertheless, in cases where the authorization (the 'verbal authorization') derives exclusively from the declaration given from the principal to the agent, the third party, even if it is in bona fide, has to respect that the order limits the power of the agent in accordance with the instruction (section 11, paragraph 2). The manifest authorization may be revoked in the same way as it has been established. An agent who assumes a professional function must be dismissed and removed from his occupation. A written declaration must be returned to the principal. A 'verbal authorization' according to section 18 is revoked by a declaration to the agent. According to section 25, in case of transgression of its authority, the agent may be liable towards the bona fide third party.

§2. Sale of Goods

I. Legislation on Sale of Goods Contracts

338. The sale of goods is comprised of the SGA[257,258] which originally came into force in 1906, codifying the existing case law at that point of time. It has been amended a limited number of times, including in 1980, when a special chapter upon consumer sale was inserted. The SGA is not applicable to contracts on services.[259] The international sale of goods is covered by a *lex specialis*, the Act on International Sale of Goods,[260] which implements the United Nation's Convention on CISG of 11 April 1980 by providing that the CISG is applicable, except for sales between the Nordic countries. International sales are sales between parties who have their place of business in different countries. In business relationships, the provisions of neither of the acts are mandatory. The parties in international contracts of sale may choose to apply domestic rules of law (SGA) instead of those of the CISG.

339. In case CISG is applicable since the parties are situated in countries which have ratified CISG, compare Article 1(1)(a) there is no need to apply private international law in order to determine which law is applicable to the case. However, if only one of the parties is situated in a country, where CISG has been ratified, the choice of law question must be solved in accordance with the Convention of The Hague of 5 June 1955 on the Law applicable to International Contracts on Sales of Goods, provided however that the jurisdiction is in Denmark.[261] At present, eight states have ratified the Convention. This Act provides for the parties to agree on the

257. Author: Kim Østergaard.
258. Consolidated Act 140/2014 (*Købeloven*).
259. UfR 2010 p. 332 (Eastern Court of Appeal).
260. Consolidated Act 1224/2014 (*International købelov*).
261. The convention is incorporated into Danish law by Consolidated Act 722/1986.

free choice of law in accordance with Section 3. If no such agreement has been made, the rules of law in the country of the domicile or the business place of the seller at the time where/when he received the order must be applied, Section 4. Thus, Danish exporters may expect Danish law, i.e., CISG, to be applicable when the contract does not contain a choice of law provision.

II. Types of Sale and Product Description in the SGA

340. The domestic SGA distinguishes between purchases made in the ordinary course of business (business sales), consumer sales and other sales. For business sales, severe remedies are provided in case of breach of contract in order to persuade the parties to fulfil their obligations. Consumer sales, which constitute sales in which the seller is a professional who acts within the line of his business and the buyer is a consumer, are to a wide extent comprised by mandatory provisions of protection, section 1, subsection 2 of the SGA.

341. The SGA establishes an important distinction between certain goods that are particularly specified and identified in the contract (specified goods) and goods that are exclusively defined in the contract by their nature (generic goods), SGA, section 3. Whereas generic goods are defined in SGA specified goods are not defined by the SGA. The distinction is basically whether the contract allows the seller to choose between more than one specified good in order to fulfil her/his obligation according to the contract correctly.

The SGA does not contain general rules on the description of goods except in consumer sales. The seller has to deliver the quality and quantity of goods on which the parties have agreed. If nothing concerning the condition of the goods is agreed or follows from the contract, goods of normal proper quality should be delivered. Sections 75a and 76 of the Act state in general terms when goods are defective in consumer sales and provide criteria applicable by analogy to sales in general. Roughly compared with the principles established in the CISG, Article 35 on the conformity of the goods with the contract both sets of rules is quite similar. However, the CISG emphasizes the purpose and the usual quality whereas the SGA, section 76, makes a point of the statements of the seller and the importance of misleading information.[262]

III. Delivery

342. The seller has to deliver the goods determined by the agreement in sufficient quantity and quality, in due time and at the right place. The seller has to do what is necessary in order to secure that the goods in question come into possession of the purchaser. The SGA, section 17, subsection 1, lays down the main rule that the seller carries the risk of the incidental loss or depreciation of the goods until delivery has taken place in accordance with sections 9, 10 or 11. It is provided in

262. UfR 2014 p. 578 (Supreme Court).

SGA, compare section 37, that in cases where the seller carries the risk and the goods cannot be delivered because of circumstances caused by the buyer (*mora creditoris*), the risk passes to the purchaser from the moment when the delivery could have taken place, provided the contract concerns specified goods. If the contract concerns generic goods (*genus*), the goods must have been clearly designated in favour of the purchaser. Otherwise, the risk does not pass to the purchaser.[263]

343. The main rule with respect to the place of delivery is laid down in section 9 of the Act, which provides that the seller has to make delivery at his business place, or if he has no business place, at the place of his domicile. The purchaser has to pick up the good, pay for costs of the transportation, and must also pay the relevant insurance in conjunction with the transportation. If the goods are sent from one place to another, it is provided according to SGA section 10 that delivery has taken place when the goods have been handed over to the first carrier who has undertaken the transportation from the place in question. In case of transportation by ship, the goods are delivered when they have been brought into the ship over the ship's gunwale. In case of local sales in a certain place, delivery has not taken place until the goods have come into the possession of the purchaser, according to the SGA section 11. In order to apply either section 10 or 11 of SGA, the parties must have agreed upon the place of delivery. Otherwise, section 9 of SGA is the default rule of SGA.

344. Concerning the costs of transportation, it is the main rule that the purchaser has to pay such costs once the goods are delivered. The SGA provides for the content of certain traditional transportation clauses. Section 62 regulates the 'free on board' clause according to which the seller has to bring the goods at his own costs to the place of shipping and to perform what normally is undertaken by a shipper in order to load the goods. The risk passes to the purchaser once the goods have passed the ship's gunwale. The purchaser has to procure ship or shipping space. According to section 63, the clause 'cost and freight', c & f or 'cf' means that the seller has to transport the goods at his own cost to the place of destination. However, the risk passes to the purchaser once the goods are handed over to a carrier or have passed the ship's gunwale in accordance with the main rule with respect to the risk issue. According to section 64, a 'cif' clause is submitted to the same rule as the 'cost and freight' clause, except that the seller has to take out a normal insurance. It must be noticed that the content of the Danish 'cf' and 'cif' clauses differs from the corresponding INCOTERMS 2010[264] as these terms are similar to the Danish 'fob' clause with the modification that the seller has to pay the costs to the place of destination

---

263. The SGA Section 17, subs. 2 lays down a special rule on specied goods which have to be picked up by the purchaser within a period at a time chosen by the purchaser. The good shall be at this party's risk from the beginning of the period, provided however that the seller has secured the good in question is ready to be picked up. Thus, the risk for an accidential occurrence passes to the purchaser at this point of time.

264. The practical discordance between the Danish clauses and the INCOTERMS is minor, as there is no difference when the goods are transported exclusively by sea or the transportation has been initiated by ship and continued by other means of transportation.

in the harbour of arrival. Section 65, provides for the clause 'delivered' (*leveret*), according to which the seller has to bear both the risk and pay the costs to the place of destination.

345. The time of delivery is determined by the SGA, compare section 12, which provides that the seller has to deliver on demand when the time of delivery is not settled within the sales agreement or can be derived from the circumstances. If the parties have agreed upon a particular period of time when delivery can take place, the seller is normally entitled to choose the time for the delivery, unless the period of time has been settled in favour of the purchaser, compare SGA section 13.

Unless the parties have agreed otherwise, the good(s) and the payment are supposed to be exchanged simultaneously. Thus, the main rule is cash payment, compare SGA section 14. According to the provision, the seller is not obliged (retention right) to deliver the good(s) unless payment is at seller's disposal at the same time, unless the parties have agreed on a respite, payment may be demanded against documents, compare SGA section 16.

IV. The Price

346. The parties would in most cases agree upon the purchase price to be paid. As a default rule, section 5 of SGA provides that the purchaser has to pay what the seller demands provided, however, that the requested purchase price is not unreasonable. Case law is rather scarce with respect to this provision. In case the seller has sent the purchaser an invoice, the purchaser has to make an objection immediately to the seller in order not to be bound by the content of the invoice unless the parties have agreed upon a lower price or the purchase price evidently is unreasonable, compare SGA section 6. For consumer sales, SGA section 72 provides that the price must be reasonable in relation to the sales object's normal price and the circumstances.

The payment must be made on demand if nothing is agreed on as regards the time of payment, compare SGA section 12. In international sales, the payment may normally be made in the currency of the seller's country if the currency has not been agreed upon.

V. Breach of Contract

A. Regulation in General

347. The SGA regulates breach of contract when the breach is due to a delay of performance concerning the goods or the payment, factual defects of the goods, or defective title. The breach of contract may constitute an actual breach or it may be evident that the obliged party will not be able to perform when the date of delivery or payment is due. It is not considered a breach of contract in Danish law when the other party does not receive delivery (*mora creditoris*). However, the seller has certain rights and obligations in accordance with SGA, Sections 33–37, including the right to resell the good and claim damages from the original purchaser. Case law is scarce and there is no recent case law.

B. Late Performance

348. The SGA Sections 21–27, lays down the general rules on late delivery, which includes no delivery at all, by the seller. Special provisions for consumer sales are laid down in SGA sections 74 and 75, which are mandatory rules of protection. The SGA Sections 21–27 are still applicable in consumer sales, but are non-mandatory rules.

When the delivery does not take place in due time, the purchaser has the choice to require specific performance or terminate the contract without notice. The purchaser is entitled to delivery in kind. In cases where delivery is or is considered impossible the seller is not obliged to deliver the object of sale, but he is obliged to pay damages to the purchaser, compare below. When the delivery is subject to a fundamental delay, the purchaser is entitled to terminate the contract without notice, provided that he did not cause the breach of contract, compare SGA section 21. A late delivery is always considered a fundamental breach in business sales, or if the contract contains a precisely fixed term for delivery, compare SGA section 21, subsection 3. When successive sales are delayed, each delivery is normally to be considered separately in accordance with SGA section 22.

349. The conditions concerning payment of damages for late delivery depend on the nature of the goods. Damages for delay of delivery of species goods may be claimed in cases in which the breach of contract is due to the seller's negligence, compare SGA section 23. As the provision presumes that the seller or his employees have been negligent, the seller has to prove his innocence (presumption of negligence). If the seller fails to do so, the seller has to pay damages. For delay of generic goods, SGA, section 24 provides the principle that the seller in breach is liable to pay damages regardless of negligence (strict liability). The seller is not liable when an exemption clause is lawfully agreed upon (i.e. if the seller did not act with intent or (as a main rule) with gross negligence) or when the seller proves that it must be considered impossible to comply with the contract because of extraordinary circumstances which were unforeseeable at the conclusion of the contract and which have caused the destruction of every object of the same nature, etc. The essence of this condition is that only 'acts of God' caused by extraordinary events having made specific performance impossible, may free the seller from liability. This is the force majeure provision of the SGA, which has been construed strictly by the Danish courts.

The damages to be paid in case of liability shall compensate the loss suffered by the purchaser caused by the breach of contract. The purchaser must be placed in a financial position identical to the situation in which the purchaser would have been, had no breach of contract taken place. Lost profit may be compensated. Furthermore, the difference in price is compensated for when the purchaser has had to purchase the goods elsewhere for a higher price than that agreed upon with the seller. Whether the purchaser requires specific performance or terminates the sales contract, the purchaser is entitled to receive damages as described above. The burden of proof that the price is reasonable is fulfilled by the purchaser when a covering purchase is made in a proper manner in accordance with section 25.

C. Examination of the Goods

350. The SGA section 47 provides that a purchaser shall show watchfulness in conjunction with the examination of the good, *(caveat emptor)* before the purchase is made or has been provided with the opportunity or the invitation to examine a sample of the good, and cannot invoke a defect afterwards which the purchaser had or ought to have discovered during such an examination, unless the seller has been acting fraudulently.

In business sales, the purchaser has to examine the goods delivered or a sample received when it follows from good business practice, compare SGA section 51. If the purchaser discovers or ought to have discovered a defect, the purchaser has to notify the seller if he wants to make a claim. In business sales, the notification must be made immediately, in sales in general without unjustified delay, compare SGA section 52. The ultimate term for notification is laid down in SGA, section 54, which provides that claims concerning defects must as a general rule be raised within two years after the goods have been handed over to the purchaser unless the seller has given a guarantee for a longer period or has behaved fraudulently.

D. Regulation of Defects

351. In case of non-conforming goods, the purchaser has different remedies at his disposal. When a defect decreases the value of the goods, the purchaser is entitled to claim a proportionate deduction of the price which the purchaser has to pay according to the contract.[265] The amount of the deduction is calculated on the basis of the relation between the value of the defective goods and the value of the goods in conformity with the requirements.

The purchaser may terminate the sales contract in question if the non-conformity (the defect) can be considered fundamental. SGA section 42 comprises specific goods as SGA, section 43 entails generic goods. In accordance with the latter provision, the purchaser is entitled to require delivery of substitute goods, provided the defect can be considered fundamental with respect to the delivered good in question.

If the quantity is too small, the purchaser is entitled to demand the rest of the delivery (specific performance). The contract may be cancelled in any case where

265. If for instance the value of the goods without defect was DKK 100 and the value of the defective goods is DKK 90, the proportionate deduction amounts to 10% of the price, which is DKK 10.

the seller has acted fraudulently. Furthermore, concerning the sale of generic goods, the purchaser may also cancel when the seller had known the defects in due time so that he could have procured goods without defects.

352. In cases where the seller is able to remedy the lack of conformity by repair before the expiration of the term of delivery, the seller has the right to do so when it is apparent it does not cause costs or inconvenience for the purchaser, compare SGA section 49. In practice, this is a very narrow possibility to exercise redress. Apart from consumer sales (compare SGA sections 78 and 79), the purchaser has no right to claim redress.

353. If the purchaser has suffered a loss caused by the defect, the purchaser is entitled to claim damages on certain conditions. In cases concerning generic goods, the seller has to pay damages even if the defect was not caused by his negligence, compare SGA section 43, subsection 3, which refers to section 24. It follows from this provision that the seller is exempted from the obligation to pay damages only when any object becomes defective due to qualified extraordinary circumstances which could not have been foreseen by the seller at the establishment of the contract, or similar events. For specific goods, it is provided in SGA, section 42, subsection 2 that the purchaser may claim damages for the loss caused by defects that already existed at the establishment of the contract when the seller has guaranteed the good in question or acted fraudulently; furthermore, damages may be claimed for goods which have become defective due to the negligence of the seller after the formation of the contract. The size of the compensation is calculated in the same way as in case of delay, according to SGA, section 45 referring to section 25.

354. The seller has to deliver the goods free from any right or claim of any third party. The starting point is of course that the purchaser gets title to the good in question. The SGA, section 59 is the only provision in the SGA dealing with this issue. The provision, in accordance with the wording, is only applicable in case, the defect in a title is originally, entirely and deals with specific goods. In such cases, the seller has a strict liability which is unconditional. It is established practice that the regulation on non-conformity may be applied analogously otherwise dealing with a defect in a title.

E. Regulation of Payment

355. The purchaser has to pay the price for the goods and to take such steps as may be required to enable payment to take place. In case of fundamental delay in payment, the seller is entitled to terminate the contract without notice. However, if the good is handed over to the purchaser, the seller is not entitled to terminate except when the seller has made a reservation to the effect that he still holds the right to the title of the good until payment is made or when the object is refused by the purchaser, compare SGA, section 28, subsection 2. In cases where the seller is obliged to or has to stick with a specific performance of the contract despite the breach by the purchaser, the seller is entitled to claim the payment and the fulfilment of the measures for enabling the price to be paid as well as an interest which compensates the loss due to the delay. The size of the interest amounts to the bank rate of the Central Bank (*Nationalbanken*) plus 8%.[266]

356. Furthermore, the seller is entitled to claim damages. The SGA, section 30 provides that in case of termination, the rule of SGA, section 24 is applied; *see* above Part I, Chapter 9, §2.IV, D. Since it is extremely rare that the conditions for exemption of liability should be fulfilled when money should have been paid, the purchaser normally has to pay damages. A case of exemption might be that the payment can be fulfilled only in a specific currency and an unexpected government order prevents any payment from being transferred from the country. However, in such cases, CISG will in most cases be applicable. When the agreed price exceeds the normal price, the seller may claim damages corresponding to the difference between the contractual price and the normal price for similar goods.

F. Anticipated Breach of Contract

357. When the parties have agreed to purchase on credit, severe economic difficulties may occur for the purchaser within the period between the conclusion of the contract and when payment is due. Even if the purchaser has not actually violated his obligations, an anticipated breach of contract can be invoked when insolvency of the purchaser is presumed and the purchaser will not be able to pay the price when it is due. According to SGA, section 39, the purchaser will be deemed insolvent when he goes bankrupt or negotiations on a compulsory arrangement are initiated, and furthermore, when the purchaser by execution has been found unable to recover his debts or, when dealing as a businessman the purchaser has stopped his payments, or his financial circumstances presumably do not permit him to pay the price at the term of payment. In suchcases, the seller is entitled to retain the goods or, when they have been sent, to prevent them from being handed over to the purchaser unless the payment is secured. When the term of delivery has arrived, the bankrupt estate may ask for a security of the payment. If the demand is not fulfilled, the contract may be terminated.

358. The SGA, section 40 entails the situation in which the purchaser has gone bankrupt. Before delivery is due, the seller may ask the bankrupt's estate to enter into the contract. If it does not enter, the seller may terminate the contract without notice. When the goods have been handed over to the bankrupt's estate after the bankruptcy was declared without payment the sale price, the seller is entitled to get the goods in question back, unless the bankrupt's estate declares to enter into the contract and places a security for the payment in accordance with SGA, section 41. When the bankrupt estate has disposed of the goods, it is assumed to have entered into the contract.

266. Consolidated Act 459/2014 on Interest Due to Delay of Payment (*Renteloven*).

G. No Obligation of the Purchaser to Take Delivery

359. There is no breach of contract where the purchaser fails to take the goods into his possession. Normally the purchaser has no direct obligation to receive the sales objects. In cases where the goods remain in the possession of the seller since the purchaser has not picked up the goods or made it impossible for the seller to hand them over to him, the seller has to hold them until the purchaser takes them into his possession, or the seller applies the right he might have because of the purchaser's non-performance of his duties to pay the price and to terminate the contract, compare SGA section 33. The seller is entitled to sell the goods when they cause him substantial costs or inconvenience, compare SGA section 34. For the costs incurred by the storage or otherwise, the seller may claim compensation, and the seller is entitled to retain the goods as security.

H. Differences Between the SGA and the CISG

360. International sales are comprised by the regulation of the GISG as mentioned above. The main outlines of the CISG are close to those laid down in the Danish SGA. However, some differences may be pointed out.

In contrast to CISG, SGA distinguishes between different types of sales and provides for significant consequences following from breach of contract on the basis of the main distinction between contracts concerning specific goods and generic goods respectively.

The CISG Article 35 lays down rules regarding the quality of the objects of sale which are not the same as those set up in the SGA, section 76, concerning consumer goods. However, the descriptions do not conflict with each other.

In case of the seller's breach of the contract caused by late delivery or non-conformance of delivery of goods, the CISG, Articles 47 and 49, entitle the purchaser to fix a reasonable period of time for performance by the seller of his obligations. This possibility does not exist under the Danish SGA (outside consumer sale).

The SGA contains no rule on formalities of termination of the contract, whereas the CISG, Article 26, lays down rules on declaration of cancellation.

Furthermore, the CISG does not limit the right for the seller to terminate in cases where the purchaser does not comply with his obligation to pay the price but nevertheless the goods have been handed over to him, *see* the provisions on cancellation, compare CISG Article 64. As mentioned above, according to the SGA, section 28, subsection 2, the seller cannot terminate and take the goods back in such cases.

With respect to defective goods, the CISG, Article 46(3), provides that the purchaser may require the seller to remedy the lack of conformity by repair and according to Article 48, the seller may remedy at his own expense any failure to perform his obligations even after the date of delivery. The SGA only gives the consumer-buyer the right to request the repair of defective goods, compare SGA, section 78, and the seller has the right to accomplish the remedy only before the agreed time for delivery.

Concerning the obligation to take delivery, it is not considered a breach of contract in Danish law when the purchaser fails to make it possible for the seller to bring the goods into the possession of the purchaser. According to CISG, Article 60, the purchaser has the obligation to take delivery.

§3. Commercial Services

I. Distribution

A. *Distribution in General*

1. Definition and Concept of Distribution

361. A distributor purchases the goods from the supplier and resells them in his own name and on his own account.[267] He decides how he will conduct his business, and he bears the full risk of loss for unsold goods and other normal business risk.

362. Exclusive rights may be transferred to the distributor by agreement. When the agreement is engaged on open exclusive distribution, the distributor holds the exclusive right within certain territory to be the only one who may procure his supplies from the supplier in order to resell the goods in the territory or to a certain group of customers. The agreement does not prevent distributors established in other territories from doing business with customers in the territory in question. The distributor obtains the full protection of his exclusive rights when it is agreed that nobody except the distributor in question is entitled to do business with the customers within the territory, which constitutes a closed exclusive distribution agreement. Both the open and the closed exclusive agreements are considered as sole distributorships (*eneforhandling*) in Danish law even if the first category only confers the distributor with a preferential position.

2. Legal Regulation

363. Agreements on distribution are subject to the general non-statutory law on contracts. Standard contracts are frequently used. Special statutory rules are provided for contracts on distribution of petrol.[268]

Distribution relationships, and in particular exclusive distribution, are subject to the public control laid down in competition law.[269]

267. Author: Peter Møgelvang-Hansen.
268. Consolidated Act 1718/2010 on petrol distribution contracts *(benzinforhandlerkontrakter)*.
269. *See* Part II, Ch. 4 on Competition Law.

364. Distributors are not within the scope of The Danish Act on Commercial Agents.[270] To some extent, the Act reflects and clarifies the same fundamental principles on collaboration. When the distributor is integrated in the distribution system of the supplier to such an extent that he has to follow instructions, which considerably limit his self-determination of the conduct of business, he may be in a position that is close to that of a commercial agent who is protected by the mandatory provisions of the Act on Commercial Agents. However, the courts are not inclined to apply the provisions of the Act analogously to distribution contracts.

3. Validity and Effects of Exclusivity Clauses

365. The exclusivity clauses restricting or eliminating the supplier's right to deal with the customers within the territory of the distributor may be set aside according to rules similar to those provided in EU Competition law. Thus, an executive order,[271] issued under the Danish Competition Act, section 10, lays down rules to the effect that the Commission Regulation (EU) 330/2010 on the application of Article 101(3) TFEU to vertical agreements and concerted practices also applies within the scope of the Danish Competition Act.[272]

4. Obligations of the Parties

366. The obligations of the distributor concerning the duty of loyalty, duty of information on relevant matters, and duty to be active in promoting sales correspond to those imposed on the commercial agents according to the Act on Commercial Agency.

A duty for the distributor to buy a minimum quantity of goods from the supplier within a certain period may be established by agreement as far as it is reasonable according to the Contracts Act, section 36. The parties may also agree on a clause allowing the distributor to deal with competing products within the contract period. Competition clauses, which defend or limit the competitive conduct of the distributor after the contract has come to an end may violate section 36 of the Contracts Act. Thus, a competition clause is void if it goes further than necessary in order to protect against competition having regard to the period of time, the place or other circumstances, or if it restricts the obliged party's access to exercise a profession in an unreasonable way.

In addition to the general contract principles, the rules of competition law apply, *see* Part II, Chapter 4, §2.

367. The obligations of the supplier correspond to those of the distributor concerning loyalty, information and the duty to place material concerning the goods at the disposal of the distributor. In principle, the supplier has no duty to provide the

270. Act 272/1990 *(Handelsagentloven).*
271. Executive Order 739/2010 on block exemption of vertical agreements and concerted practices.
272. *See* Part II Ch. 4 on competition law.

distributor with goods for resale. Even if the distributor is obliged not only to buy the goods exclusively from the supplier but also to take certain quantities of goods, the supplier may keep the liberty to decide how to conduct his business. However, a refusal of supply may be considered a breach of contract if it is unfair or creates unequal conditions for doing business.

5. Termination of the Distribution Relationship

368. When a contract is fixed for a determinable period, it expires automatically. If the parties continue their collaboration according to the contract terms, the relationship may be considered an indeterminate contract which cannot be terminated without notice. When a contract has been agreed for an indeterminate period, it is the general rule that reasonable notice has to be given.

As a general rule, the 'reasonable length' of the notice period under distributor contracts of long duration seems to be six months.[273] In a Supreme Court decision, two months were considered to be the 'reasonable length' in a case where the distributorship lasted less than one year.[274] When the termination is due to a breach of contract, it may be cancelled without notice. Compensation for loss caused by the termination with or without too short notice and other breaches of contract may be claimed according to the general rules laid down in the contract law.

369. The question of whether the sole distributor may have a claim on goodwill indemnity when the relationship is terminated by notice and a claim of indemnity has not been agreed between the parties has been debated and also submitted to the courts in a number of cases. According to the rulings of the Supreme Court, indemnity *(godtgørelse)* is normally not available in such cases[275] but only allowed in special cases where the distributor has worked up a clientele, from which the supplier can immediately benefit at the expense of the distributor when the distributor, for instance, because of the short duration of the distributorship, has no possibility to recover his costs in future sale.[276]

370. In contract practice, a variety of clauses exists. The model contract elaborated by The Danish Chamber of Commerce lays down a clause on goodwill indemnity corresponding to the gross profit in one year, when the termination of the agreement has not been caused by the breach of contract of the distributor.

273. Danish Supreme Court decision reported in UfR 2004.148. The case concerned a forty-year-old distributor contract. Six months was also the result in the Supreme Court decision reported in UfR 2000.567/2 concerning a distributorship that lasted for eight years.
274. Decision reported in UfR 2000.1581/2.
275. Supreme Court decisions reported in UfR 2000.567 and UfR 2000.1543.
276. Supreme Court decision reported in UfR 2000.1581/2.

B. Contracts on Distribution of Petrol

371. Distributors of petrol enjoy special protection under the Act on Petrol Distribution Contracts.[277] The Act provides *inter alia* that the contract may bind the distributor for a maximum period of three years. After this term, the period of notice for termination is maximum one year. Clauses and declarations on opening hours, minimum sales and competition clauses concerning terms and places are void. The Act also provides for leaseholders of filling stations. Furthermore, the Act is applicable on contracts including declarations registered on real property which confer the supplier with a sole right to provide petrol for resale from the property, also in cases where no actual petrol distribution is going on there, as well as declarations on options to purchase the property.

C. Franchise Contracts

372. A franchise contract constitutes an agreement according to which a supplier, the franchisor, transfers the right and the duty to produce or to sell the goods in accordance with the business concept to the franchisee. The parties use a common name and mark in order to get a uniform appearance. The franchisor transfers know-how to the franchisee and confers him with commercial or technical assistance within the contract period. The object of the contract constitutes a totality of industrial or intellectual property rights.

Franchise contracts are not regulated as such under Danish law. The franchisee is normally a self-employed businessman, often a sole distributor. But the instructions and the clauses of the contract may be so strict that the franchisee is considered an employed person. This situation might create problems of liability for the franchisor. He is not liable for the self-employed franchisee, but risks to be bound according to the general principles of contract law if it is not communicated to third parties that the liability for the business is placed on the franchisee.[278]

It is a characteristic feature of the franchise contract that the parties have to accept restrictions in their liberty to act in order to create a uniform appearance with the purpose of promoting the sale and augmenting a competitive market. Franchise contracts are within the scope of Executive Order 739/2010 on block exemption of vertical agreements and concerted practices, *see* paragraph No. 365 and *infra* Part II, Chapter 4.

D. Selective Distribution

373. Distributors who enter into a selective sales system have to fulfil certain requirements in order be considered able to collaborate with the supplier. The requirements typically relate to the situation of the business plant, its inventory the

277. Consolidated Act 1718/2010 *(Benzinforhandlerkontrakter)*.
278. Cf. Eastern High Court decision reported UfR 1994.146.

quality of the products and the professional skills of the distributor. The requirements may be imposed only when they are objective and important for the marketing, and they should be applied to the applicants in an equal and uniform way, without discrimination. In the absence of statutory contract law rules, the general principles and rules of contract law apply. As far as regulation under competition law is concerned, *see* Executive Order 739/2010 on block exemption of vertical agreements and concerted practices, compare paragraph No. 365 and *infra* Part II, Chapter 4.

II. Middlemen or Intermediaries

A. *General Survey*

374. The law on intermediaries[279] deals with the relationships in which a contract is not established directly between the offeror and the offeree, but is made by an intermediary who is acting either on behalf of one of the parties or brings the parties together on a neutral basis. Two relationships may be distinguished; the internal one between the principal and the intermediary regulated by the law of intermediaries, and the external one between the intermediary and the third party which depends on the extent of the power of attorney conferred to the intermediary by the principal. The latter relationship is regulated mainly by the general rules of power of attorney according to The Contracts Act[280] Chapter 2.

The special regulation of middlemen is mostly established in order to regulate the internal relationship between the principal and the intermediary complementary with certain provisions concerning the adaptation of the rules on authority. The most important categories of commercial middlemen from an economic point of view are the distributors and commercial agents. However, platform intermediaries are playing an increasing role, both nationally and internationally. A *lex specialis* is issued only for the commercial agents and travellers and for commission agents. For the other categories of brokers and agents, there are established provisions mainly regulating public requirements within their trade line.

B. *Commercial Agents*

375. The regulation of commercial agency is laid down in the Act on Commercial Agents and Commercial Travellers (CAA),[281] which constitutes the implementation of the Directive on self-employed commercial agents.[282] The CAA introduces

279. Author: Kim Østergaard.
280. Consolidated Act 193/2016 (*Aftaleloven*).
281. Act 272/1990 on Commercial Agents and Commercial Travellers (*Lov om handelsagenter og handelsrejsende*).
282. Council Directive of 18 Dec. 1986 on Approximation of Laws of the Member States Relating to (Self-Employed) Commercial Agents (86/653EEC), O.J. 1986 L. 382/17.

mandatory provisions in accordance with the rules of the Directive in order to protect the commercial agent who is considered to be the weak party to the contract.

1. Definition of a Commercial Agent

376. According to the CAA, section 2, the commercial agent is defined as a self-employed intermediary who, against remuneration, is acting continuously for sale or purchase of goods by taking orders or concluding transactions in the name and for the account of the principal. The power to conclude transactions requires that the authority has been conferred to the agent by agreement with the principal, according to the CAA, section 16. The commercial agent without authority has to concentrate on promotion activities in order to facilitate the connection between the client and principal where the latter concludes the transaction directly with the client.

377. The commercial agent may, by agreement, obtain a sole agency within a certain territory, a certain part of a territory, or regarding a certain clientele.

378. The commercial agency contract requires no form. However, if the agent or the principal demands a contract in writing such requirement must be met, compare CAA, section 3. This provision is mandatory. The Act is silent as regards the consequences in case of non-compliance with this requirement. Even though the requirement is not met the contract is still binding.

2. Obligations of the Parties: Right to Commission

379. Concerning the rights and duties of the parties, CAA, sections 4 and 5 closely follow the provisions laid down in the directive, compare Articles 3 and 4. The parties have an obligation of loyalty and integrity to each other. The commercial agent has to make efforts to promote the business of the principal. The principal has to provide relevant information about the goods in question, including samples of goods. Furthermore, the principal must inform the agent if the turnover in the relevant territory is expected to decrease. Depending upon the authority, the commercial agent is entitled to negotiate the sale or purchase of goods or even to negotiate and conclude the sale or purchase of the goods on behalf of the principal.

Furthermore, the commercial agent may have the obligation to achieve a minimum turnover, typically on an annual basis, as far as the agreement thereon is fair according to the Contracts Act, section 36. The CAA, section 8 provides that the agent has the right to get the usual commission in case the parties have not agreed upon this issue. That is an unlikely scenario, however. As stated in CAA, section 9, no. 1, compare the directive, section 7, the commercial agent is entitled to a commission on transactions brought about by his activities during the contract period, provided that the agreement is concluded by the principal and the third party, i.e., the customer. The commercial agent also gets a commission for transactions concluded without his cooperation when the principal concludes an agreement with a third party who has been the commercial agent's 'customer' concerning similar transactions in accordance with CAA, section 9 no. 2. Concerning the commission for direct transactions related to a certain territory, Denmark has chosen to implement the option of the directive in Article 7, subsections 2, 1st indent in the Danish Act. The CAA, section 9, no. 3 provides that the agent to whom a geographical territory or a determined clientele is transferred is entitled to commission for transactions with the customers belonging to the territory even if the commercial agent does not have exclusive rights. In case of termination of the agency contract, section 10 provides that the commercial agent is entitled to a commission for agreements performed within a reasonable time after the termination when the orders – which may have been concluded directly or indirectly – have reached the commercial agent or the principal before the termination of the contract. When the agent has been active in bringing about a transaction within the contract period, he is also entitled to a commission when the order arrives only after the termination, provided that the transaction is performed within a reasonable time.

There may be some deviation from the provisions in CAA, sections 8, 9 and 10 by, provided the parties have agreed otherwise.

The commission becomes payable when the goods are or ought to have been delivered or the third party has paid or ought to have paid the price, and a notice of the due commission should be sent to the agent at the latest on the last day of the month after the quarter within which the commission has become payable, according to CAA, sections 11 and 12 which follow the rules of the directive, Articles 10 and 12. It is the same for purchase transactions. The rule of the directive, Article 11 according to which the commercial agent in case of non-performance of the transaction gets no commission when this is not due to the principal, has been adopted in CAA, section 14. In accordance with CAA, section 14, subsections 2 and 3, the commercial agent is entitled to a commission in cases where the principal grants a respite of payment to a customer without the consent of the commercial agent and the payment is not performed. In cases of part performance, the corresponding commission for the performed part is paid or shall be paid to the commercial agent.

According to CAA, section 15, the commercial agent is entitled to demand all relevant information from the principal with respect to the calculation on the commission obtained. The provision is mandatory.

380. The CAA, sections 16–21 regulate the authority of the commercial agent. The CAA, section 16, subsection 2 and section 17, subsection 1 deal with cases where the commercial agent has transgressed his authority or the principal does not want to accept an offer received by the commercial agent. In such cases, the principal has to give notice thereon to the third party without undue delay. If the principal does not, the principal is bound by the agreement. According to CAA, section 20, the commercial agent is not entitled to receive payment, grant a price reduction, or to grant a respite without authority from the principal. Complaints from the customers concerning delivered goods may be pointed directly to the commercial agent, provided (that) the commercial agent has participated in the formation of the contract with the customer, compare CAA, section 21.

3. Termination of the Commercial Agency Contract

381. The agency contract may be concluded on a determinate or indeterminate basis. When the contract is concluded for a certain term, it lapses without further notice at the end of the term. If the contract without a fixed termination date, the parties are obliged to terminate with a certain notice. The mandatory period of notice is set out in section 22 of the CAA. It provides for a notice period of one month within the first year of the commercial agency contract. The period of notice is prolonged with one month for each year which the contract has been in effect. The maximum period of notice is, however, six months no matter how long the commercial agency contract has been in force. It may be agreed that the commercial agent may terminate the contract with a three-month notice period even though the commercial agency contract has been in force for three years or longer in accordance with CAA, section 22, subsection 2. If the parties agree on a longer period of notice, the principal may not benefit from a shorter period than the commercial agent. The periods of notice run from the end of a calendar month if nothing else is agreed.

The CAA, section 24 provides that each party may terminate the commercial agency contract without notice when the other party has breached the commercial agency contract in such a manner that the breach must be considered fundamental.

4. Right to Goodwill Indemnity

382. At the termination of the contract, the agent is entitled to goodwill indemnity for the loss of clientele. Denmark has chosen the system of indemnity laid down in the directive Article 17(2). The CAA, section 25, states two conditions that must be met. First, the commercial agent must have brought new customers to the principal or significantly increased the volume of business with existing customers. Substantial benefits for the principal has to derive from the continued business with these customers. Second, the amount of indemnity has to be reasonable, having regard to all the circumstances, in particular, the loss of commission suffered by the commercial agent, as the commercial agent is deprived of doing business with these customers in the future. The claim on indemnity also exists in case of the death of the agent when the conditions laid down in CAA, section 25, subsection 2, compare subsection 1 are fulfilled. The maximum amount of the indemnity is fixed as the average annual remuneration calculated on the basis of the preceding five-year period, compare CAA, section 26. The gross remuneration should be applied. It comprises not only the commission but also transport, marketing and office expenses. According to CAA, section 27, the commercial agent is not entitled to indemnity when the principal terminates the commercial agency contract due to a fundamental breach of contract originating from the commercial agent.

The commercial agent also loses the right to indemnity if he terminates the contract, except when the termination is justified because of circumstances caused by the principal or is due to the age or the health conditions of the commercial agent. When the agent transfers the agency to a succeeding agent he is not entitled to indemnity. The claim on indemnity has to be raised less than one year after the termination of the contract. Otherwise, the commercial agent loses the right to goodwill indemnity, compare CAA, section 28. CAA, Sections 25–28 cannot be deviated from unless it is in favour of the commercial agent.

5. Competition Clauses

383. Within the contract period, the agent is not prevented from dealing with competing products. However, he has to comply with the obligation of loyalty, and a prohibition of competition may be agreed upon. A competition clause concerning the period after the contract has been brought to an end may be imposed on the agent for a maximum of two years after the expiration of the commercial agency contract. Such a provision between the parties must be in writing and must be limited to the clientele and the territory conferred to the agent as well as to the goods comprised by the commercial agency contract in accordance with CAA, section 30.

C. Commercial Travellers

384. Commercial travellers are comprised of Chapter 3 of CAA. They are employees who promote the trade by contacting customers and being active for sale or purchase of goods which they do not possess or have in stock. The CAA, section 32, lays down a general prohibition of dealing with competing activities conducted by the commercial traveller. With respect to commission and the authority related to third parties, CAA is applicable.

D. Commission Agents

385. Commission agents are comprised by the Commission Act (Hereinafter 'CA').[283]

The commission agent is an agent who sells or purchases goods, securities and other movables for the account of the principal, but in his own name. When a tradesman has made it his business to act as a commission agent, he is designated a commercial commission agent. The goods received by the commission agent for sale remain the property of the principal until they are acquired by the customer.

1. Obligations of the Parties

386. The commission agent has to follow the instructions given by the principal. He has to act loyally and must comply with his duties in relation to the principal. The CA section 54, states that in cases where the commission agent retains

283. Consolidated Act 332/2014 (*Kommissionsloven*).

the goods of the principal and sells them under an imposed minimum price or purchases them over a maximum price, the third party may claim the rights set out in the sales agreement made with the commission agent, provided that the third party has ignored or could not have known that the commission agent had seriously disregarded the interests of the principal. The customer keeps the goods, and the commission agent has to compensate for the loss which the principal has suffered, compare CA, section 15, subsection 2. The commission agent may be submitted to a '*del credere*' obligation following from an agreement or usages, which signifies that he becomes surety for the customer. A commercial commission agent is not obliged to inform the principal on behalf of the customer. But in cases where he does not disclose the name, the principal may demand the commission agent to comply with the agreement. It is a general rule set out in CA, section 17, that the commission agent who does not comply with his duties has to pay damages to the principal for the economic loss. The commission agent is entitled to receive a commission for the agreements concluded on the account of the principal on the condition that the third party fulfils the agreement, unless the non-performance is caused by the principal. The commission agent may be reimbursed for such expenses as phone calls, letter postage, etc.

The commission agent may enter into contracts on his own behalf when it follows from agreement or usages. He has to inform the principal expressly of the fact that the commission agent himself acts as seller or purchaser, compare CA, section 40, and he has to sell or to buy within the limit of the current price at the time of the transaction, compare CA, section 42.

2. Termination of the Commission Contract

387. The contract on commission agency may be terminated by one of the parties at any time. When the contract has been established for a definite period of time or for bringing about a certain transaction, or a period of notice has been agreed, the commission agent may claim compensation for the loss he suffers when the contract has been terminated too soon. The party who withdraws without respecting the terms of the contract has to pay compensation to the innocent party.

E. Brokers

388. Brokers constitute a diversified category of intermediaries. However, it is a common feature that brokers bring the contracting parties together and they negotiate the agreement with the customer on the basis of their specialized knowledge of the sales object/service and the conditions and usages within the trade line. In general, intermediaries do not represent one of the parties, and they negotiate in a neutral way.

The broker's contract is submitted to the general contract law, and the public requirements concerning access to the profession and the execution of business activities are laid down in the legislation concerning their field of trade. As part of the tendency to liberalize commercial life, the specialized legislation for brokers dealing with goods and ship brokers has been abolished. As professional advisers, a broker is responsible in accordance with the default rule of damages in Danish law based on negligence.

F. Forwarding Agents

389. The forwarding agent, who is forwarding goods in his own name and for the account of the client, is normally comprised by NSAB 2015. The starting point is, however, the principle of freedom of contract. NSAB 2015, section 2 contains a number of obligations a forwarding agent can deal with.

III. Insurance

390. Insurance law makes a distinction between indemnity insurance, where compensation is paid for a certain economic loss assessed in the concrete case, for example, a fire insurance *(skadesforsikring)* and personal insurance *(summaforsikring)* based on valued policies, where the agreed insurance sum, without evaluation of the loss, is paid at the occurrence of the insurance event, for example, life insurance.[284] Special considerations must be observed for the latter category such as protection of the integrity of the insured person and the regulation of access for creditors, heirs and other third parties to get into possession of the insurance sum. Insurance contracts are submitted to the Act on Insurance Contracts,[285] which lays down general provisions applicable for all categories of insurances and special rules on insurance of transportation, fire, cattle and liability as well as on personal insurance. The Act dates back to 1930 and is an early example of legislation protecting customers (not only non-business policyholders, i.e., 'consumers') by mandatory rules securing a minimum of protection against unfair contract terms.

391. An insurance contract is normally prepared by an insurance agent, who has no authority to accept the offer. The company decides on the entering into the contract and issues the policy, which is binding for the company from the moment when it is sent from the company to the policyholder. The Act on Insurance Contracts provides for the obligations of the company in cases where the policyholder, before the issuance of the policy, has given incorrect information or has failed to give information. The company is not bound to the contract when the policyholder, fraudulently or contrary to honesty, has given incorrect information or has kept silent about relevant information, unless the company knew or ought to have known about the information, sections 4 and 9. If the insured has given the incorrect information in bona fide, the liability of the company is not affected, but the company may give termination to the contract by notice, section 5. The rule is the same when the insured, by carelessness other than gross negligence keeps silence about information, section 7. In other cases of negligence, concerning incorrect information or

284. Author: Peter Møgelvang-Hansen.
285. Consolidated Act 1237/2015 *(Forsikringsaftaleloven)*.

failure of information, the Act lays down principles in section 6 according to which the company may be bound to the extent to which it would have accepted the conditions. The provisions of section 5 and sections 7–9 are mandatory in favour of the policyholder.

If the policyholder intentionally has provoked the insurance event, the company is not obliged to pay compensation except in cases of self-defence or actions in order to prevent damages. When the policyholder has provoked the event by gross negligence, it depends on the concrete circumstances whether the company has to pay compensation. However, when the contract concerns life or liability insurance, the company as a general rule has to pay full compensation, sections 18–20. If the policyholder fails to inform the company of the occurrence of the insurance event without delay, the compensation may be reduced or may be lost, sections 21–23.

392. Concerning insurance of property, the Act on insurance contracts, section 37 lays down the principle that the value of the insured goods is equivalent to the purchase price reduced by the decreased value caused by age and use. The Act provides for problems of under-insurance and double insurance, sections 40–44, and for cases of increased risk within the contractual period, sections 45–50. Sections 51–52 regulates the steps that must be taken by the policyholder in order to limit the damage when the insurance event has occurred. Furthermore, section 54 provides that insurance of property covers everybody who has a right in the insured goods.

Liability insurance covers only the insured party who has become liable, not the injured third party. However, section 95 provides that in cases where the liability is proved and the amount of the compensation is fixed, the injured party takes over the claim of the insured party against the company.

Product liability insurance is not subject to special regulation. In order to solve some of the problems which follow from this type of liability, a model standard contract has been elaborated by the Danish Association for Non Life Insurance *(Dansk Forening for Skadesforsikring, SKAFOR)* in collaboration with Danish Industry *(Dansk Industri)*.

393. Life insurance is an important type of personal insurance. The most important special rules which deviate from the general provisions concern failure to inform to the company, cessation of paying of the premium, provocation of the insurance event and appointment of a beneficiary. The policy may be transferred to a third party, and it may be subject to trade. In principle, the rights of the policyholder and the beneficiary cannot be attached by creditors, according to section 116. However, section 117 provides that in cases where the policyholder goes bankrupt and it is proved that within the last three years he has expended an extraordinary amount on payment of premiums in consideration of his economical circumstances, the bankrupt estate may demand payment of the exceeding amount, if it can be covered from the value of the insurance.

394. The Act on Liability for Damages[286] provides for the right of recourse. Section 19 lays down the general principle that the tortfeasor is not liable to pay damages if a claim is covered by the injured party's property insurance or business interruption insurance. Thus, the damage must be covered through the insurance, and the insurance company has no right of recourse. The principle does not apply if the tortfeasor caused the damage by intent or gross negligence. Neither does it apply to damage caused in connection with carrying out business or public activities. Special rules to the same effect are established concerning damage caused by employees.

IV. Financial Services

395. The banking and credit sector[287] is subject to a general regulation in accordance with the EU harmonization laid down in the Financial Business Act.[288] The financial institutions are controlled by the DFSA *(Finanstilsynet).See infra* Part II, Chapter 2, §3 on the general regulation of the financial sector.[289]

396. The sole right of directing to the public the offer to receive deposits is granted to the financial institutions and to foreign credit institutions holding a permit or allowed according to the EU-rules to do business in Denmark. The EU Directive on deposit-guarantee schemes[290] is implemented by Danish Guarantee Fund for Depositors and Investors which is a private independent institution established by statute.[291] The rules of the Guarantee Fund apply to both private individuals and business enterprises that have deposited money and securities with Danish financial institutions. The Guarantee Fund covers losses in case of bankruptcy, etc. of the financial institution. Cash deposits are generally covered up to EUR 100,000 whereas some special deposits are fully covered without deduction of any debt to the bank. Such special deposits include savings schemes established by law, and various pension accounts, etc.

397. Legislation on payment cards was introduced in 1984.[292] After further development, the rules are now part of the Payment Act[293] implementing the EU Directives on the subjects.[294]

---

286. Consolidated Act 1070/2018 *(Erstatningsansvarsloven).*
287. Author: Peter Møgelvang-Hansen.
288. Consolidated Act 457/2019 *(Finansiel virksomhed).*
289. *See also supra* Part I. Ch. 8 on stock and commodity exchanges.
290. Directive 1994/19/EC as amended by Directive 2009/14/EC.
291. Consolidated Act 1155/2018(*Garantifonden for indskydere og investorer*) and Executive Order 1483/2016.
292. Cf. Peter Møgelvang-Hansen *Danish Law* 264–267 (Børge Dahl et al., ed., Thomson 2002).
293. Consolidated Act 652/2017 (*Betalingslov*).
294. Directive 2015/2366 of the European Parliament and of the Council of 25 Nov. 2015 on payment services in the internal market,

A. *Leasing*

1. The Leasing Concept

398. Leasing is established by an agreement according to which the owner of the contractual object, the lessor, hires (leases) the object out to the lessee. Danish law contains no statutory rules dealing with leasing contracts as such. The characteristic feature is that the object is handed over to the lessee for a certain period on payment of a periodical fee, which is based on the price of the object plus the costs of financing, spread over the entire leasing period. Within that period, the agreement is not terminable. Ownership remains with the lessor. When operational leasing is agreed, the owner of the object, for example, the producer or the supplier, represents the lessor who leases the object directly to the lessee. When a leasing contract constitutes an arrangement of financing, the lessor represents a financing institution or a leasing company.

2. Relation Between the Lessor and the Lessee's Creditors

399. In relation to the creditors of the lessee, the lessor has the prior claim on the leasing object. The lessor is entitled to take the object back in case of breach of contract even if it is subject to a mortgage unless the mortgaged object is incorporated in real property. When it is part of the building, it is submitted to the Land Registration Act,[295] section 38, according to which, it, when installed in the building, becomes part of the mortgaged real estate, and the retention of ownership cannot be maintained. As far as real estate organized for business purposes is concerned, it is laid down in the Land Registration Act, section 37 that business inventory and material of business belonging to the owner is submitted to the registered mortgage when nothing else is agreed with the creditor. Consequently, when the owner establishes a sale-and-lease-back arrangement where such inventory or part of it is sold to the lessor and leased back to the owner, the leased objects are still part of the mortgage when nothing else has been agreed with the creditor, who therefore retains the prior claim.

3. Obligations of the Parties

400. The duty of maintenance is placed on the lessee, and normally he has to take out full insurance. Eventually, the lessor takes out the insurance both as the policyholder and as the secured part. Frequently, the rights of use may not be transferred to others without the consent of the lessor. The fee is normally paid per month. The basic contractual period is normally from two to seven years, most frequently from three to five years. Even if the leasing contract is interminable, it may be terminated in case of serious breach of contract. The lessor may take the object

295. Consolidated Act 1075/2014 (*Tinglysningsloven*).

back and claim compensation for the non-paid present and future fee as well as the interest and the costs following from the breach. If it has been the intention of the parties from the very start that the 'lessee' shall become owner of the object, the contract constitutes a hire purchase agreement in the sense of the Credit Contracts Act,[296] section 4 no. 16. In that case, the procedure and calculation concerning repossession laid down in the Act on Credit Contracts Act apply, which normally is in favour of the lessee not only in consumer contracts but also in business relationships. When the lessee is entitled to continue the contract for a reduced fee or to purchase the object at the market price, the agreement is normally not submitted to Act on Credit Contracts.

401. A leasing agreement may stipulate a cut-off clause according to which the lessee cannot raise a claim against the lessor concerning defects of the object. In a financial leasing contract, it is considered reasonable to insert such a clause in order to prevent the lessee from presenting a claim to the lessor, which might reduce the value of the object and the amount of the fee. But the clause must be emphasized in the contract, and it is submitted to the Contracts Act, section 36 on regulation of unfair contract terms.[297]

B. Factoring

1. The Concept of Factoring

402. Factoring includes different types of agreements between an enterprise and a factoring company, the factor, according to which the factor purchases or mortgages the claim of the enterprise on the clients according to the invoices. Danish law contains no statutory rules dealing with factoring contracts as such. The general statutory and non-statutory rules on assignment of claims of apply.[298]

The genuine type is the agreement where the factor purchases the claims on the clients and takes over the risk of payment. But the most common type is the one where the factor mortgages the claim, normally about 80% of the full claim, without taking over the risk of payment. Such an agreement is part of a global arrangement of mortgage on invoices within a total maximum of the loan. A security account may be established in relation to the agreement. A similar type of agreement concerns the factor's purchase of the claim on the client without taking over the risk, where the factor is entitled to cancel the purchase in case of insolvency of the client, and the part of the claim already fulfilled should be paid back. Normally, a security account is established in connection with this agreement.

403. It is a characteristic feature of factoring that it constitutes a systematic arrangement for a plurality of claims. In relation to the clients, the factoring may be open, half open or closed. In case of an open agreement, the client is informed on the transfer (*denunciation*) and has to pay the debt to the factoring company only.

296. Consolidated Act 1336/2015 *(Kreditaftaleloven).*
297. *See supra* §1.
298. *See infra* Part I. Ch. 10 on commercial security.

When the agreement is half open, the client is informed, but temporarily continues to pay to the enterprise. This type requires intensive control measures taken by the factoring company. When the agreement is closed, the client is informed neither on the transfer nor on the place of payment. According to Danish law, the closed agreement does not establish the title to property for the factor, neither to ownership nor to a mortgage.

Another characteristic feature is that the factoring company takes over functions of administration or collection of debts. The reward for the factoring company may be an amount paid at one time. But most common is the reward based on the calculation of an interest. Frequently, a fee is paid for administrative functions and similar services, as well as the taking over of risks. It may be stipulated that certain types of claims or clients are not submitted to the agreement. The security account typically constitutes 20% of the claim. The security account may be mortgaged to the factoring company.

2. Relations to the Clients

404. The clients may raise objections regarding the goods or services for which the invoices have been established. Cut-off clauses are not binding on consumers[299] but are normally enforceable in commercial contracts, if they are sufficiently clear.

The factoring company has no duty to examine the solvency of the clients. But in cases where the company is aware of something suspicious, it has a duty of diligence according to which it has to warn the enterprise against dealing on terms of credit with the clients in question.

V. Carriage by Land, Sea and Air

A. General Survey

405. The Transport Law regulates the transport of persons and goods.[300] In the following, the transport of goods in business relationships is primarily addressed. The national regulation of transport law is to a great extent based on international conventions. A division may be made between sea transport law, road transport law, railway transport law and air transport law according to the different sets of rules to which they are submitted. However, it must be emphasized that the aforementioned rules are developed with unimodal transport in mind, which is hardly the main principle today, since most goods are carried as multimodal transport.

In principle, the division could be reduced to two areas, the air and sea law on the one hand and the road and railway law on the other; (as) the air law originally was based on the law of the sea. The system of liability, within these two areas, has reflected the traditional principle of fault and negligence (*culpa*). The Convention on International Carriage of Goods regulating the Law of Roads is based on the

299. The Consolidated Credit Contract Act 1336/2015 *(Kreditaftalelov)* Sections 32 and 33.
300. Author: Kim Østergaard.

Convention on the Carriage of Goods by Rail which regulates the railway law. This legislation provides for liability even if no fault or negligence has been committed. Thus, it is a strict liability. However, besides the similarities, there are other rules which differ within each field of law, such as the rules on limitation of liability, on notice of claims and on the period of prescription.

The agreement on transport provides for the delivery of the goods to the place of destination according to the contract terms. In relation to the parties, the means of transportation are subordinated in relation to the terms of the agreement. Frequently, different means of transportation are applied for bringing the goods to the destination, and agreements on transportation are established between contracting carriers who arrange the transportation and carriers who execute the physical transportation.

406. The Danish contract law of transportation is based on the general principle of freedom of contracting when it comes to the transportation of goods, but characteristic features may be emphasized. As this field of law is important for international relationships, it has been necessary to set up certain uniform, mandatory rules. The aim of the rules is to prevent exemption clauses of liability established by the carriers and to secure that documents are transferable, in particular, to maintain the negotiability of the bill of lading. The rules concerning liability in transportation law are more strict than the general culpa principle, as the provisions lay down a culpa rule with a reversed onus of proof or a strict liability. However, besides the mandatory rules on limitation of liability, there is a favourable calculation of compensation. Frequently, these rules are standardized and the calculation is based on the value of the damaged goods, not on the individual loss of the damaged party.

Furthermore, the compensation may be limited to a maximum. However, limited liability cannot be claimed by a carrier who has acted intentionally or with gross negligence. As a counterpart to the liability on a strict basis, there are rules of periods for notice of claims which are short compared to the Danish rules in general. Similarly, the delays of prescription are usually one year in transport law, whereas the general rule in Danish law concerning services is three years according to the Act on Prescription.[301]

The specific documents applied in transport law are also a characteristic feature of transport law.

B. Sea Transport Agreements

407. Sea transport agreements are regulated by Chapter 13 in the Maritime Act.[302] Chapter 13 in the Maritime Act (MA) is to a great extent based on the Bills of Lading Convention of 25 August 1924 (the Hague Rules), as amended by the

301. Cf. Consolidated Act 1238/2015 (*Forældelsesloven*) Section 3. The Act contains other rules on prescription differing from the main rule of prescription contained in Section 3.
302. Consolidated Act 1505/2018 *(Søloven)*.

Supplementary Protocol of 23 February 1968 (the Visby Rules) and the 1979 Protocol. Denmark has ratified the Rotterdam Rules which, most likely, will be enacted into the MA at some point.

The majority of the sections in the MA may be deviated from by agreement(s) concerning transport of goods, except for rules based on The Hague and the Visby Conventions. The mandatory rules comprise: the liability of the carrier, the obligation of the carrier to issue a bill of lading, liability for damage and liability for legal deviation, compare MA, section 254. Furthermore, the carrier is obliged to take care of the goods. The opportunity to agree on deviations from non-mandatory provisions is frequently applied by the parties.

According to the MA, section 292, subsection 3, the bill of lading sets out the terms for transport and delivery of the goods. Other terms are not valid unless the bill of lading comprises such issues. The bill of lading serves as proof that the carrier has received and loaded the goods as described in the bill of lading, if nothing else has been proved in accordance with MA section 299, subsection 1. The carrier is responsible for the accuracy of the information laid down in the bill of lading concerning the goods. When the carrier knows or ought to have known that information relating to the goods is wrong, the carrier cannot claim the incorrectness of the bill of lading unless he has expressly made a notice (thereupon/thereof/of it) in the document, according to MA section 299, subsection 3.

408. The liability of the carrier in relation to goods under his charge is set out in the MA section 274, subsection 1. The carrier is liable while the goods are in the possession of the carrier. Traditionally, this time span covers the period when the goods are in the possession of the carrier in the port of loading, during the course of transportation and in the port of discharge. The carrier is liable for loss caused by damaged or perished goods, compare MA section 275, subsection 1, or caused by late delivery of the goods, compare section 278, subsection 1. The carrier is subject to the 'culpa' rule with a reversed onus of proof, compare MA section 275, subsection 1. The carrier has to prove that the loss was not caused by fault or negligence committed by himself or by those under his charge, or by contribution from them. Furthermore, the carrier is also liable as a master for those who are working in the service of the ship, unless the liability concerns faults and negligence related to the navigation or the management of the ship or to a fire. According to MA section 276, subsection 2, the carrier is liable for loss following from the lack of seaworthiness of the ship at the commencement of the voyage, as he and his crew have to exercise reasonable care for the seaworthiness at this point of time. The onus of proof is placed on the one who claims freedom from liability. The liability of the carrier may be reduced or set aside if the carrier proves that the charterer or his crew, by fault or negligence, have committed or contributed to the damage.

409. The value of the goods is standardized according to MA section 279, as it is calculated on the basis of the usual value of goods of the same nature in the same place and at the time of discharge. The value may not exceed SDR 667 (Special Drawing Rights) per kilo or other unit of the goods or SDR 2 per kilo gross weight of the goods which are lost, damaged or delayed depending on which of the amount has the greater value. The transport unit, for example, a container, is considered as a unit if nothing else has been noted in the bill of loading, compare MA section 281.

C. Agreements on Transport by Road

1. Legislation

410. National and international transport by road is regulated in different ways according to Danish law. National transport by road is based on the general principles of contract. Thus, between the parties, there is the principle of freedom of contract. Whereas international transport by road is subject to the CMR-Convention,[303] which is enacted into Danish law.[304]

411. According to CMRA, section 1 subsection 1, the Act is applicable when the contract concerns the transport to or from Denmark or takes place between two foreign countries, where at least one of the countries has ratified the CMR Convention. The CMRA is also applicable when a vehicle loaded with goods is transported by ship, railway or aircraft during a part of the journey, compare CMRA, section 3, subsection 1, provided the goods stay on board the vehicle during the course of the journey. Certain exceptions are laid down in CMRA, section 3, subsection 2. In accordance with CMRA, section 1, subsection 3, the Act is mandatory apart from certain exceptions concerning the division of compensation among liable carriers.[305] The CMRA may be applied in relation to other parties who may raise claims based on the transport contract even if they are not contracting parties, such as the sender and the consignee.

412. National road transport is based on the general principles of contract law, as mentioned above. Consequently, the parties are subject to freedom of contract. Standard conditions may be applied, for example, the General Terms adopted by the Nordic Association of Freight Forwarders in 2015. The provisions of the Road Traffic Act[306] concerning the liability for damages to goods are applicable when nothing else has been agreed upon by the parties.

---

303. Geneva Convention of 19 May 1956 on the Contract for the International Carriage of Goods by Road.
304. Cf. Consolidated Act 1122/2015 on the Contract for the International Carriage of Goods by Road *(CMR-loven),* [hereinafter *CMRA*).
305. Cf. CMRA Section 46, subs. 3.
306. Consolidated Act 1324/2018 (*Færdselsloven*). Especially Section 101 attracts interest, when it comes down to the question about liability.

2. The Transport Contract

413. The transport contract in international transport is confirmed by a consignment note, compare CMRA section 5, subsection 1. However, even though the parties have not established a CMR waybill or the CMR waybill does not concur with the minimum content in accordance with CMRA section 7, or the CMR waybill has vanished, the contract is still considered valid and subject to the CMRA according to CMRA section 5, subsection 2.

The Act lays down detailed provisions for the establishment of the CMR waybill and the information to be included, compare CMRA section 7 and optionally such information where it is relevant in accordance with CMRA section 8. According to CMRA section 9, the sender is liable for the costs and damages inflicted on the carrier when it follows from the fact that the sender has given incorrect or incomplete information to be applied for the establishment of the CMR waybill.

When the carrier takes over the goods for transportation, the carrier has to verify that the number of pieces and their marks and numbers are correct, as well as the visible condition of the goods. When correctly issued, the CMR waybill shall be the evidence of the formation of the transport contract and the receipt of the goods by the carrier. Counter evidence may be produced.

414. In national transport, a waybill is rarely issued, and in case of application, the carrier frequently establishes the document without providing information from the sender.

3. Liability

415. In international transport, the CMRA section 24, subsection 1 provides that the carrier is liable for loss and damage to the goods incurred during the period from the taking over of the goods until the time of delivery. Furthermore, he is liable for delay in delivery. The carrier is subject to a strict liability. According to CMRA section 4, the carrier is liable for the acts and omissions caused by the employees and/or any third party engaged by the carrier to participate in the fulfilment of the transport contract. The CMRA section 24, subsection 2 sets out particular reasons exonerating the carrier from liability, if he is able to prove that the loss or damage was due to circumstances which were unavoidable for the carrier and the consequences of which he was not able to prevent. In case law, the conditions for exoneration seem to be treated like acts of force majeure.[307] For instance, only robbery involving violence, not theft of the vehicle and loading, seems to fulfil the conditions.[308]

416. The liability for defects of the vehicle used for the transportation is strict. The CMRA, section 25 enumerates 'special dangers' which exonerate the carrier for liability, if the carrier can prove that the loss or damage might have been caused by

307. *See* for instance UfR1989.1086 H and UfR 1990.240 H.
308. *See* for instance UfR 1983.585 SH and UfR 1989.820 H.

these particular situations. The causation between the danger and the loss or damage need not be proven, as the connection is presumed. In case law, the rule of exoneration has been construed in the sense that the driver has the obligation to control the loading and stowage. The carrier cannot expect to be exonerated when no reservation has been taken in case of evident defaults of loading, traffic dangers at the loading, or expert knowledge in relation to the employees and a third party related to the sender.[309] The carrier may not invoke provisions on exoneration, limitation of his liability, or modifications of the burden of proof when the carrier or his employees have acted intentionally or with gross negligence according to CMRA section 37.

417. The compensation is computed as the value of the goods or depreciation of value in the place and at the time of the handing over (of) the goods for transportation in accordance with CMRA section 29, subsection 1 and section 31, subsection 1. Furthermore, only carriage rates, customs and other costs involved in the transport may be compensated in accordance with CMRA section 29, subsection 3. The 'individual' loss is not subject to compensation. In case of loss or damage to the goods, a maximum limit of SDR 8.33 per kilo is used in accordance with compare CMRA section 29, subsection 2, and section 31, subsection 2. In case of delay, the compensation is not limited to the value of the goods or the depreciation. Lost profit and other damages following from the delay may also be compensated. The maximum amount may not exceed the carriage charge, compare CMRA section 32.

A compensation based on a value exceeding the maximum amount, according to CMRA section 29, subsection 2, may be obtained as compensation for a supplementary remuneration, provided the parties have agreed upon this, compare CMRA section 30 and section 33. The loss of the whole consignment is not considered to be a delay. The CMRA lays down specific provisions with respect for time limits for notification of claims which must be met in order to make an objection against the carrier, compare CMRA section 38.

418. Liability for national transport is regulated by the general rules of contract law. In accordance with Danish law, the carrier is subject to the 'culpa' rule with a reversed onus of proof. There is no standardized compensation or maximum limit.

D. Contracts on Transport by Railway

419. Denmark is, along with forty-six other countries, a Member State to Convention concerning International Carriage by Rail (COTIF) of 9 May 1980 in the version of the Protocol of Modification of 3 June 1999. The change of the COTIF-Convention came into force 1 July 2006, including the CIM rules (CIM)[310] listed in Appendix B. In accordance with the Act on Railway (RA)[311] section 25, subsection

309. *See* UfR 1984.531 H.
310. *See* http://www.otif.org/fileadmin/user_upload/otif_verlinkte_files/07_veroeff/03_erlaeut/rpex99-ru-cim-e.pdf, which includes the explanatory report.
311. Consolidated Act 686/2015 on railways *(jernbanelov)*.

1, the Minister for Transport has the authority to conclude conventions about the carry of persons, luggage and goods. Once such conventions have been announced in the Official Law Gazette in Denmark, they become a part of Danish Law. The COTIF Convention with later amendments as mentioned above has been announced in the Official Law Gazette.[312]

Formally, only international railway transport is entailed by the COTIF Convention. However, in accordance with RA section 17, subsection 3, the issue of liability in national railway transport is entailed by CIM rules with the exception that the maximum compensation is subject to the rules in the CMR-Convention.

Consequently, the regulation of national and international railway transport is nearly identical, when Danish Law is applicable.

The CIM Article 6 deals with the question of the contract of carriage, which is a consensual contract. The consignment note is only a documentary proof. It provides the necessary proof of the conclusion, the content of the contract and the taking over of the goods by the carrier. The requirements concerning the consignment note are set out in Article 7. Compared to the requirements in CMR, the list of data required in the consignment note is quite comprehensive.

In accordance with CIM Article 17, the carrier must deliver the consignment note as well as the goods to the recipient at the planned point of delivery against unloading and payment of any resulting credits for the contract of carriage.

420. The issue of liability concerning the carrier is regulated in detail in accordance with CIM Articles 23–41. However, with respect to the basis of liability and the general rules of liability the rules are set out in Articles 23 and 25. As a starting point, the carrier has a strict liability for damages resulting from the total or partial loss or from damages to the goods. The RIM Article 23, subsections 2 and 3 contain exemptions, where the carrier is not responsible. In accordance with RIM Article 25, subsection 1, it is the carrier who has the burden of proof with respect to the listed situations in RIM Article 23, subsection 2. If the case entails one of the special risks listed in RIM Article 23, subsection 3, it is the carrier who has the burden of proof with respect to the presumption, that one of these special risks is the cause. The claimant will, however, maintain the right to prove that the damage has not been totally or partially caused by one of these risks. The CIM Articles 30–37 contains many (and) very detailed provisions regarding whether the compensation should be computed and how the compensation may not exceed the amount fixed.

As a main rule, any demand arising from the carriage of transportation is prescribed in one year in accordance with RIM Article 48, subsection 1. Other demands will be prescribed in two years, compare RIM Article 48, subsection 1, litra a)–c).

312. Cf. The official law gazette C, statutory order no. 71 of 18 Sep. 1985, statutory order no. 30 of 14 Mar. 1991, statutory order no. 68 of 27 Jun. 1991, statutory order no. 69 of 8 Jun. 1995, and statutory order no. 1 of 1 Feb. 2007.

E. Contracts on Air Transport

421. Air transport is regulated by the Carriage by Air Act.[313] The International Civil Aviation Organization (ICAO) has passed a number of multilateral air law conventions.[314] Originally the Carriage by Air Act implemented the 1929 Warsaw Convention,[315] the 1955 Hague Protocol,[316] and the Guadalajara Convention.[317] However, the Warsaw system, so to speak, was to some extent replaced by the highly successful Montreal Convention, which was enacted into the Carriage by Air Act and came into force in 2004.[318] There are still some countries which have not signed the Montreal Convention, but where the Warsaw system still applies. The Carriage by Air Act is applicable within Danish territory in accordance with section 1, and to Danish aircraft outside Danish territory according to section 4, unless the rules are contrary to foreign law, which are applicable according to international conventions or in relation to fundamental principles of law. The Minister for Transportation and Energy may state, in accordance with an agreement with a foreign State, that certain provisions of the Carriage by Air Act should be applied on aviation by an aircraft registered in that State but placed at the disposal of a Danish user, compare Carriage by Air Act section 4, subsection 2.

422. Chapter 9 of the Carriage by Air Act deals with air transport of passengers, luggage and goods. In accordance with section 90, subsection 1, no 1 and 2, the chapter is applicable to domestic flights and for international flights between countries, which have signed the Montreal Convention. In case the aircraft is flying between Denmark and a country which has not signed the Montreal Convention, then the exhibit to RAA is applicable. This means basically that Danish law contains two different sets of rules for international flights, depending on whether the aircraft is flying from or to Denmark from a country, which has signed either the Montreal Convention or the Warsaw system. Below is only dealt with the rules in Chapter 9 of the Carriage by Air Act.

423. The Carriage by Air Act sections 94–97 entail the requirements to the documents of transportation which must be issued in conjunction with the transportation of goods. Even though the requirements are not fulfilled in accordance with the aforementioned provisions, the agreement on air transport is still valid and the provisions in sections 94–97 are still applicable. An air waybill must be issued and in three originals. In accordance with section 97, the air waybill and a cargo receipt,

313. Consolidated Act 1149/2017 on Carriage by Air *(Luftfartsloven).*
314. *See* http://www.icao.int/secretariat/legal/Lists/Current%20lists%20of%20parties/AllItems.aspx (accessed May 2019).
315. Convention for the Unification of Certain Rules Relating to International Carriage by Air, Warsaw, 1929.
316. Protocol to amend the Convention for the Unification of Certain Rules Relating to International Carriage by Air signed at Warsaw 12 Oct. 1929, The Hague, 1955.
317. Convention Supplementary to the Warsaw Convention, for the Unification of Certain Rules Relating to International Carriage by Air Performed by a Person Other than the Contracting Carrier, Guadalajara, 1961.
318. Act 1074/2002 amending the Carriage by Air Act came into force on 28 Jun. 2004, cf. Executive Order 549/2004.

which must contain information about: (1) the place of departure and destination; (2) if there is an agreed place of landing en route, provided the place of departure or destination is placed in the same country and if one or more landing en route in another country is agreed on; and (3) the weight of the goods to be transported.

424. The Act provides for the principle of strict liability for transport of persons, registered luggage and goods, but with certain exemptions, for example of acts of God in relation to damage caused by delay of the transport.[319] The compensation for damage on passengers, luggage or goods may be reduced or annulled when the one who has suffered damage, intentionally or by negligence, has contributed to the damage in accordance with compare Carriage by Air Act section 110.

425. The computation of compensation for goods is fixed to a maximum of 19 SDR per kilo, compare Carriage by Air Act section 111, subsection 5.[320] More compensation may be agreed upon when the amount is based on a specific interest indicated at the delivery to the carrier and a surcharge is paid. Agreements on a lower amount of liability or other exemptions are not valid unless the loss or damage is due to the quality or defect of the goods in accordance with Carriage by Air Act section 112. Section 113 allows agreements on higher levels of damages than those maxima set out in section 111. The act provides a term of fourteen days for prescription of claims, calculated from the day on which the goods have been received, and twenty-one days by late delivery in accordance with section 115, subsection 2, unless the carrier has acted fraudulently. Furthermore, the injunction must take place within two years from the point of time when the aircraft arrived at the point of destination or should have arrived, or when carriage was discontinued.

F. Other Contracts on Transport

426. A Through Bill of Lading is submitted to the general rules on bills of loading according to the Maritime Act, section 293. Within the fields of land and air transport, the normal documents of transport are applied to similar transports.

427. Combined transport executed by succeeding carriers (multimodal transport) is not submitted to the transport legislation. In principle, the agreement is subject to freedom of contract. However, the CMRA, section 3 provides for transport by sea, railway or air situated between two transports by road, provided the vehicle is loaded during the time when the intervening transport is going on. Furthermore, as mentioned above, the Rotterdam Rules will entail multimodal transport, and the rules are supposed to be enacted in the MA by 2013 or 2014.

319. *See* Carriage by Air Act ss 106 et seq.
320. For passengers, the maximum is in general SDR 113,000 per person. *See* Carriage by Air Act, Section 111, subsections 1–3.

VI. Other Services: Construction Contracts

428. Construction contracts *(entreprise)* are regulated by contracts which constitute a special field of contract law.[321] The contractor undertakes the performance of the project and the contractual responsibility for the work which is made for the client. Usually, the work is transferred to a general contractor *(hovedentreprise)*, who divides the contract into minor parts for distribution of the different works to sub-contractors. Thus, with a general contract the client contracts with only one contractor on a particular project, with the details specified in advance. The general contractor undertakes the entire performance of all the specialized works. This type of contract is subject to competition primarily on the price.

A total contract *(totalentreprise)* is used when the contractor undertakes the entire performance of the project. The contract does not specify the construction and elaboration. The contractor may construct and execute the project in his own way. This type of contract is subject to competition between the contractors both on price, architecture/projection and on period of time.

Construction contracts as such are not regulated by statute. The general non-statutory principles of contract law apply. The contract usually refers to the Standard Terms of 2018 on General Conditions Concerning Works and Deliveries within the Building and Construction Activities Line, an agreed document referred to as *AB 18*).[322] AB 18 is an agreed document made by trade and business organizations representing various constructors' and clients' interests and constitutes a set of terms that by and large reflects the general principles of construction contract law.

321. Author: Peter Møgelvang-Hansen.
322. *Almindelige betingelser for arbejder og leverancer i bygge – og anlægsvirksomhed af 1992.*

Chapter 10. Commercial Securities

§1. Types of Securities

429. Securities may be applied in order to obtain performance of an obligation in cases where the debtor does not comply with his obligations.[323] Two instruments are applicable in general: the surety or guarantee, (*kaution*), and the pledge or mortgage (*pant*). The agreement on *kaution* confers the creditor with the right to get satisfaction through the fortune of a third person, whereas specific items, for example, goods or real property, constitute the objects of satisfaction when the security is obtained through *pant.* In special contracts such as sale of goods, a security may be obtained through the agreement on the seller's right of repossession of the goods in cases where the buyer omits to pay the amount due. Banker's credit or documentary credit (*remburs*) constitutes a security which is frequently applied in international sales. In the present chapter, only general instruments are treated.

§2. Surety or Guarantee (Kaution)

430. There is no general legislation concerning *kaution.*[324] Rules thereon are established by case law. *Kaution* is a type of security according to which a third party, who may be a physical person, e.g., the majority shareholder of a company, or a legal person, e.g., a bank, guarantees the fulfilment of an obligation, for example, the payment of a loan or a service.

There are two types of guarantees, depending on the moment from which the guarantor becomes liable. The first type constitutes the simple guarantee (*simpel kaution*). In this case, the debtor must be sued before a claim can be alleged against the guarantor. Only when the obligation has been submitted to exhaustive legal prosecution without result the guarantor may be sued for the debt. The second type is the suretyship (*selvskyldnerkaution*), where the guarantor in the case of non-payment is liable for the payment as soon as the day of maturity has passed. The guarantor enters into the debt as if he had obligated himself as debtor, and the creditor is not required to raise a claim before the courts in order to obtain satisfaction. The parties may agree on the type of liability they prefer. If nothing else is agreed, the agreement on *kaution* is considered a simple guarantee. However, the Act on Commission,[325] section 14, provides that in cases where a commission agent acts *del credere*, the agent has assumed the liability of suretyship (*selvskyldnerkaution*).

The parties may agree that a guarantee is limited to a determined amount or to a part of the debt. If nothing else is agreed, the guarantor is liable for the total debt. However, If a guarantee is provided for a loan granted by a bank as creditor outside

323. Author: Camilla Hørby Jensen.

324. B. Iversen & L.L. Petersen, *Danish Business Law*, 6th edition, pp 503–508 (DJØF Publishing 2015).

325. Consolidated Act 332/2014 on Commission (*Kommissionslov*).

a commercial relationship, the guarantor may not be liable for an amount greater than the principal of the loan or the maximum credit on establishment of the guarantee agreement.[326]

An agreement may be concluded between the creditor and more guarantors on joint surety. If nothing else is agreed, they are all jointly and severally liable. A subsequent liability may also be agreed. In such case, the guarantors agree with the creditor that the first guarantor has to fulfil the obligation completely. Only when he is unable to pay the second guarantor becomes liable. An agreement on counter security may also be concluded between the debtor and the guarantor. Such an obligation does not confer the creditor with any claim against the guarantor, which may be asserted by the debtor only.

431. The guarantee is binding through an agreement concluded between the guarantor and the creditor. The agreement may in principle be concluded orally or in writing. However, if a guarantor outside a commercial relationship has provided a guarantee for a loan granted by a bank the agreement shall be in writing to be valid.[327] Minor and incompetent persons may not assume the guarantor's liability, even with the consent of the guardian.[328]

432. The guarantor is free when the secured debt is paid or the obligation is otherwise performed, or the debt has disappeared because of limitation or foreclosure. However, if the debtor has obtained a compulsory arrangement with his creditors on reduction or abolition of the debt, the guarantor remains liable for the dishonoured part of the debt. The guarantee itself disappears in case of limitation of the guarantee promise. Furthermore, if, *within a commercial relationship*, a guarantee is provided for a loan granted by a bank as creditor and the debtor neglects to pay the principal, instalments or interest, a written notification shall be forwarded to each guarantor, no later than six months after the due date of the relevant repayment. The bank's mission to do so shall imply that the bank loses its claim against the guarantors to the extent that the guarantors' recourse claim against the debtor has been impaired by the omission.[329]

433. If the guarantor in the same situation is *outside a commercial relationship*, the written notification by the bank shall be forwarded to the guarantor no later than three months after the due date of the relevant repayment. This provision applies correspondingly if the bank grants the debtor an extension of time without the specific consent of the guarantor. If the three months is exceeded, the obligations as guarantor shall only apply to the guarantor for the amount of the debt of the debtor after the secured amount that would have been outstanding if all instalments had been paid on time up to a date three months prior to the date notification was issued.

---

326. Consolidated Act 1140/2017 on Financial Business (*Finansiel virksomhedslov*) as most recently amended by Act 1520/2018, section 48 para 4.
327. Consolidated Act on Financial Business, section 48 para. 3.
328. Consolidated Act 1015/2007 on Guardianship (*Værgemålslov*) as most recently amended by Act 1722/2018, section 27.
329. Consolidated Act on Financial Business, section 47.

Further, the bank shall lose its claim against the guarantors to the extent that the recourse claim of the guarantors against the debtor has been impaired by the omission.[330]

434. When the guarantor has complied with his obligations, he has recourse against the debtor. The guarantor enters directly into the rights of the creditor against the debtor including accessory rights. If, for example, the creditor's claim is preferential, the guarantor has the same right.

435. In case of joint security, the creditor may claim the total payment from any one of the guarantors. When one guarantor has paid, he may claim the share from the others for which each of them is liable. When nothing else is agreed, they all have equal shares. If one of them cannot pay his share, the payment thereof is distributed between the others according to the agreement on distribution of liability.[331] If the liability of each guarantor is different in relation to the creditor, it is presumed that the mutual distribution of liability is made in relation to their liability regarding the creditor.

§3. Pledge and Mortgage (Pant)

436. A pledge (*håndpant*) and a mortgage (*underpant*) allows the possessor of the right to obtain satisfaction for a debt by disposing over the objects covered before the debtor's other creditors.[332] Real property as well as goods, promissory notes, other kinds of claims and intellectual property rights may be subject to a pledge or a mortgage. Furthermore, a floating mortgage can be established in different kinds of assets owned by businesses as company mortgage. Typically, goods are subject to pledge whereas real property and debts never can be pledged.

437. The pledge and the mortgage are established by an agreement. In certain relationships, the establishment is based on statute. For example, State and county taxes and certain supply fees which are charged on the real property are subject to mortgage according to the Land Registration Act,[333] section 4 paragraphs 1 and 2, without agreement or registration.

The pledging is completed when the object of pledge is handed over to the pledgee or when the pledgor is deprived of the disposal thereof. The mortgage is completed by registration of the right. Contrary to the pledgor, the mortgager is still free to de facto dispose of the property with certain exceptions.

---

330. Consolidated Act on Financial Business, section 48 para 6–8.
331. Consolidated Act 333/2014 on Promissory Notes (*Gældsbrevsloven*), sections 2 and 61.
332. *See* B. Iversen & L.L. Petersen, *Danish Business Law*, 6th edition, pp 469–501 (DJØF Publishing 2015).
333. Consolidated Act 1075/2014 on Land Registration (*Tinglysningsloven*) as most reccently amended by Act 1722/2018.

I. Pledge and Mortgage on Movable Property

A. Pledge

438. Normally, movable property is subject to pledge but can also be subject to mortgage. Hence automobiles, ships of a certain size and aeroplanes, as well as other items subject to certain conditions, will often be 'pawned' by way of mortgage.

The security for movable property given in pledge is established in favour of the creditor when the transaction act has been observed. The traditional transaction act, created through usages and case law, is performed when the pledgee has got the item into his possession. However, the pledging is considered valid as long as the pledgor is unable to dispose of the item. It may be deposited by a third person acting on behalf of the pledgee, or it may be kept under lock and key in a way that deprives the pledgor of the disposal of the item.

When the pledgor does not comply with his obligations, the pledgee may dispose of the pledge in satisfaction of his claim. Normally, he has to put the pledge up to public auction. Before this action, he has to inform the pledgor thereon in order to give him the opportunity to redeem the pledge. When the auction brings more than the amount of the pledgee's claim, the surplus has to be paid to the pledgor. When the auction shows a deficit, the pledgor is liable for the remaining debt to the creditor.

The pledgor is free of the debt in cases where the pledgor is not identical with the debtor, but is a third person, who has given the item in pledge. The parties are free to agree on other ways of performance. For example, the pledge may be sold in private, or it may be transferred to the pledgee as his property, normally after valuation.

B. Mortgage

439. The item subject to mortgage remains at the mortgager's disposal. The transaction act for mortgage on movable property is completed by digital registration of a dematerialized document. An authorized standard form should be applied for this purpose and the mortgager may not be a minor or incompetent person.

440. According to the Land Registration Act, section 47b, the document must include a specified identification of each item. Exception is made for equipment and material concerning business exercised from rented property. For agricultural holding exercised from rented property, exception is also made for stock, dressing, yield and other products, even if they are removed as part of the farming. Furthermore, in case of company mortgage it is sufficient just to mention the type of assets included, cf. Land Registration Act, section 47c. Otherwise, it is not allowed for the mortgager to give mortgage in his total current or future property, cf. Land Registration Act, section 47a.

The mortgage for movable goods and company mortgage is entered into a central register called 'The Book of Persons' (*Personbogen*). However, automobiles must be entered into a special register called 'The Motorcar Book' (*Bilbogen*).

Mortgage of ships of twenty gross register tonnes or more is established by the entering of the ships into 'The General Ship's Register' (*Det almindelige Skibsregister*). Each ship has its own sheet in the register. Ships that weigh less than twenty tonnes but more than five tonnes may be entered into the register. The mentioned ships cannot be subject to pledge, even if they are handed over to the pledgee. They should be registered. However, ships weighing less than five tonnes may be subject to pledge.

441. As a general rule, unless renewed the mortgage disappears automatically after ten years, cf. Land Registration Act, section 47, paragraph 9 and section 47e, paragraph 4. However, the debt remains until it is paid, or the time of limitation has arrived. If the mortgager does not comply with his obligations, the mortgagee may obtain satisfaction through the mortgaged item. He is not required to bring his claim before the courts but may seize the items in execution and may sell them by a forced sale.

II. Mortgage on Real Property

442. Security in real property is obtained by mortgaging. There should be a document which constitutes both a promissory note concerning the loan and a mortgage deed on the property. Registration of the document is done digitally. The document is entered into 'The 'Land Registry' (*Tingbogen*) which is kept at the jurisdiction of the Registration Court. The legal effects operate from the moment of entry into the Land Registry.

443. Mortgage in real property may be obtained for a continuous credit in the form of a so-called letter of indemnity (*skadesløsbrev*). A document like this has to include the maximum amount of the credit in order to be entered into the Land Registry because of the legal priority effects of the registration.

444. The mortgager is also entitled to issue a mortgage deed to himself, a document of 'owner mortgage deed' (*ejerpantebrev*). This document may be registered on the same conditions as other mortgage deeds. The owner may use the document as security for, for example, a bank loan. The security is established as the transfer of the document is registered.[334]

III. Negotiable Securities and Promissory Notes

445. Negotiable securities in the form of paper documents or dematerialized documents can be subject to pledge, provided that a prohibition against has not been

334. Consolidated Act on Land Registration (*Tinglysningsloven*), section 1a.

agreed.[335] The pledging of a negotiable security in the form of a paper document is completed when such a document is removed from the disposal of the pledgor by handing it over to the pledgee.[336] For dematerialized bonds and shares which are registered in a central securities depository, the pledgee's right must be registered in the central securities depository.[337].

Security concerning promissory notes and other kind of debts is obtained by notification of the pledgee's right of security to the debtor.[338]

335. *See* B. Iversen & L.L. Petersen, *Danish Business Law*, 6th edition, pp 453–468 (DJØF publishing 2015).
336. *See* for example, Consolidated Act on Promissory Notes (*Gældsbrevsloven*), section. 22.
337. Consolidated Act 12/2018 on Capital Markets (*Kapitalmarkedsloven*) as most recently amended by Act 1520/2018, section 184.
338. *See* for example, Consolidated Act on Promissory Notes (*Gældsbrevsloven*), section 31.

Part II. Economic Law

Chapter 1. State Intervention in Economic Activities

§1. Institutional Framework

446. Intervention of the public sector into economic activities is based on 'the principle of legality' (*legalitetsprincippet*).[339] The public sector comprises the State, the Regions (Municipal Counties) and the municipalities, as important activities have been placed and executed on a local level. In 2018 the Government suggested to shut down the Regions as part of a reform of the public health sector. If so the tasks of the Regions will be divided between State and the municipalities. It follows from the requirement of legality that the administration should be in accordance with the law. Consequently, every concrete decision should be based on a statute passed by the Danish Parliament *(Folketinget)* but may also be based on an equivalent norm. Frequently, the statutes lay down provisions in general terms and leave the application to the discretion of the administration. On this basis, the administration may issue Executive Orders *(bekendtgørelser)* which interpret and complete the statutes. The administrative liberty of action is also reflected in the discretionary considerations of the concrete cases which are laid down in the administrative practice which, when it is established, is issued by the authorities in government circulars *(cirkulærer).*

State enterprises are mostly based on a specific act regulating the enterprise. Some state enterprises have been privatized and listed. The state may have retained part of the shares. Regions and municipalities must find the legal basis for involvement into economic activities in general legislation such as the act on the municipalities execution of tasks for other public authorities and the municipalities and the regions' collaboration with Companies[340] or on a court develop tradition for the limits of the municipalities' economic activities (the so-called *kommunalfuldmagt*). It specifies a number of legal principles that define what is lawful for the municipality to use funds when moving outside the area of legislation, i.e. in relation to tasks not imposed on the municipality by law. Within the utility sector, the municipalities can normally base their engagement on special provisions in legislation governing a specific supply sector such as electricity, district heating, natural gas or water.

339. Author: Bent Ole Gram Mortensen.
340. Act 548/2006 most recently amended by Act 740/2015 *(om kommuners udførelse af opgaver for andre offentlige myndigheder og kommuners og regioners deltagelse i selskaber)*.

447. Together with the development towards internationalization and augmented competition, it has been necessary to dispose of private as well as public resources in a rational way. Currently, the public administration not only makes the decisions on the benefits and limitations for the individuals, but it also exercises activities in order to cover the collective or individual requirements of the society. There is no sharp demarcation between the exercise of the power of decision in order to authorize certain business activities of the citizens and approve environment conditions of a private enterprise on the one hand and to exercise economical activities by the authority itself on the other hand. Traditionally, the public sector takes care of schools, hospitals, transport, utilities, police functions, etc. Normally the activities are submitted to a ministry or a municipal board. Overall, there are no requirements for the public sector's choice of organizational form. The leadership may have been assigned to an independent entity or to a special department such as the Danish Railways (*De Danske Statsbaner*; DSB) which is submitted to the minister of transport. Some economic activities are organized as integrated parts of the public administration. Others are organized in independent structures. The State-owned enterprises DSB (Danish Railways), Energinet.dk and Naviair are so-called independent public enterprises. They are not private companies, but they are fairly independent of the minister and the established administrative hierarchy. The form of the enterprise may also be a private company, for example, the limited company of Storebælt *(A/S Storebælt)* which constructed the bridge over the water of the strait Great Belt (*Storebælt*) between Sealand and Funen and the Danish national energy company Ørsted A/S. Both are now partly privatized with the Danish State still owning the majority of the stocks. Other State-owned enterprises can be independent institutions. An example is the Danish National Bank *(Danmarks Nationalbank)*, which is an independent institution organized as a private foundation.[341] The tendency has been to augment the involvement of the public sector in certain business activities as traditional fields of public service have been abandoned and transferred to the private sector.

§2. Planning

448. The yearly planning of the incomes and expenses of the State is laid down in the State Budget.[342] It is established according to the requirements of the Constitution, which provides in section 46 paragraph 2, that no expense may be paid when it is not in accordance with the Budget or a supplementary or preliminary appropriation act concerning incomes, the Constitution, section 43, provides that taxes may be imposed only by statute. According to section 46 paragraph 1, taxes may not be collected before the Budget or a preliminary appropriation act has been passed by the Danish Parliament. A great deal of the public economy is not subject to the Budget, as a quantity of public services has been transferred to the municipalities in consequence of a municipal reform in 1970. The public activities have been divided between the State, the regional and the municipal entities, so that most

341. Act 116/1936 *(Danmarks Nationalbank)* most recently amended by Act 579/2010.
342. Author: Bent Ole Gram Mortensen.

of the services within the social sector, health and teaching are provided by the regions and the municipalities, whereas the State holds the fields where direct subsidies are given to the citizens and the enterprises such as unemployment benefit, systems of business subsidies and old-age pension. In order to recover the service expenses, the municipalities collect the incomes not only from taxes. State subsidies are provided mainly in the following forms: block subsidies are transferred as a yearly compensation for the augmented expenses to services which the municipalities have undertaken in consequence of the municipal reform. Furthermore, a reimbursement is paid for certain expenses paid in advance by the municipalities such as payments in relation to old age pensions. Finally, the State compensates expenses following from a legal regulation which imposes augmented expenses on the municipalities. In return the municipalities have to pay the State if the legal regulation introduces reduced expenses, the so-called principle of total balance. The collaboration between municipal services and the enterprises in order to develop the local economic life is continuously being augmented. The nature of the State expenses has to be determined in the Budget as well as the foundation of the appropriation. For this purpose, the Budget is structured with a systematic index containing every proposal of appropriation, the proposals laid down in sections where each section corresponds to a ministry and notes which are part of the text. The Act is supplemented by additional remarks. The Budget concerns regular subsidies which are previously laid down in the legislation and normative expenses which are proposed to be granted.

449. According to the Constitution, section 45, the Budget proposal for the coming financial year should be introduced to the Danish Parliament not later than four months before the beginning of the financial year. Normally it is introduced by the Minister of Finance.[343] When the readings cannot be expected to be terminated within this period, a proposal for a preliminary act of appropriation should be introduced. When a new regulation requiring State expenses has been passed after the Budget has been introduced or the expenses have been otherwise known by the Danish Parliament, the appropriation is granted by a supplementary appropriation act, according to the Budget, section 45. In practice, the grants are given by the Financial Committee, a permanent committee composed of members of the Danish Parliament, which also may grant appropriation of expenses without budgetary recovery required by a minister, when the conditions for the appropriation are judged to be well founded. The Public Accounts have to be introduced to the Danish Parliament not later than six months after the expiration of the financial year, according to the Constitution section 47 paragraph 1.

450. The economic development of Denmark is surveyed by the Economic Council *(Det Økonomiske Råd)*, which has to contribute to the coordination of the different economic interests. The Council was originally established in 1956. In 2007, it was supplemented by the Environmental Economic Council. Both councils

343. The Ministry of Finance elaborates a budget guidance, which lays down rules and indications concerning the system of budget and appropriation.

are subject to legal regulation[344] Both councils are established by the Minister of Economy. The Economic Council is directed by three experts of national economy (in popular parlance called 'the three wise men') and is composed of twenty-four members belonging to different business lines and interest groups. After deliberations in the Council, the directors offer a report addressed to the government. The Council does not take decisions. It is an independent entity which has to analyse and evaluate the economic development and to deal with questions in relation to the economic interests of the society. The objective of the Environmental Economic Council is to examine the interaction between the environment and the economy and to assess the efficiency of the Danish environmental policy. The Council consists of chairmanship and. has twenty-four members representing unions, employers, NGO's and the Danish Government.

451. The spatial planning of the land territory is regulated by the Act on Planning,[345] which gathers the former legislation on urban and rural zones, on national and regional planning, on municipal planning, and on summer houses and camping. According to section 1, the Act provides for a spatial planning of the interests of society concerning application of the area and protection of nature and the environment in order to promote a sustainable development for human beings, animals and plants. Special attention shall be given to a development based on macroeconomic considerations, the creation and conservation of valuable buildings and areas, the prevention of pollution and noise, and promotion of the participation of the public in the planning activities. The municipalities are the primary authority regarding spatial planning. A special regulation is established on protection of nature[346] and on preservation of the forests.[347] The legislation provides for a sustainable development within these fields. Outside the land, territory planning are done by the State. It may be based on provisions in special legislation or based on the more general Act on maritime spatial planning[348] implementing EU Directive 2014/89/EU.

§3. State Shareholdings

452. The State may own undertakings or part of undertakings.[349,350] The decisive factor for ownership and shareholdings is political, and it requires adoption of legal basis by the Parliament. During the last two decades, liberalization at EU level has had an impact on State shareholdings. There is no common approach to State ownership of undertakings or shareholdings;[351] solutions and legal basis are created

344. Consolidated Act 181/2017 *(Det Økonomiske Råd og Det Miljøøkonomiske Råd) as* amended most recently by Act 384/2017.
345. Consolidated Act 287/2018 *(Planlov).*
346. Consolidated Act1122/2018 *(Naturbeskyttelseslov)* as amended most recently by Act 1518/2018.
347. Consolidated Act 122/2017 *(Skovlov) as* amended most recently by Act 720/2018.
348. Act 615/2016 (M*aritim fysisk planlægning*) as amended most recently by Act 1714/2018.
349. Author: Grith Skovgaard Ølykke.
350. *See also* Part II, Ch. 3, §3.
351. For example, the Danish State owns part of Copenhagen Airport (39.2%) https://www.cph.dk/om-cph/investorer/aktieinformation (accessed Feb. 2019); part of Scandinavian Airlines (14.2%) http

for the specific situation.[352] Ultimo 2017, the State-owned shares in ten limited companies, ten independent public undertakings, as well as six limited companies three partnerships (*interessentskaber*) where the state owned less than 50% of the company.[353] Three of the limited companies were public limited companies.

453. The approach to privatization and liberalization has been a gradual approach, either through reduced shareholdings and liberalization of markets,[354] or creation of competition through public procurement (e.g., public transport). A special problem in connection to transforming departments of the State into public undertakings under private law (e.g., as limited companies) has been the status and compensation of civil servants who have hitherto enjoyed special job security and pensions.[355] This has been solved through creation of 'independent public undertakings', where civil servants can be employed. Independent public undertakings in Denmark include Naviair, providing air navigation services, Energinet.dk, providing electricity and gas transmission services, Danske Stats Baner (DSB), providing passenger transport by railway. Post Danmark, providing postal services, was previously an independent public undertaking, but, in 2003, it was converted into a limited company and in 2009 it was merged with the Swedish Postal operator to form PostNord AB which is co-owned by the Danish and Swedish States. Transfer of civil servants as part of privatization and compensation for extra costs in this context was an aspect of the *Combus* judgment from the General Court of the European Union in 2003.[356] The General Court found that the compensation paid as bonuses to the employees who volunteered to change their status from civil servant to employees on contractual basis did not involve State-aid contrary to Article 107(1) TFEU.

454. Regions and municipalities can also own and operate companies; the latter may also provide services for other municipalities.[357] Service provision for other municipalities can only take place if the value of the contract is below the thresholds which triggers an obligation to advertise the procurement at EU level; i.e. municipalities are not allowed to participate in EU level procurement procedures (unless they participate in companies).[358] Regions' and municipalities' ownership of companies is somewhat limited, as they may only be involved in activities based on

---

s://www.sasgroup.net/en/shareholders/ (accessed Feb. 2019); and, part of Ørsted (former DONG Energy) (50%), *see* annual report for 2018 at: https://orsted.com/-/media/Annual_2018/Orsted_Annual_report_2018.ashx?la=en&hash=A64F4AF34FD9CA0EEE78FE7FA690B484 (accessed Feb. 2019).

352. For example, Consolidated Act 844/2011 (*Post Danmark A/S*); Consolidated Act 997/2018 (*Energinet.dk*); Consolidated Act 1184/2010 (*DSB lov*); Act 232/1995 (*DSB Busser A/S*).
353. https://www.fm.dk/publikationer/2018/statens-selskaber-2018, p. 9 (accessed Feb. 2019).
354. An example of full privatization is the sale of TDC – the national telecom operator – in 1997–1998, subsequent to the liberalization of the telecom sector at EU level.
355. Consolidated Act 488/2010 (*Tjenestemandslov*).
356. Case T-157/01 *Danske Busvognmænd* (2003) ECR II-917, paras 52–60.
357. Act 548/2006 (*Kommuners udførelse af opgaver for andre offentlige myndigheder og kommuners og regioners deltagelse i selskaber*) as amended by Act 620/2011.
358. Act 548/2006 (*Kommuners udførelse af opgaver for andre offentlige myndigheder og kommuners og regioners deltagelse i selskaber*) as amended by Act 81/2014, s. 2.

locally/regionally created knowledge and know-how, or in activities concerning fulfilment of their own demand.[359] This requirement limits Regions' ownership to companies in the healthcare, transport and social services sectors. The companies in which regions and municipalities participate must have at least 25% private ownership.[360] Moreover, the companies may only receive 50% of their income from other customers than the region/municipality.[361] Municipalities may collaboratively provide services through municipal cooperatives.[362]

455. The State and municipalities could also jointly own companies. A prominent example of this is the Metroselskab constructing and operating and the Metro in Copenhagen.[363] The Metroselskab is owned jointly by the Municipality of Copenhagen (50%), the Municipality of Frederiksberg (8.3%) and the Ministry of Transport (41.7%). Another example is By & Havn which is a company operating for the purpose of developing the part of Copenhagen called Ørestad and operating the Port of Copenhagen.[364] It is owned by the Ministry of Transport (5%) and the Municipality of Copenhagen (95%).[365]

§4. Basic Principles of Economic Law

456. Since 1973, Denmark has been a member of what is now the EU. Hence, the basic principles of economic law generally reflect the open market economy on which the EU is founded.[366] Certain sectors are regulated, for example, with regard to access to do business, quality requirements or educational requirements. For example, the Consolidated Act on Land Surveyors requires a certain education and reserves some services exclusively for land surveyors.[367] The sector regulation has been amended to ensure compliance with EU law, notably the Services Directive.[368] Another example is the pharmacy sector, which is regulated with regard to territorial availability, and where each pharmacist may only own and operate one pharmacy.[369] Since 2001, other shops than pharmacies have been allowed to sell medicine for which prescription is not required. Another example is the taxi sector,

359. *Ibid.*, s. 3.1.
360. *Ibid.*, s. 4.
361. Act 548/2006 (*Kommuners udførelse af opgaver for andre offentlige myndigheder og kommuners og regioners deltagelse i selskaber*) as amended by Act 1234/2012, s. 5.1.
362. Consolidated Act 47/2019 (*Kommunernes styrelse*) s. 60. Such collaborative cannot carry out tasks involving exercise of public authority.
363. The company was established by Act 551/2007 *(Metroselskabet I/S og Arealudviklingsselskabet I/S), see also* www.m.dk (accessed Feb. 2019).
364. The company was established by Act 551/2007 (*Metroselskabet I/S og Arealudviklingsselskabet I/S*). *See also* http://www.byoghavn.dk (accessed Feb. 2019).
365. Act 551/2007 (*Metroselskabet I/S og Arealudviklingsselskabet I/S*) as amended by Act 156/2015.
366. Author: Grith Skovgaard Ølykke.
367. Consolidated Act 680/2013 (*Landinspektørvirksomhed)* ss 1 and 4.
368. The Act *ibid.*, implements Directive 2005/36/EC on the recognition of professional qualifications, OJ (2005) L 255/22 and Directive 2006/123/EC on services in the internal market, OJ (2006) L 376/36.
369. Consolidated Act 801/2018 (*Apoteksvirksomhed*) s. 15.1. Dispensation could allow pharmacists to own up to four pharmacies, cf. s. 15.2.

where previously a limited number of licenses with geographical limitation have been available. From primo 2018, among others, these restrictions have been removed by amendments to the regulation of the taxi sector.[370] Hence, there are trends towards liberalization of regulated sectors.

I. Import and Export of Goods and Capital

A. *General Regulation*

457. Import and export of goods is regulated by EU law as implemented in national law.[371] Hence, it is only relevant to consider rules on import and export of goods from/to third countries. The Consolidated Act on Application of Certain EU Legislative Acts Regarding Economic Relations to Third Countries concerns the measures available, for example, boycott of goods from third countries, and prohibitions on technical assistance for development of certain military technologies.[372]

B. *Foreign Exchange of Capital*

458. For the purpose of regulating foreign exchange, a distinction between transactions made by residents and non-residents is made in the Executive Order on Foreign Exchange.[373] For companies, the requirement for being a resident with regard to foreign exchange is permanent establishment (in the sense of EU law).[374] The Executive Order also defines foreign exchange dealers as: 'Financial institutions, which on a commercial basis settle payments between residents and non-residents via accounts held in or on behalf of foreign banking institutions (correspondent banks).'[375] The National Bank of Denmark may on the basis of negotiation with the Ministry of Economic and Business Affairs issue rules on the business of foreign exchange dealers and on reporting requirements for foreign exchange.[376] Residents, in the sense of the Executive Order, may be fined if they do not provide the required information in time or if they provide false information.[377]

370. Act 1538/2017 entered into force 1. Jan. 2018.
371. However, Consolidated Act 279/1988 on Foreign Exchange *(Valutaforhold m.v)* concerns certain provisions on limitations of import and export of goods, in ss 3–6. The rules provide for repeal of such measures and their practical importance is probably limited.
372. Consolidated Act 635/2011. Further details are available in Executive Order 301/1988 on the administration of certain EU measures on import and export of goods.
373. Executive Order 658/1994 (*Valutaforhold*).
374. *Ibid.*, s. 1.3.
375. *Ibid.*, s. 2.
376. *Ibid.*, s. 3. The rules may be obtained from the National Bank of Denmark.
377. *Ibid.*, s. 5.

459. The Consolidated Act on Foreign Exchange delegates the adoption of further regulation of foreign exchange to the Minister of Economic and Business Affairs.[378] No rules have been issued on this basis.

II. Labour Forces

460. The labour market is organized according to a model based on collective bargaining between organizations representing the employers and employees (unions). All EU law concerning the labour market is implemented by law; however, collective agreements may provide employees more advantageous terms than required by law. In 2017, approximately 67% of employees were members of a union.[379]

461. The system of collective bargaining was in 2007 challenged by the *Laval* judgment of the Court of Justice of the EU. In order to adhere to the *Laval* judgment,[380] the Act implementing the Directive on Posting of Workers has been amended to ensure free movement of services.[381] In 2008, the following wording was inserted in the Consolidated Act on Posting of Workers:[382]

> Section 6 a. In order to ensure posted workers a wage corresponding to the wage Danish employers are obliged to pay for performance of similar work, collective action may be taken against foreign service provides in the same way as against Danish employers, in order to support a demand of entry into a collective agreement; however, see subsec. 2. 2. Collective action as mentioned in stk. 1 may only be initiated if the foreign service provider has been informed of the provisions of the collective agreement entered into by the most representative labour market organizations in Denmark, and which apply in all geographical areas of Denmark. The relevant collective agreement must be sufficiently clear on the aspect of wage to be paid.[383]

462. The Danish labour market model may be characterized as 'flexicurity' model.[384] The flexicurity model implies a relatively low level of security in employment, combined with a high level of unemployment benefits. However, rights for employees have been increased through EU legislative acts.[385]

---

378. Consolidated Act 279/1988 *(Valutaforhold)* ss. 7 and 8.
379. https://www.etui.org/Publications2/Books/Benchmarking-Working-Europe-2017 (accessed Feb. 2019).
380. Case C-341/05 *Laval* (2007) ECR I-11767.
381. Directive 96/71/EC concerning the posting of workers in the framework of the provision of services, OJ (1997) L 18/1, the Directive is implemented by Act 933/1999 *(Udstationering af lønmodtagere)*. The Act has been amended several timers. Currently, the Consolidated Act 1144/2018 applies.
382. By the amendment Act 1394/2008.
383. Author's translation.
384. On flexicurity, *see* Ruth Nielsen, *EU Labour Law*, 2th ed., Jurist- og Økonomforbundets Forlag 2013, chapter 7.
385. *Ibid.*

III. Facilities for Development

463. The access to financing for start-ups is available through private venture capital investors and the State-owned Growth Foundation.[386] The venture capital provided by the Growth Foundation is defined as capital:[387]

- available for young growth companies with a significant growth potential;
- very risk prone and patient;
- available as convertible loans or equity;
- is involved in the strategic decision-making of the company;
- is supervised by persons with an insight in the company's business activities.

464. Various State-owned foundations provide financing for innovation, notably for projects involving cooperation between private companies and Universities.[388]

IV. Global and Local Planning

465. The Consolidated Act on Planning from 2009 has been amended several times – these amendments will be incorporated in the description of the Act.[389] The objective of the Consolidated Act on Planning is to:[390] 'Ensure coherent planning which unites the interests of the society in the utilisation of land, contributes to preserving the nature and environment in the country and creates a framework for growth and development of the entire territory to enable development of the society on the basis of sustainability, respect for the conditions of life for humans, preservation of wildlife and vegetation as well as increased economic welfare.'[391]

Planning takes place at three levels: by the Minister of Environment and Food, the regions and the municipalities. The Consolidated Act on Planning distributes the competence for planning at the three levels[392] and lays out the rules for adoption of regional and local planning decisions.[393]

466. The country is divided into zones: city zones, summerhouse zones and rural zones (the latter being the residual category).[394] Planning of city centres and shopping facilities is delegated to the municipalities. However, Chapter 2d of the Consolidated Act on Planning limits the discretion of municipalities' planning. The size and number of shops are restricted relative to the population in the relevant geographical area.[395] Planning in summerhouse zones and coastal areas is restricted in

386. For further on support for entrepreneurs, *see* Part II, Ch. 3, §1. B.
387. www.vf.dk (accessed Feb. 2019).
388. https://ufm.dk/en/research-and-innovation?set_language=en&cl=en (accessed Feb. 2019).
389. Consolidated Act 287/2018 *(Planlov)*.
390. *Ibid.*, s. 1.
391. Author's translation.
392. Cf. e.g., *ibid.*, ss 5j and 5k.
393. *Ibid.*, Ch. 6.
394. *Ibid.*, s. 34.
395. *Ibid.*

order to take into account environmental factors and tourism.[396] Special restrictions are placed on planning in rural areas.[397] The Consolidated Act also contains provisions on expropriation of private property.[398]

V. Means of Communication

467. The competence to provide, finance and regulate means of communication is split between the State, the regions and the municipalities.

A. *Railways*

468. The railway sector has been liberalized further than required by EU law. The physical network is managed by Banedanmark (a public authority), who owns, maintains and develops the rail network.[399] The State-owned provider of passenger transport by railway, DSB, is an independent public undertaking regulated by the Consolidated DSB Act.[400] The DSB provides public service traffic under contracts negotiated directly with the Ministry of Transport, Building and Housing/the Danish Transport Authority.[401] A few local routes are served by railway companies owned jointly by regions, municipalities and private parties.

469. In addition to the vertical separation of network and service provision, a few routes have been opened to competition by public procurement. In 2001–2002, the first public procurement procedure was conducted concerning passenger transport by railway on routes in Jutland; re-tendering of the routes in Jutland was carried out in 2009. Furthermore, a public procurement procedure for passenger transport by railway has been carried out in 2007–2008 for provision of passenger transport by railway on routes linking to Sweden, and in 2018, the Minister of Transport, Building and Housing delegated the responsibility for procurement of passenger transport services on that route to Skånetrafiken (a Swedish public authority).[402]

396. *Ibid.*, Ch. 2a and Ch. 8.
397. *Ibid.*, ss. 35–38.
398. *Ibid.*, Ch. 11. For further on expropriation, *see infra* Part II. Ch. 3. §1. E.
399. https://uk.banedanmark.dk/ (accessed Feb. 2019).
400. Consolidated Act 1184/2010 *(DSB-lov)*.
401. In accordance with EU law, notably Regulation 1370/2007 on public passenger transport services by rail and by road and repealing Council Regulations (EEC) Nos 1191/69 and 1107/70, OJ (2007) L 315/1, as amended by Regulation (EU) 2016/2338 of the European Parliament and of the Council of 14 Dec. 2016 amending Regulation (EC) No 1370/2007 concerning the opening of the market for domestic passenger transport services by rail, OJ (2016) L 354/22.
402. https://www.trm.dk/da/publikationer/2018/aftale-med-skaanetrafiken--overdragelse-af-trafikkoeber ansvar (accessed Feb. 2019).

470. Freight transport by rail has been fully liberalized, and many different operators have licence to carry out freight transport on the Danish rail network.[403]

B. Aviation

471. The aviation sector is regulated at EU level, notably safety, security and international relations. In addition, *inter alia*, access to carrying out transport by aviation (licensing) and safety is regulated in the consolidated Act on Aviation, however, explicitly without prejudice to EU regulation of the sector.[404] Copenhagen Airport is a public limited company (the Danish State owns 39.2% of the shares); other (local) airports are public undertakings and are owned by municipalities, according to location.

C. Roads

472. Public roads are roads, streets, bridges and squares open for normal traffic, administered by the State or the municipalities. The State administers main roads of importance for national traffic, and municipalities administers roads of importance for local and regional traffic.[405] The Consolidated Act on Public Roads allocates competences, requires the relevant authority to maintain roads and to ensure that appropriate safety measures are taken, and delegates the competence for planning traffic to the Minister of Transport, Building and Housing.[406]

473. In case a road is categorized by the Municipality as a private common road (i.e., it is of minor importance for local traffic), citizens and businesses owning property along the road may have to pay for its maintenance (incl. snow removal) and lighting.[407] The municipality may maintain the road and charge the relevant citizens, if appropriate, in rates. The municipality may decide to charge citizens and businesses owning property along public roads in city zones where private common roads are located, for maintenance of the public roads in that area as well.[408]

D. Postal Service

474. The postal sector has been liberalized at EU level. The Postal Act outlines requirements for access to deliver postal services.[409] In 2009, the previous national monopolist, the State-owned limited company Post Danmark A/S, merged with the

403. https://www.bane.dk/da/Jernbanevirksomhed/Jernbanevirksomheder-paa-Banedanmarks-infrastruktur#accordion= (accessed Feb. 2019).
404. Consolidated Act 1149/2017 *(Luftfartslov)* s. 1.
405. Act 1520/2014 *(Offentlige veje)* ss. 1 and 2.
406. *Ibid.*
407. Act 1234/2015 *(Private fællesveje)* ss. 6–8.
408. Act 1520/2014 Ch. 4.
409. Consolidated Act 1040/2017 *(Postlov).*

Swedish Posten AB and formed PostNord, which is owned by the Danish State (40%) and the Swedish State (60%).[410] The business of Post Danmark A/S is regulated in the Consolidated Act on Post Danmark A/S.[411] In accordance with EU law, Post Danmark A/S is assigned a public service obligation (carrier of last resort) obliging it to collect and distribute mail in Denmark, at transparent and non-discriminatory prices reflecting costs.[412]

475. Mail to businesses and citizens from public authorities is sent by electronic means. The Act on Public Digital Mail requires citizens and businesses to hold so-called e-box, where they receive all correspondence and bills from public authorities and utilities.[413]

E. Telecommunication

476. The telecommunications sector has been liberalized at EU level. The previous national monopolist, TDC was privatized in 1997–1998 when it entered into a strategic partnership with Ameritech, and subsequently bought off the remaining shares from the Danish State.[414] The TDC owns the cobber network. The telecommunication sector is regulated in the Act on Electronic Communication Networks and Services.[415] The Act provides *inter alia* for: consumer rights; data protection; public service obligations; price regulation; the telephone number system; and, conditions for access to provide services and access to the network. Supervision is carried out by the Danish Business Authority.[416]

F. Radio Communication

477. Transmission of radio programmes is regulated in the Consolidated Act on Radio and Television,[417] and requires permission from the Radio and Television Board under the Danish Agency for Culture.[418] Permissions are tendered as concessions, and one of the award criteria is the concession payment offered by the potential provider.[419] Danmarks Radio is one of the State-owned providers TV broadcasting, and is on the basis of a contract assigned public service obligations for the transmission and production of radio programmes.[420] The public service

410. http://www.postnord.com/ (accessed Feb. 2019).
411. Consolidated Act 844/2011 *(Post Danmark A/S).*
412. Consolidated Act 1040/2017 *(Postlov)*, s. 15.2.
413. Consolidated Act801/2016 *(Offentlig Digital Post)*, s. 3.
414. https://tdcgroup.com/da/m%C3%B8d-tdc-group/historie (accessed Feb. 2019).
415. Consolidated Act 128/2014 *(Elektroniske kommunikationsnet og –tjenester)* s. 18. 1 on compensation for public service obligations.
416. https://danishbusinessauthority.dk/telecom (accessed Feb. 2019).
417. Consolidated Act 115/2019 *(Radio- og fjernsynsvirksomhed).*
418. *Ibid.*, s. 3. On the Radio and Television Board, *see* Ch. 7.
419. *Ibid.*, s. 4.
420. *Ibid.*, s. 12.

activities are financed through TV and Radio license fee payment by users.[421] Advertising in the different media is also regulated in the Consolidated Act on Radio and Television. As a general rule, advertisements may be sent for twelve minutes per hour on the radio.[422] Digital radio transmission was introduced for the public in 2001–2002, on the basis of the Digital Audio Broadcasting technology. Analog radio is gradually being out phased.

478. Radio frequencies are a scarce resource, and the use of frequencies is regulated by the Act on Radio Frequencies.[423] Use of radio frequencies requires permission from the Danish Energy Agency.[424]

G. Building Regulation

479. The objective of the Consolidated Act on Construction is to: promote security with regard to fire, health and safety; ensure satisfactory quality in the context of the intended use of the building; enable sound maintenance; ensure reparation of building damages; promote constructions enabling access for handicapped; promote architectural quality; increase efficiency in construction; encourage measures intended to reduce waste of resources; and encourage measures intended to reduce the waste of raw material.[425] The Act applies to new constructions, conversions, demolition and refurbishment. Permission is needed for construction.[426] Competence to give permission is vested in the municipalities. For new constructions, access to an authorized road, drainage, water supply and authorized means for fire extinguishing must all be supplied before the building is used.[427] More detailed rules for the construction of buildings can be found in the Building Rules,[428] which are issued on the basis of the Consolidated Act on Construction. Municipalities may make their authorizations for construction contingent on esthetical factors.[429]

421. *Ibid.*, s. 11 .7 and ss. 69–70.
422. *Ibid.*, ss. 74–75.
423. Consolidated Act 1100/2016.
424. *Ibid.*, s. 6.
425. Consolidated Act 1178/2016 *(Byggelov)* s. 1.
426. *Ibid.*, s. 16. 1.
427. *Ibid.*, s. 4.
428. http://www.bygningsreglementet.dk/ (accessed Feb. 2019).
429. Consolidated Act 1178/2016, s. 6D.

Chapter 2. Law of Establishment and Supervision of Commercial Activities

480. Section 74 of the Constitution provides for the free and equal access to exercise a profession, limited only by restrictions following from the public well-being.[430] On this basis, a large number of requirements are laid down for special professions. It is the aim of the legislation to establish a proper balance between the freedom of doing business and limitations concerning the public security, health and order, as well as an efficient utilization of the resources of the country.

481. The Act on services in the internal market[431] implements parts of the EU Service Directive 2006/123. It gives service providers that are citizens of or established in another EU/EEA country access to establish in Denmark[432] and service providers established in another EU/EEA country a right to perform services in Denmark,[433] all in accordance with the Directive. The Portal 'Business in Denmark'[434] run by the Business Authority (*Erhvervsstyrelsen*) is the point of single contact, *see* Article 6 of the Directive. It contains information on authorization schemes and requirements according to Danish law for services covered by the Service Directive.

§1. Requirements for Professional Qualifications and Exercise of Trade

I. General Requirements

482. The rules regulating specific professional activities often lay down personal requirements regarding age, majority and authority, diplomas and/or training, and good conduct. Furthermore, the place of residence, the citizenship, solvency and the importance of debts due to the public sector are considered. Normally the execution of the profession depends on an authorization, which may be used by the public authorities as an instrument for a qualitative and quantitative regulation of certain professions, taking into account the EU-rules on free movement. For some examples, *see infra* Part II, Chapter 2, §1.II–§1.IV.

483. The Act on Recognition of Professional Qualifications[435] implements the Directive 2005/36 on the Recognition of Professional Qualifications as amended most recently by Directive 2013/55. It gives EU/EEA citizens access to exercise activities within certain professions regulated by law. According to section 3 of the

430. Author: Peter Møgelvang-Hansen.
431. Act 384/2009 (*tjenesteydelser i det indre marked)* as amended most recently by Act 1871/2015.
432. Sections 9 and 10 of the Act implementing the Directive's Chapter III on freedom of establishment.
433. Sections 11 and 12 of the Act implementing the Directive's Chapter IV on free movement.
434. https://danishbusinessauthority.dk/business-denmark. (accessed Apr. 2019)
435. Act 1871/2015 (*Anerkendelse af visse uddannelses- og erhvervsmæssige kvalifikationer*).

Act, non-employed as well as employed persons subject to the rules are admitted to exercise the regulated professions on the same terms as Danish citizens. The access to each of the regulated professions is administered by the relevant competent public authority. The Ministry of Higher Education and Science (*Ministeriet for uddannelse og forskning* is designated coordinator and designated contact point according to Articles 56–57 of the Directive.[436]

II. Liberal Professions

A. Advocates

484. The requirements for advocates (solicitors, barristers, in Danish *advokater*) are laid down in the Administration of Justice Act,[437] Chapters 12–15b. The advocates are admitted to the bar by the Minister of Justice. The requirements for being an advocate are full legal capacity, solvency, a Danish bachelor and master degree in law (*juridisk kandidateksamen*),[438] three years of practical juridical training, and a completed theoretical basic education and a passed examination in matters of special importance to the profession of advocate as well as a passed practical test in litigation, section 119. Other conditions relate to good conduct and no major debt to the public sector, section 121. In order to ensure the necessary knowledge of Danish procedural law and of the Danish language at a level that enables the proper conduct of oral proceedings the Ministry of Justice may fix a trial period as a condition for authorization as an assistant attorney of persons who hold a master degree in law from one of the EU/EEA Member States that corresponds to the level of the Danish degree. The ministry may also otherwise, to the extent needed for fulfilling EU obligations, exempt candidates from the requirement that they must hold a Danish degree in law, including fixing a trial period as a condition, section 135a.

Practising law is incompatible with a legal position at the courts of justice, the prosecution service or the police and as a main rule any position in public service, section 122. Apart from lawyers acting as sole practitioners or in a grouping of lawyers, only professional corporations of lawyers in the form of public limited, private limited or limited partnership companies may practise law. The only permitted object of a professional corporation of lawyers shall be to practise law, section 124. With a few exceptions, advocates hold a sole right to appear in court for others, section 131. Every advocate has to be a member of The Danish Bar and Law Society (*Det Danske Advokatsamfund*), section 143.

---

436. Detailed information (in English) is available at http://ufm.dk/en/education /recognition-and-transparency/regulated-professions (accessed Apr. 2019) including a list of 130 professions regulated by law, each accompanied by information on the competent authority, relevant legislation, documentation requirements, etc.

437. Consolidated Act 1284/2018 (*Retsplejeloven*).

438. *See infra* on Section. 135a concerning persons who hold a Master's degree in Law from one of the other EU Member States.

B. Auditors

485. The conditions for approval and registration of auditors and audit firms, and for the performance of audit assignments, etc. are found in the Act on Approved Auditors and Audit Firms.[439] The Act implements the Directive on Statutory Audits of Annual Accounts and Consolidated Accounts and relevant parts of the Regulation on Specific Requirements regarding Statutory Audit of Public-interest Entities .[440] The Act applies to the auditor's provision of financial statements, and other assurance reports that are not exclusively meant for the principal's own use. According to section 3, the Business Authority (*Erhvervsstyrelsen*) may approve a person as a State-authorized public accountant or a registered public accountant if the person in question resides in Denmark, in another EU/EEA country, has full legal capacity, is not insolvent, has passed a special examination,[441] has, unless exemption is granted, participated, for at least three years in the performance of assignments that concern audits of financial statements, etc. and is insured against claims for damages that may be made in connection with the performance of assignments. Other conditions relate to good conduct and no major debt to the public sector.

Persons who have concluded a study programme or training programme abroad, which can be equated with the study and training programme mentioned above, have knowledge of Danish legislation and meet the other conditions may also be approved as auditors. And where special circumstances apply, the Business Authority (*Erhvervsstyrelsen*) may, moreover, permit foreign auditors to handle specific tasks for which a State-authorized public accountant or a registered public accountant is required in accordance with the existing legislation, section 10. According to section 11, auditors that are authorized according to Directive 2006/43 and established in another EU/EEA Member State and have registered a declaration that they intend to provide temporary or occasional services in Denmark,[442] are also permitted to handle tasks other than statutory audit.[443]

In audit firms, the majority of the voting rights must be held by auditors or audit firms that are approved in pursuance of rules implementing the Directive on statutory audits of annual accounts and consolidated accounts. The same requirement applies to the majority of the members of the supreme management body of the audit firm, section 13(2) and (5) of the Act.

C. Real Estate Agents

486. Real estate agents are subject to the Act on Real Property Transactions.[444] The Act regulates a register for real estate agents and provides for mandatory

439. Consolidated Act 1287/2018 (*Revisorloven*) as amended most recently by Act 1716/2018.
440. Directive 2006/43, as amended by Directive 2014/53, and Regulation 537/2014.
441. Executive Order 1045/2016 issued under Section 33(2) of the Act.
442. Executive Order 966/2016.
443. Exempted according to Art. 3(1) of Directive 2006/43.
444. Act 526/2014 (*lov om formidling af fast ejendom*) as amended most recently by Act 503/2018

consumer protection rules concerning the exercise of the professional activities as intermediary concerning real estate transactions.

487. The access to deal in real property as an intermediary is regulated by section 6 of the Act. It provides for the exclusive right of mediation for registered real estate agents, advocates and temporary service providers established as real estate agents in other EU/EEA Member States that have registered a declaration that they intend to provide temporary or occasional services in Denmark during the following year.[445] A security covering indemnity for loss inflicted on a consumer has to be provided.

488. The requirements for registration as a real estate agent are laid down in the Act's section 5. The register is kept by the Business Authority (*Erhvervsstyrelsen*). Only persons entered in the register are entitled to use the designation of *'ejendomsmægler'* (real estate agent) or a similar name which could be mixed up with the designation.[446] The admission to the register requires residence in Denmark or in another EU/EEA country, personal capacity and solvency. The real estate agent may not exercise professional activities which are incompatible with the agency business. Professional skill requirements on theoretical and practical knowledge are established by the Business Authority *(Erhvervsstyrelsen)*.[447] The condition of no major debts to the public should be fulfilled by the estate agents. Besides the conditions of registration and access to do business, the Act[448] lays down mandatory provisions for the exercise of the professional activities in relation to consumers.

III. Self-Employed Trade

489. Whereas self-employed business as retail trader generally does not require a licence according to the general Trade Act,[449] rules to that effect can be found in specific legislation, for example, service of hard liquor requires a special licence *(alkoholbevilling)* under the Act on Restaurants.[450]

445. See Section 13 of the Act and Executive Order 6/2016 implementing Art. 7 of Directive 2005/36 on the Recognition of Professional Qualifications.
446. Section 7. According to Section 22(2) of the Act, under certain conditions a real estate agent is entitled to choose the designation as an independent real estate agent when it has not bound itself to be active for transactions with financial products or other products related to transactions concerning real property and directs any provision, etc. from a provider of financial products to the consumer and the business is conducted in a way that does not cause doubt as to its independence. Section 22(1), lays down that a connection between a financial institute, a mortgage credit institute or an insurance company and a real estate agency has to appear directly in the name of the estate agency or has to be added to the name.
447. *See* Executive Order 6/2016.
448. *See also* Executive Order 1230/2014.
449. Consolidated Act 595/2011 *(Næringsloven)*.
450. Consolidated Act 135/2010 (*Restaurationsloven*) as amended most recently by Act 1665/2017.

IV. The Health Sector

490. The administration and supervision of the health sector are regulated by the Act on Health[451] and the Act on Authorisation of Health Persons.[452] The National Board of Health (*Sundhedsstyrelsen*) submitted to the Ministry of Health *(Sundhedsministeriet)* acts as supervisor of health conditions and of persons who are dealing with health activities.

The Act on Authorization of Health Persons lays down requirements for authorization of *inter alia* doctors, nurses, dentists, chiropractors, midwives, occupational therapists and opticians. The authorization generally gives the holder the right to exercise the health activity in question and to use the designation in question. Section 3 of the Act provides for the access for health persons from for EU/EEA citizens to exercise professional activities in Denmark.[453] The special conditions for exercising the specific professions are provided in Chapters 8–25 of the Act.

§2. Quantitative Limitation of the Number of Enterprises

491. Generally there are no quantitative restrictions but within some sectors there is specific regulation to this effect, *see infra* No. 492 – 494 for examples.

492. It is the general purpose of the regulation within the agricultural sector that the natural resources should be exploited and developed in an appropriate way in accordance with environmental and economic considerations and in order to keep rural districts populated, etc., compare the Act on Agricultural Holdings[454] section 1. Chapters 7–9 of the Act contain detailed rules on the acquisition of agricultural holdings in land zones.

493. The Act on Fisheries[455] implements EU-regulations and authorizes the Minister of Food, Agriculture and Fisheries to issue executive orders restricting the commercial exploitation of fish resources.[456]

494. The Act on Chemists' Activities,[457] section 4 provides that the Minister of Health decides on establishment, abolition or removal of pharmacies.

---

451. Consolidated Act 1286/2018 *(Sundhedsloven) as* amended most recently by Act 730/2018.
452. Consolidated Act. 13/2018 *(Autorisation af sundhedspersoner)* as amended most recently by Act 1555/2018.
453. Cf. Executive Order 49/2010, as amended by Executive Order 61/2016, implementing Directive 2005/36. Executive Orders 1372/2010, 97/2011 and 478/2013 provide rules on authorization of doctors and dentists and other health persons from non-EU/EEA countries.
454. Consolidated Act 27/2017*(Landbrugsejendomme).*
455. Consolidated Act 261/2019 *(Fiskeriloven).*
456. Cf. Executive Order 1270/2018.
457. Consolidated Act 801/2018 (*Apoteksvirksomhed*).

§3. Supervision of Credit Institutions, Insurance Companies, etc.

495. The supervision of the various financial undertakings is carried out by the DFSA (*Finanstilsynet*). The DFSA is a separate agency within the Ministry of Industry, Business and Financial Affairs *(Erhvervsministeriet)*. The DFSA supervision comprises not only the financial undertakings but also the securities market. As far as the supervision of the securities market is concerned, *see supra* Part I, Chapter 8.

496. The supervision of financial undertakings comprises mainly credit institutions, mortgage credit institutions, insurance companies, pension funds, insurance brokers, investment companies and investment associations (UCITS). The financial institutions are highly regulated, not only at the national level but also within the EU. The great majority of rules are found in the Financial Business Act.[458] The Act implements the EU directives concerning the financial institutions, including the principles of Home State control and single licence.

497. The overall aim of the DFSA supervision is to ensure that the financial institutions observe the various provisions set out in mainly the Financial Business Act. The supervision also includes protection of consumers and investors.[459]

Traditionally the most important supervisory activity is monitoring that undertakings have adequate own funds to cover their risks (supervision of solvency). In the wake of the financial crisis, the Financial Business Act has been amended frequently and a more proactive approach has been adopted. The supervisory activities of the DFSA now go beyond monitoring that the undertakings meet the statutory demands, in that they also include assessment of the undertakings' ability to manage the risks connected with their business models.

458. Consolidated Act 457/2019 (*lFinansiel virksomhed*).

459. Executive Order330/2016 on Good Business Practice for Financial Undertakings, issued under s. 43(2) of the Financial Business Act.

Chapter 3. State Incentives for Economic Activities

§1. Subsidies

498. The term 'subsidies' is in the following given the same legal content as the term 'State aid', which is used in EU law, and in national law.[460,461] State aid is State resources transferred by the Member State in any form whatsoever which distorts or threatens to distort competition by favouring certain undertakings or the production of certain goods, insofar as it affects trade between Member States.[462] State aid is as a main rule prohibited in the EU and must be notified to the EU Commission.[463] Only State aid compatible with the Internal Market is approved.[464] All official subsidy schemes or individual grants of subsidies in Denmark are hence approved by the EU Commission.

499. In 2017, the Danish State spent 1.56% of GDP on State aid (less aid to railways).[465] The subsidized sectors are illustrated below in Figure 4:

Figure 4 Subsidized sectors in Denmark, 2017

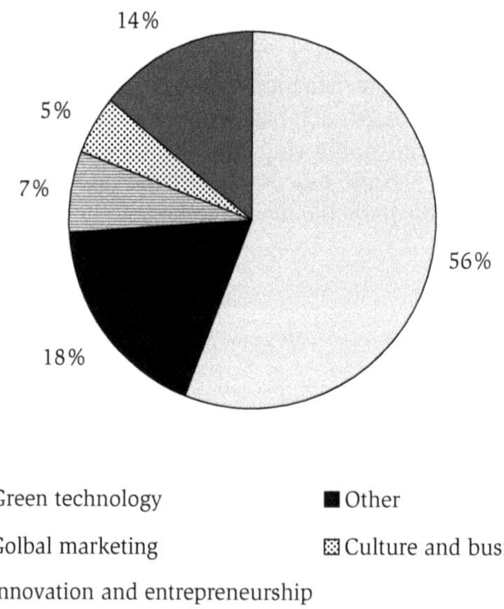

460. Author: Grith Skovgaard Ølykke.
461. Cf. Part II, Ch. 4, §2. I, where it is mentioned that the Consolidated Competition Act includes a provision on prohibition of State aid (§11a).
462. Article 107(1) TFEU, and C-482/99 *Stardust Marine* (2002) ECR I-4397.
463. Article 108(3) TFEU.
464. Article 107(2) and (3) TFEU.
465. 2018 State aid Scoreboard, http://ec.europa.eu/competition/state_aid/scoreboard/index_en.html (accessed Feb. 2019).

Source: Ministry of Economic and Business Affairs' Report on subsidies for promotion of businesses (https://em.dk/media/9696/05-17-erhvervsfremme-og-stoette.pdf, accessed February 2019), p. 5, translated and modified by the author.

500. In 2018, a general sanitation of subsidy schemes in the agricultural, fisheries and environmental areas was carried out and several schemes were terminated;[466] the historical measures are not considered below.

I. The Agricultural Sector

501. Subsidies for the agricultural sector must be in compliance with EU's common agricultural and rural development policies, and international obligations, notably the WTO Agreement on Agriculture. There are two levels of subsidies for the agricultural sector, subsidies granted and financed by the EU and subsidies granted and financed by the Member States. EU Regulations on subsidies for the agricultural sector are implemented by the Consolidated Act on the Administration of the European Communities Regulations on the Common Agricultural Policy Financed by the European Agricultural Guarantee Fund.[467] National subsidies must be notified to the EU Commission.[468] Both types of subsidies are administered by the Danish Agricultural Agency under the Ministry of Environment and Food.[469]

502. A list of current subsidy schemes is available at the website of the Danish Agricultural Agency.[470]

503. Amongst the objectives of the Act on Green Development and Demonstration Program in the Food, Agricultural, Fisheries and Aquaculture sectors is a competitive and sustainable food and non-food production and the further development of a market-driven organic food sector.[471] The Act delegates to the Board of the Program to implement subsidy projects.

II. The Sector of Fisheries

504. The sector is regulated at EU level. There are two levels of subsidies for the Fisheries sector, subsidies granted and financed by the EU and subsidies granted and financed by the Member States. Both types of subsidies are administered by the Danish Fisheries Agency under the Ministry of Foreign Affairs.[472]

466. Act 1551/2018.
467. Consolidated Act 231/2018.
468. Cf. Regulation 1305/2013 on support for rural development by the European Agricultural Fund for Rural Development (EAFRD) and repealing Council Regulation (EC) No 1698/2005, OJ (2013) L 347/487, Art. 82 read in conjunction with European Union Guidelines for State aid in the agricultural and forestry sectors and in rural areas 2014 to 2020, OJ (2014) C 204/1, Sc. 2.5.
469. Executive Order 1273/2017 (*Landbrugsstyrelsens opgaver og beføjelser*) s. 2. 1, no. 1 and 2.
470. https://lbst.dk/tilskudsguide/ (accessed Feb. 2019).
471. Consolidated Act 23/2017, s. 1 and Executive Order 1069/2017.
472. Executive Order 983/2018 (*Fiskeristyrelsens opgaver og beføjelser*) s. 2.1, no. 1.

505. The Consolidated Act on Structural Measures for the Fisheries Sector has the objective of promoting change and structural adjustments in commercial fishery, aquaculture and manufacture and marketing of the products. Furthermore, its purpose is to promote conversion of the areas economically reliant on fishery.[473] The Act delegates the competence to implement subsidy schemes with the mentioned objectives to the Minister of environment and Food. A list of current subsidy schemes is available at the website of the Danish Fisheries Agency.[474]

506. Previously, the Fisheries Bank of the Kingdom of Denmark would provide for financing for fishermen.[475] However, in 2008, the Fisheries Bank was closed and the engagements were transferred to the State, new loans are not provided for.[476]

III. The Environment

507. Regulation of environmental issues mainly takes place at International and EU level, and national measures must be in accordance with EU law.

508. Regarding subsidies for green energy, the Transmission System Operator, Energinet.dk (an independent public undertaking)[477] is assigned public service obligations (PSOs) comprising of *inter alia* security of supply, payment of an additional price subsidy for green energy, and research and development in sustainable production technologies for electricity.[478]

509. International and EU obligations (notably the EU Commission's Natura 2000 initiative)[479] require Denmark to identify geographical areas worthy of protection.[480] In order to realize the environmental targets for preserving nature, the Consolidated Act on Protection of Nature provides for compensation to property owners which are ordered to fulfil the action plans in order to achieve the environmental targets pursued in *inter alia* the Natura 2000 initiative.[481]

473. Consolidated Act 35/2017.
474. https://fiskeristyrelsen.dk/tilskud/tilskudsguide/ (accessed Feb. 2019).
475. The Bank was established in 1978, by Act 54/1978 *(Kongeriget Danmarks fiskeribank).*
476. Executive Order 1149/2008, s. 1, as amended by Executive Order 1176/2016.
477. Cf. Part II, Ch. 1, §3.
478. Consolidated Act 52/2019 on Electricity Supply *(Elforsyningsloven)* s. 8 read in conjunction with the mentioned provisions on Promotion of Sustainable Energy.
479. On the Danish activities concerning the Natura 2000 agenda, *see* the webpage of the Environmental Protection Agency https://mst.dk/natur-vand/natur/natura-2000/ (accessed Aug. 2012).
480. Which is implemented by Executive Order 1595/2018.
481. Consolidated Act 1122/2018 *(Naturbeskyttelseslov)* s. 19h.

IV. Trade and Industry Subsidies

A. *Protection of Trade and Industry in General*

510. Generally, sectorial subsidies to certain industries or undertakings are subject to approval by the EU Commission. According to the Ministry of Economic and Business Affairs' Report on subsidies for promotion of businesses, in 2017, such subsidies amounted to DKK 25.9 billion.[482] For lists of the included subsidies, refer to Annexes 3 and 4 of the Report.

511. On the basis of the Act on Promotion of Business, in 2018 the Danish Board on Promotion of Business was established.[483] One of the tasks of the Board is to administer EU funded subsidies for growth initiatives.[484] Furthermore, Municipal Business Houses which will implement initiatives locally.[485]

B. *Subsidies for New Enterprises*

512. The Growth Foundation administers several financing schemes for entrepreneurs: growth guarantees on loans/credits/etc.; start loans; subordinated loans; and growth loans for companies which have already received venture capital.[486] General support for entrepreneurs is provided by 'StartGrowth' (*Startvækst*), administered by the Danish Business Authority.[487]

C. *Export Credit*

513. The Export Council of the Ministry of Foreign Affairs was established in 2001 by Act on Certain Aspects of the Export Credit Council's Business.[488] Assistance from the Export Council normally costs DKK 995 per hour.[489]

514. The Export Credit Foundation provides for guarantees in cases of extraordinary risks which are not covered by private banks or insurance companies.[490] Guarantees are given to the Danish undertaking's bank in order to facilitate financing of, for example, production for export or payment of the price by the foreign

482. https://em.dk/media/9696/05-17-erhvervsfremme-og-stoette.pdf, p. 5 (accessed Feb. 2019).
483. Act 1518/2018 *(Erhvervsfremmelov)*, Ch. 3.
484. *Ibid.* s. 9.1. no. 3.
485. *Ibid.* Ch. 12.
486. https://www.vf.dk/ (accessed Feb. 2019). On venture capital, *see* Part II. Ch. 1. §4. III.
487. https://startvaekst.virk.dk/ (accessed Feb. 2019).
488. Act 53/2001 as amended most recently by by Act 361/2014, *see also* https://thetradecouncil.dk/ (accessed Feb. 2019).
489. Guideline 1513/2018 for the Executive Order on Payment for Services provided by the Ministry of Foreign Affairs, s. 9.
490. Act 104/2016*(Dansk Eksportkreditfond)*, as amended by Act 1549/2017, s. 2.4. For access to the English translation of the legal bases of the Export Credit Foundation, *see* http://www.ekf.dk/en/about-ekf/ekfs-legal-basis/Pages/EKFs-lovgrundlag.aspx (accessed Feb. 2019).

buyer. All transactions are on 'market terms' in the sense of EU State-aid rules, as the risk of each order is individually assessed on the basis of, for example, the amount, sector, time horizon, the bank's risk assessment and the relevant buyer's country.

D. *Regional Measures*

515. The Act on Promotion of Business allows municipalities to provide business development services, such as: innovation, sharing of knowledge, application of new technologies, establishment and development of new undertakings, development of human resources including development of regional and local competences, growth and development of tourism and development activities in rural areas.[491] The services must be relevant to a wide range of businesses, and may not distort competition in relation to private providers of similar services. Moreover, municipalities may provide and finance business service activities. The services must be relevant to a wide range of businesses, and may not distort competition in relation to private providers of similar services.[492] The Consolidated Act on Urban Regeneration and Development of Urban areas allows municipalities to finance public works for the purposes of urban regeneration and development.[493] On the basis of application, the State may subsidize half of the costs of the projects.[494]

516. For the period 2014–2020, a number of municipalities and small inhabited islands qualify for different degrees of regional aid under EU law (corresponding to 7.9% of the Danish population).[495]

E. *Measures Relating to Compensation of Loss*

517. The Consolidated Act on Employees Guarantee Foundation implements the EU Directive on the position of employees in case of the employer's insolvency.[496] Employees' loss on wages is compensated up to a maximum of DKK 160,000.[497]

518. The Consolidated Act on Expropriation of Real Estate provides for payment of damages for expropriation to the owner, at a level assessed by an independent committee in each individual case.[498]

491. Act 1518/2018 *(Erhvervsfremmelov)* ss. 14.
492. *Ibid.*, s. 14.4–5.
493. Consolidated Act 1228/2016 *(Byfornyelseslov)*, as amended.
494. Consolidated Act 1228/2016 *(Byfornyelseslov)*, as amended by Act 1562/2017,., ss. 7.
495. http://europa.eu/rapid/press-release_IP-14-525_da.htm (accessed Feb. 2019).
496. Consolidated Act 686/2011 *(Lønmodtagernes Garantifond)* implementing the codifying Directive 2008/94/EC on the protection of employees in the event of the insolvency of their employer, OJ (2008) L 283/36.
497. *Ibid.*, s. 3.1 read in conjunction with Executive Order 653/2009 s. 1.
498. Consolidated Act 1161/2008 *(Fremgangsmåden ved ekspropriation)*.

519. The Act on Storm Surge provides for subsidies to cover the value of non-insured goods, property and certain types of forest damaged by surge or flooding.[499] Surge and flooding are defined as levels of water which statistically only occur every twenty years.[500]

F. Other State Subsidies

520. The State subsidizes distribution of newspapers, in order to promote diversity of the press.[501] In accordance with EU legislation, the Act on Operational Aid for Shipbuilding Contingent on the Presence of a Contract allows the Minister of Economics and Business Affairs to provide subsidies of 4.5% of the contract value, if the contract value is less than DKK 10 million, and of 9% of the contract value, if the contract value is more than DKK 10 million.[502]

V. Subsidies for Vocational Training and Education

521. The Consolidated Act on Subsidies for Adult Education has the purpose of facilitating further education of adults with short educations, at secondary school, upper secondary school and higher level.[503] This is done by provision of a higher monthly State-paid allowance for adults (over 25 years), on certain conditions, for example, it is required that the person has been employed for a period of time, prior to the start of the education.

§2. Tax Incentives

522. The tax system gives several different incentives. It is given both to businesses in general and to motivate certain industries to expand[504].

523. The Act on State Tax, section 6, paragraph 1, Schedule A, admits deductions of operating costs spent by persons or enterprises. The notion of operating costs *(driftsudgifter)* constitutes costs which have been spent within a certain period, normally only one year in order to acquire, secure and maintain the taxable income.[505]

---

499. Consolidated Act 281/2018 *(Stormflod og stormfald)* s. 1.
500. *Ibid.*, s. 2.
501. Act 1604/2013.
502. Act 1009/1998 s. 2.
503. Consolidated Act 480/2018 *(Statens voksenuddannelsesstøtte)* s. 1.
504. Author: Jane Bolander.
505. Act 149/1922 on State Tax *(Statsskatteloven)* as amended by Act 428/2005.

I. Tax Relief Concerning Enterprises

524. The Act on State Tax, section 6 paragraph 2, includes a distinction between normal costs relating to the run the business and costs related to the source of the income. The acquirement or argumentation of the foundation of the income has, in principle, no importance for the statement of income. The costs to be deducted concern the consumption of the enterprise and the attribution and depreciation of the assets. It may be difficult to discern costs of establishment from costs concerning running the enterprise. Normally, costs of establishment are not deductible, but they may be deducted when there is a natural connection between the costs and the management of the enterprise. Examples of this kind of deductions are costs concerning market analyses of new markets and rent of premises before the opening of the business. Expenses for vocational training in order to get established are not deductible.

525. It is characteristic of operation costs that they are usual, normal or necessary for the management and, therefore, these distinctions are normally sufficient evidence. Certain types of costs are normally regarded as operation costs, for example, wages and other costs of the staff, rent of premises and real property, office expenses, insurance expenses, research costs, advertising and subscriptions concerning trade organizations. Expenses for education and vocational training may be deductible when they are mainly related to the management of the enterprise, such as follow-up courses arranged by the trade organizations. Expenses concerning losses in relation to the running of the business are considered deductible when they follow from the natural business risk. Such expenses may be theft, destruction or waste of the stock-in-trade or payment of compensation related to the business risk.

526. If the taxable income shows a loss, this loss can be carried forward infinite to be set off against later year's profit. In 2012, the Parliament decided to limit the right to use carried forward losses. It was decided that losses from previous years can be fully deducted up to an amount of DKR 7.5 million. Additional losses can only deduct the taxable income to 60%. If there is still further losses to be deducted it can be carried forward to the next year.

527. Depreciation *(afskrivning)* is admitted in order to allocate the asset costs to different periods. Environment investments and research costs may also be depreciated. When the enterprise has received public subsidies for making such investments, the amount of the subsidies is taxable, but the investment costs may be depreciated to the extent to which the subsidies have been used for the realization of the investment. In The Tax Assessment Act, section 8 X, the enterprise is given the opportunity to get paid 25% of the losses from deduction of costs from experiment and research. In 2012, there was established at short-term opportunity to make depreciation for 115% of the initial costs for new assets purchased before the 31 December 2013.[506] The regulation of deduction distinguishes between different types of assets, such as ships and buildings, and lays down rules on the periods of

506. Act 592/ 2012.

deduction and the methods of depreciation. Normally the depreciation rate for operating equipment's and ships is 25% and for buildings 4%. The Consolidation Act on the Investment Foundations[507] allows persons engaged in business to deduct amounts at the time of deposit on a special account for later depreciation. For example, a part of the profit of the year may be deducted from the income of that year when it is placed and bound on a special bank account. The amount is released when an asset, which may be depreciated, is acquired.

Wage earners who are taxable in Denmark are entitled to deposit a part of their wages in an account for later establishment of an independent undertaking. The system is identical to the investment foundations system.

II. Tax Reliefs Concerning Persons

528. The system of tax on persons distinguishes between wages, working income and other personal income on the one hand and income deriving from capital on the other hand.[508]

529. A person engaged in business may deduct operating costs of the enterprise, contributions to a superannuation scheme and transportation expenses from the taxable income as well as from his personal income. Deductions may be made from the capital income for expenses incurred in order to acquire, secure and maintain the income. Expenses involving interests and commission as well as deficit related to certain owner-occupied habitations are deductible.

§3. The State as Shareholder

530. There is no common approach to State ownership of undertakings or shareholdings; solutions and legal basis are created for the specific situation.[509,510] The Auditor General audits the accounts of companies where the State is shareholder.[511] Public undertakings operate on commercial terms, meaning that they do not have posts on the State budget and their capital and assets are separated from the Treasury.[512] All types of public ownership imply certain rights and obligations of the State as owner, such as voting rights, inspections, etc.[513]

507. Consolidated Act 922/1993 on Investment Foundations (*Investeringsfonds*) as amended by Act 1344/2008.
508. Consolidated Act 102/1994 on Personal Income Tax (*Indkomstskat for personer*) as amended by Act 433/2012.
509. Author: Grith Skovgaard Ølykke.
510. Further on the shareholdings of the State, *see* Part II, Ch. 1, §3.
511. Consolidated Act 101/2012 s. 2.
512. https://www.fm.dk/publikationer/2015/statens-ejerskabspolitik (accessed Feb. 2019).
513. *See* generally *ibid.*

Chapter 4. Competition Law

§1. Introduction

531. Business conduct in the market is regulated by the Consolidated Competition Act and the Consolidated Act on Marketing.[514,515] Certain sector regulation also exits in accordance with EU law. In 1997, the Competition Act was fundamentally amended to mirror what is currently Articles 101 and 102 TFEU. The Act on Marketing has continuously been amended to conformity with EU law as interpreted by the Court of Justice of the EU.

§2. Regulation of Anti-competitive Practice

I. The Danish Competition Act in General

532. In 1997, the first Competition Act reproducing the wording of the competition rules in EU law was adopted; it entered into force in January 1998.[516,517] The purpose of the amendment was among others to:[518] *'As far as possible ensure free and effective competition....The purpose is furthermore to create a good relation between national and EU competition law and to ensure that the conditions for competiiton in this country are not very different from what applies according to EU competition law. At the same time, this entails that undertakings should only adjust to one set of rules'*.[519]

The 2018 Consolidated Competition Act[520] contains, e.g. prohibitions against anti-competitive agreements (and possible exemptions, sections 6–8, stk. 1) and abuse of dominance (section 11), competences to require repayment of State aid (section 11a) and provisions on merger control (sections 12–12g).

II. The Purpose of the Competition Act

533. In the 2018 Consolidated Competition Act, the purpose of the Act is reiterated in section 1: 'The purpose of the Act is to promote effective allocation of resources in the society through workable competition for the benefit of undertakings and consumers.'

---

514. Author: Grith Skovgaard Ølykke.
515. Consolidated Competition Act 155/2018 (*Konkurrenceloven*) and Marketing Act 426/2017 (*Markedsføringsloven*).
516. Author: Grith Skovgaard Ølykke.
517. Competition Act 384/1997 (hereinafter *the 1997 Competition Act*).
518. Preparatory works of the 1997 Competition Act.
519. Author's translation
520. Consolidated Act 155/2018.

III. The Scope of the Competition Act

534. The 2018 Consolidated Competition Act applies to undertakings' distortion of competition where the trade between EU Member States is not affected by the anti-competitive agreement or behaviour.[521] The Competition Council is competent to apply Articles 101 and 102 TFEU in cases where an effect on trade is or may be present.[522]

535. The scope of the 2018 Consolidated Competition Act is outlined in section 2–3 and 5 of the Act. The 2018 Consolidated Competition Act applies to all kinds of economic activity and aid granted through public resources to undertakings (State aid). The Act does not apply to wage or conditions for employment, and it does not apply to agreements between companies related through ownership (concerns).

536. Section 2. 2 of the 2018 Consolidated Competition Act explicitly provides that the prohibitions on anti-competitive agreements and abuse of dominance do not apply if the distortion of competition is necessitated by public measures. It is emphasized that a distortion of competition necessitated by measures adopted by a Municipal Council only is necessitated, in the way required by the Competition Act, if it is necessary for the Municipal Council's fulfilment of tasks which it is assigned by legislation. In section 2. 4, it is stipulated that the relevant Minister decides whether particular distortions of competition are necessary according to the Competition Act. The Competition and Consumer Authority may address the relevant Minister to obtain the Minister's assessment. Moreover, the Competition and Consumer Authority may address the relevant Minister if it finds that public measures or aid may distort competition or hinder efficient allocation of resources; the Competition and Consumer Authority may propose competition-enhancing measures in this context.[523]

IV. Institutional Provisions

537. The Competition and Consumer Authority administers the Act. The Competition Council has the overall responsibility for the Authority's administration of the Act.

The Competition Council has seven members. It is composed of four members with insight into competition matters or other appropriate academic background, two members with experience from business management, and one member with specialized knowledge of consumer affairs. The Minister for Business, industry and Financial Affairs sets up a Consultative Group composed of up to ten members who

521. Regulation 1/2003 on the implementation of the rules on competition laid down in Arts 81 and 82 of the Treaty, OJ (2003) L 1/1, Art. 3(1).
522. *Ibid.*, and 2018 Consolidated Competition Act, s. 24.
523. 2018 Consolidated Competition Act, s. 2, stk. 5.

as a group possess broad knowledge of private and public undertakings as well as legal, economic, financial and consumer affairs.[524]

Decisions of the Competition Council or the Competition and Consumer Authority may be appealed to the Complaints Board for Competition,[525] And they cannot be tried in court until the Complaints Board has reviewed the case.[526]

538. It is, however, possible to jump administrative enforcement and file the case directly before the courts. The Maritime and Commercial Court (*Sø- og Handelsretten*) is a specialized court, and a first instance in cases concerning commercial aspects, *inter alia* cases concerning competition law. If cases are filed at any other court, i.e., District Courts (*byretter*) or Western High Court/Eastern High Court (*landsretterne*) one of the parties may request the case to be transferred to the Maritime and Commercial Court.[527] Judgments from the District Courts may be appealed to one of the High Courts, and judgments from the High Courts and the Maritime and Commercial Court may be appealed to the Supreme Court.[528]: The Act on damages in competition cases includes a specific provision, on collective redress (class actions):[529] '*If several persons have claims to damages due to a breach of the Competition Act or Articles 101 and 102 TFEU, the Consumer Ombudsman may be appointed to represent the group in collective redress suit concerning the claims, cf. Administration of Justice Act, ch.. 23a.*'[530]

Chapter 23a of the Administration of Justice Act contains general rules for collective redress,[531] which allows for both opt-ins and opt-outs. It also contains provisions on procedural rules, publicity and costs. As the Consumer Ombudsman is granted the right to represent groups in other areas of law, the Act on damages in competition cases makes this possible in the field of competition law as well.

---

524. 2018 Consolidated Competition Act s. 14.5.
525. *See* further Part II, Ch. 4., s. V. D.
526. 2018 Consolidated Competition Act s. 20.1.
527. Consolidated Administration of Justice Act 1284/2018 (*Retsplejeloven*) s. 225.
528. *Ibid.*, s. 368. 1 and 3.
529. Act 1541/2016, s. 16. The Act implements Directive 2014/104/EU of the European Parliament and of the Council of 26 Nov. 2014 on certain rules governing actions for damages under national law for infringements of the competition law provisions of the Member States and of the European Union, OJ (2014) L 349/1.
530. Author's translation.
531. Part 23a of the Administration of Justice Act was introduced by amendment Act 181/2007. In the preparatory works to this amendment Act, cases in the area of competition law was mentioned as an example where class actions might be useful, cf. Parliamentary Bill 2006/1 Lovforslag 41, s. 3.1.3. *See also infra* Part II. Ch. 5. §2. VII. on group actions.

V. Substantive Provisions

A. *Market Transparency*

539. Even after the abolition of the obligation to notify anticompetitive agreements to the EU Commission which entered into force in May 2004,[532] it is still possible for undertakings to notify agreements to the Competition and Consumer Authority.[533] The notification entails immunity to fines.[534]

540. In addition to the general right to access to documents and information relevant for investigations of the Competition and Consumer Authority,[535] a special provision in section 10a of the 2018 Consolidated Competition Act allows the Competition Council to issue an enforcement notice on dominant undertakings to submit their trading conditions to the Council. Such a notice may only be issued if:

(1) a substantiated complaint has been submitted by a competitor;
(2) special conditions are present in the market; and;
(3) on the basis of these conditions there is a special need for the Competition and Consumer Authority to gain insights in the pricing behaviour and rebates of the dominant undertaking.[536]

541. All decisions of the Competition Council and the Competition and Consumer Authority, verdicts of the Complaints Board for Competition, judgments on Competition law, fines imposed, etc. are published on the website of the Competition and Consumer Authority.[537]

542. The Competition and Consumer Authority may conduct sector inquiries and public reports on the findings.[538]

B. *Measures Against Harmful Effects of Anti-Competitive Practice*

543. In order to stop anti-competitive practices, the Competition and Consumer Authority may issue enforcement notices requiring the implicated undertakings to abstain from the relevant violation of the Competition Act.[539] The enforcement notice may include provisions requiring:

---

532. Regulation 1/2003 on the implementation of the rules on competition laid down in Arts 81 and 82 of the Treaty, OJ (2003) L 1/1.
533. 2018Consolidated Competition Act, §8. *See also* Executive Order 171/2013 on Rules for Notification of Agreements to the Competition Authority).
534. 2018 Consolidated Competition Act, §23. 2.
535. *Ibid.*, s. 17.
536. Author's translation.
537. *Ibid.*, s. 13. The website of the Competition and Consumer Authority is: www.kfst.dk (accessed Feb. 2019).
538. *Ibid.*, s. 15d.3.
539. *Ibid.*, s. 6.4 and s. 16.4, read in conjunction with s. 16.

(1) Full or partial abolition of agreements, decisions and conditions of trade, etc.
(2) Maximum prices, profits or special rules for calculating prices or profits.
(3) Obligation to supply to specific customers on normal trading conditions. The undertaking is nevertheless allowed to require cash payment or security for payment.
(4) Provision of access to facilities essential to supply a particular good or service.[540]

544. The Competition and Consumer Authority may accept commitments from undertakings which remove the competition concerns of the Authority. The Authority may make the commitments binding upon the undertakings.[541] Decisions to make commitments binding may be revoked where there has been a material change in any of the facts on which the decision was based; where the undertakings concerned act contrary to their commitments; or, where the decision was based on incomplete, incorrect or misleading information provided by the parties.[542]

545. The Minister of Business Industry and Financial Affairs may impose administrative fines on undertakings (or decide to delegate this task),[543] if they neglect to: 'provide the information which may be required according to the Act, by the Competition Council or the Competition and Consumer Authority; abide by conditions or enforcement notices; or, abide by binding commitments … '.

C. Appeal

546. The decisions of the Competition and Consumer Authority may be appealed to the Complaints Board for Competition. Cases decided by the Competition and Consumer Authority become final if they are not appealed to the Complaints Board for Competition within four weeks. Verdicts by the Complaints Board for Competition become final if they are not appealed to the courts within eight weeks.[544]

D. Penalty Provisions

547. In addition to the mentioned administrative fines, criminal fines may be imposed on legal persons.[545] The competence to impose criminal fines is vested with the public prosecutor for economic crime. The period for limitation is five

540. Author's translation.
541. 2018 Consolidated Competition Act, s. 16a.1.
542. *Ibid.*, s. 16a. 3.
543. *Ibid.*, s. 22. From 2013 to 2015 the task was delegated to the Director of the Competition and Consumer Authority, cf. Executive Order 173/2013. This Executive Order was repealed by Executive Order 981/2015.
544. *Ibid.*, s. 20.1–3.
545. *Ibid.*, s. 23.

years.[546] Furthermore, the 2018 Consolidated Competition Act provides for criminal sanctions, i.e. imprisonment for up till one year and six months, but only for participation in anticompetitive agreements (i.e. a cartel).[547]

548. The 2018 Consolidated Competition Act includes rules on leniency. If cartel members assist in investigation of the cartel, they may receive immunity for fines or reduction of fines subject to their contributions to the investigation and their cooperation.[548]

§3. The Law of Unfair Competition and Trade Practices

I. Introduction

549. Marketing and advertising (commercial practices) play a fundamental role in a market economy.[549] Advertising provides information about products and their attributes, which helps consumers choose between various products. In conventional economics, it is assumed that people are rational agents.[550] The primary purpose of marketing law is to ensure that competition is fair and honest – usually by prohibiting unfair commercial practices and by imposing information requirements. Usually the aim is to protect both those who are targeted by the marketing (consumers and businesses alike) and those competitors who may lose revenue or esteem due to the unfair practice. In some States, including Denmark, the legislation on marketing law protects also more general societal interests.

550. The primary Danish legislation on marketing law is the Danish Marketing Practices Act.[551] The Act which is discussed further below regulates unfair competition and trade practices in Denmark. Prior to 1974, marketing practices were regulated in the Danish Unfair Competition Act. The first Marketing Practices Act in Denmark is from 1974, and it has since been revised in 1994, 2005 and 2017. In addition to the general Act, there are a number of more specific acts regulating marketing in specific media or the marketing of specific products. National marketing law in the EU is to a large extent regulated by EU law, including in particular the Unfair Commercial Practices Directive and the Misleading Advertising Directive which are addressed immediately below.

546. *Ibid.* s.23.6.
547. *Ibid.* s. 23.3.
548. *Ibid.*, §23a.
549. Author: Jan Trzaskowski.
550. *See* in general Jan Trzaskowski, 'Behavioural Innovations in Marketing law' in Hans Micklitz, Anne-Lise Sibony & Fabrizio Esposito (eds), *Handbook of Research Methods in Consumer Law* (Edward Elgar Handbook series on research methods in law, 2018), pp. 296–333, and Jan Trzaskowski. *Behavioural Economics, Neuroscience, and the Unfair Commercial Practices Directive*, J. Consumer Policy. 3 (Sep. 2011).
551. Act 426/ 2017.

A. European Marketing Law

551. European marketing law has gradually grown to an expansive regulation of commercial practices. The two main Directives on this matter are the Unfair Commercial Practices Directive (2005/29/EC) and the Misleading and Comparative Advertising Directive (2006/114/EC, codified version). The Directives deal with the protection of consumers and traders, respectively.[552]

The purpose of the Misleading Advertising Directive is to protect traders against misleading advertising and the unfair consequences thereof and to lay down the conditions under which comparative advertising is permitted. It should be stressed that 'advertising' is a more narrow concept than commercial practices as dealt with in the Unfair Commercial Practices Directive. The Directive provides minimum harmonization of national legislation of misleading advertising. This entails that Member States may maintain stricter provisions in national law. However, the requirements for lawful comparative advertisement is fully harmonized in the Directive, and Member States may thus not add further requirements for allowing comparative advertising.

The Commercial Practices Directive provides full harmonization of unfair business-to-consumer (B2C) commercial practices concerning the economic interests of consumers. The Directive introduces a general prohibition of unfair commercial practices (Article 5). A commercial practice is unfair if it: (1) is contrary to the requirements of professional diligence; and (2) materially distorts or is likely to materially distort the economic behaviour with regard to the product of the average consumer whom it reaches or to whom it is addressed, or of the average member of the group when a commercial practice is directed to a particular group of consumers. In particular, commercial practices are unfair if they are misleading (Articles 6 and 7) or aggressive (Articles 8 and 9). Further, in Annex I of the Directive is found a list of commercial practices which in all circumstances are to be regarded as unfair, i.e., without considering the economic affect on consumers (per se prohibitions).

The Unfair Commercial Practices Directive provides full harmonization within its broad scope of application. The full harmonization of marketing law in the Internal Market is important for clarity and foreseeability in the businesses' market behaviour. Self-regulation, the Consolidated ICC Code of Advertising and Marketing Communication Practice[553] in particular, may be an important instrument to provide some foreseeability in the interpretation of the Directive – in particular, the requirement of 'professional diligence'. It is mentioned in recital 20 that:

> It is appropriate to provide a role for codes of conduct, which enable traders to apply the principles of this Directive effectively in specific economic fields. In

552. It should be mentioned that there is no general regulation that regulates more general societal interests (legal requirements related to taste and decency) and the protection of public authorities outside the capacity of being a trader.

553. *See* www.iccwbo.org. *See also* Jan Trzaskowski, 'Interpretation and Assessment under the Unfair Commercial Practices Directive – the ICC Code for Advertising and Marketing and the Commission's Staff Working Document' in Ulf Bernitz & Caroline Heide-Jørgensen, *Marketing and Advertising Law in a Process of Harmonization* (Hart Publishing 2017), pp 85–103.

sectors where there are specific mandatory requirements regulating the behaviour of traders, it is appropriate that these will also provide evidence as to the requirements of professional diligence in that sector.

In addition to the two general Directives concerning marketing, there are a number of more specific Directives that will apply, particularly depending on media, product and commercial practice. It is important to note that in the case of conflict between the provisions of the Unfair Commercial Practices Directive and other Community rules regulating specific aspects of unfair commercial practices, the latter is to prevail and apply to those specific aspects.[554] It goes too far in this context to provide an extensive account of all regulation concerning particular products such as tobacco,[555] medicine[556] and foodstuff.[557] The 2000 E-Commerce Directive[558] provides a broad regulatory framework for so-called Information Society Services, which in broad terms comprise all online activities as well as e-mail communications.[559] The definition does, however, not extend to those broadcast services covered by the Audiovisual Media Services Directive.[560]

II. The Danish Marketing Practices Act

A. *Scope of Application*

552. The Danish Marketing Practices Act applies to commercial activities whether it is carried out by a private or a public business as long as the product (in broad terms) is offered on the market. The law applies to all commercial activities including advertising, distribution, sale and consequently service and collection of debt. The activity must not necessarily be connected to the sale of a product, but it

554. Unfair Commercial Practices Directive, Art. 3(4).
555. *See* Directive 2014/40/EU on the approximation of the laws, regulations and administrative provisions of the Member States concerning the manufacture, presentation and sale of tobacco.
556. *See* Directive 2001/83/EC concerning medicinal products for human use and Regulation (EC) No 726/2004 laying down Community procedures for the authorisation and supervision of medicinal productsfor human and veterinary use and establishing a European Medicines Agency.
557. *See* in general Directive 2000/13/EC concerning the labelling, presentation and advertising of foodstuffs as amended by Directive 2003/89/EC.
558. Directive 2000/31/EC on certain legal aspects of information society services, in particular electronic commerce, in the Internal Market (Directive on electronic commerce).
559. The definition is according to Art. 2(a) derived from Directive 98/34/EC as amended by Directive 98/48/EC (laying down a procedure for the provision of information in the field of technical standards and regulations), as any service normally provided for remuneration, at a distance, by electronic means and at the individual request of a recipient of services. An indicative list of services not covered by this definition is set out in Annex V of the Directive, excluding *inter alia* telephone services and traditional radio and television broadcasting services. The definition of 'television broadcasting' referred to in the predecessor to the Audiovisual Media Services Directive was not defined by opposition to the concept of 'information society service'. (Case C-89/04, *Mediakabel BV v. Commissariaat voor de Media*, para. 25).
560. Directive 2010/13/EU on the coordination of certain provisions laid down by law, regulation or administrative action in Member States concerning the provision of audiovisual media services (Audiovisual Media Services Directive) as amended by Directive (EU) 2018/1808.

must have some relation to the market in broad terms. The Act applies to activities in the Danish market. However, obligations in the Internal Market limits the extent to which requirements under Danish law may be imposed on businesses established in other EU Member States.

B. The Average Consumer and Children

553. The European protection of consumers against unfair commercial practices takes its starting point in an average consumer-test. Thus commercial practices may not distort the economic behaviour of: (1) the average consumer to whom it reaches; or (2) is addressed; or (3) the average member of the particular group of consumers to whom the commercial practice is directed.[561] It is provided in recital 18 that 'the average consumer test is not a statistical test', and that national courts and authorities will have to exercise their own faculty of judgment, to determine the typical reaction of the average consumer in a given case. Danish marketing law must be interpreted accordingly.

554. It follows from the Danish Marketing Practices Act that marketing directed at children and young people shall be framed with specific reference to their natural credulity and lack of experience and critical sense, as a result of which they are readily influenced and easy to impress (section 3(2)). This provision concerns marketing directed at people under 18 and entails a 'stricter' interpretation of all the provisions of the Act when this group of people is targeted. In section 11, it is further, under criminal liability, provided that marketing directed at children and young people must not directly or indirectly incite them to violence or other dangerous or inconsiderate behaviour, nor make unwarrantable use of violence, fear or superstition in order to influence them. In addition, it follows from section 11(2) that such marketing may not mention or contain pictures of or make reference to intoxicants, including alcohol.

C. Substantive Provisions

1. The General Clause

555. Sections 3 and 4 of the Danish Marketing Practices Act provides that businesses must act in accordance with good market behaviour. This general clause is a central part of the Act that is both the main provision and serves a residual purpose to the more specific provisions of the Act. There has been a general clause on good market behaviour since 1937. The provision was introduced on the background of Article 10*bis* on unfair competition in the Paris Convention. In 2017, the general

561. Article 5(2)(b).

clause was divided into two sections applying to issues falling inside (section 4) or outside (section 3) the scope of the Unfair Commercial Practices Directive.[562]

The purpose of a flexible general clause is to create space for an ongoing adjustment of its interpretation in light of societal developments. The broad and dynamic nature of the general clause does not always guarantee foreseeability and is for that reason not sanctioned with fines. Failure to comply with the general clause may lead to injunctions and damages, but notably not criminal sanctions such as fines. The general clause can be used to prevent *inter alia* unfair contract terms and marketing, counterfeit products, parasitic marketing, personal integrity and the privacy. In the interpretation of the general clause, the courts may also consider the norms for marketing practices laid down in ICC's Code of Advertising and Marketing Communication Practice.[563]

The general clause protects both consumers, competitors and more general societal interest. The consideration of these three purposes is weighed equally in the interpretation of the provision. The balancing of the three considerations is generally carried out in the Danish Consumer Ombudsman's administration of the Act and in last instance by the Danish courts. The protection of general societal interests (taste and decency falling outside the scope of the Unfair Commercial Practices Directive) includes protection against practices that violates social responsibility or incite hate based on race, religion or nationality. Marketing should also not exploit fears, sickness, unfortunate circumstances, superstition or incite violence or behaviour that is detrimental to health.

556. Consumers are *inter alia* protected against marketing that violates the personal integrity and the right to privacy, but also marketing that is importunate, aggressive, exploitive, disturbing or in other ways insulting or offensive. This includes aggressive marketing practices such as sending product that the consumer has not ordered. The consideration concerning competitors protects against unfair competition, including violation of other businesses' rights to names, design, trade secrets, etc. The provision can also be used against disparaging remarks and unfair parasitism on a competitor's goodwill. The general clause aims at protecting business' efforts related to product development and advertising. Therefore the general clause is often used in cases concerning enforcement of intellectual property rights.

2. Misleading and Aggressive Marketing

557. The general clause is supplemented by a number of more specific provisions in the Act. For practices concerning misleading aggressive practices falling within the scope of the Unfair Commercial Practices Directive, Chapter 2 applies

---

562. This division is introduced to ensure proper implementation of the Unfair Commercial Practices Directive, however, to the detriment of a coherent legal framework.

563. *See* Jan Trzaskowski, 'Interpretation and Assessment under the Unfair Commercial Practices Directive — the ICC Code for Advertising and Marketing and the Commission's Staff Working Document' in Ulf Bernitz & Caroline Heide-Jørgensen, Marketing and Advertising Law in a Process of Harmonization (Hart Publishing 2017), pp 85–103.

(sections 4–9). In other instances (e.g. B2B), section 20 prohibits misleading and aggressive practices. The purpose is to ensure that traders do not use misleading or undue indications or omit material information if this is designed to significantly distort consumers' or other traders' economic behaviour on the market. Further, marketing whose content, form or method used is misleading, aggressive or subjects the consumers or traders to undue influence, and which lends itself to significantly distorting their economic behaviour, is not permitted. In contrast to the general clause, the use of this provision requires some kind of possible 'commercial effect' set forth in the requirement of distortion of economic behaviour. This provision does not protect general societal interests, and infringement may lead to both criminal and civil law sanctions.

The Danish provisions on misleading and aggressive marketing (sections 5–6 and 7, respectively) must be interpreted in accordance with the Unfair Commercial Practices Directive, and the thirty-one per se bans in the Annex (*see* section 9).

It follows further from section 13 that where factual statements are made, these must be capable of being substantiated by documentation. This entails that the business carries the burden of proof for statements of a factual nature. This does not prevent users from what in the Unfair Commercial Practices Directive has been denoted 'common and legitimate advertising practice of making exaggerated statements or statements which are not meant to be taken literally'.[564]

3. Identification of Commercial Intent

558. Section 6(4) of the Danish Marketing Practices Act provides that commercial intent must be made clear, which should be read in conjunction with Article 7(2) of the Unfair Commercial Practices Directive: it shall be regarded as a misleading omission when the trader fails to identify the commercial intent of the commercial practice if not already apparent from the context – and where this causes or is likely to cause the average consumer to take a transactional decision that he would not have taken otherwise. This is supplemented by Item 11 of the blacklist which provides that '[u]sing editorial content in the media to promote a product where a trader has paid for the promotion without making that clear in the content or by images or sounds clearly identifiable by the consumer (advertorial)' is an unfair commercial practice.

4. Comparative Advertising

559. Provision on comparative advertising is found in section 21 of the Danish Marketing Practices Act. The provision covers 'any advertising which explicitly or by implication identifies a competitor or products or services offered by a competitor', and it must be interpreted in accordance with the full harmonization found in

564. Article 5(3).

Article 3a of the Misleading Advertising Directive. It provides that comparative advertising must, as far as the comparison is concerned, be permitted when the following conditions are met:

(a) it is not misleading within the meaning of Articles 2(2), 3 and 7(1) of this Directive or Articles 6 and 7 of Directive 2005/29/EC of the European Parliament and of the Council of 11 May 2005 concerning unfair B2C commercial practices in the internal market;
(b) it compares goods or services meeting the same needs or intended for the same purpose;
(c) it objectively compares one or more material, relevant, verifiable and representative features of those goods and services, which may include price;
(d) it does not discredit or denigrate the trademarks, trade names, other distinguishing marks, goods, services, activities, or circumstances of a competitor;
(e) for products with designation of origin, it relates in each case to products with the same designation;
(f) it does not take unfair advantage of the reputation of a trademark, trade name or other distinguishing marks of a competitor or of the designation of origin of competing products;
(g) it does not present goods or services as imitations or replicas of goods or services bearing a protected trademark or trade name;
(h) it does not create confusion among traders, between the advertiser and a competitor or between the advertiser's trademarks, trade names, other distinguishing marks, goods or services and those of a competitor.

5. Unsolicited Communication with Specific Customers

560. It follows from section 10 of the Danish Marketing Practices Act that '[a] trader must not approach anyone by means of electronic mail, an automated calling system or facsimile machine with a view to the sale of products, real property, other property, labour and services unless the party concerned has requested him to do so'. These rules are the Danish implementation of now repealed Distance Selling Directive[565] and the E-Privacy Directive.[566] The ban under national law protects 'anyone' and not just consumers or subscribers/users (as used in the E-Privacy Directive).

There is in subsection 2 an exception to the general prohibition which provides that 'a trader that has received a customer's electronic contact details in connection

565. Directive 97/7/EC of 20 May 1997 on the protection of consumers in respect of distance contracts. Now replaced by Directive 2011/83/EU of 25 Oct. 2011 on consumer rights, amending Council Directive 93/13/EEC and Directive 1999/44/EC of the European Parliament and of the Council and repealing Council Directive 85/577/EEC and Directive 97/7/EC of the European Parliament and of the Council.

566. Directive 2002/58/EC of 12 Jul. 2002 concerning the processing of personal data and the protection of privacy in the electronic communications sector (Directive on privacy and electronic communications). *See* Art. 13 as amended by directive 2009/136/EC of 25 Nov. 2009.

with the sale of products or services may market his own similar products or services to that customer by electronic mail'. It is required that the customer has the option, free of charge and in an easy manner, of declining this both when giving his contact details to the trader and in the event of subsequent communications.

For other means of remote communication with a view to sales, Subsection 3 provides that a trader must not approach a specific natural person using such means if the person concerned has declined such communications from the trader. The trader must also consult a Robinson-list prepared each quarter by the Central Office of Personal Registration (CPR) to ensure that the person concerned has not declined communications for such marketing purposes. This requirement does not apply if the person in question has previously requested the communication from the trader. The first time a trader makes such a communication with a specific natural person who is not on the CPR list, the trader must inform him clearly and comprehensibly of his right to decline communications from the trader as referred to above. At the same time, the person concerned shall be offered an easy manner of declining such communications.

Telephone communications are also subject to the regulations governing unsolicited communications in the Act on Certain Consumer Contracts.[567] This law bans with a few exceptions (*inter alia* the sale of books, newspapers, etc., insurance, and certain rescue services) in section 4 the use of unsolicited telephone calls for direct marketing purposes.

6. Price Indications

561. It follows from the general assessment of marketing that the price or the manner in which the price is calculated, or the existence of a specific price advantage is an important factor in determining whether marketing is misleading.[568] However, it follows from the Unfair Commercial Practices Directive that a commercial practice in order to be misleading must be likely to deceive the average consumer and be likely to cause him to take a transactional decision that he would not have taken otherwise. In Danish law (Executive orders issued according to section 14), there is a general obligation to provide clear information by labelling, signing or otherwise as to the overall price of the product, including fees, costs, VAT and all other expenses. This is required when products are offered for sale to consumers (this does not include the sale of products by auction). Taxes or costs which the trader is not obliged to collect directly from the consumers are not covered by the requirement, but must be indicated separately.

The requirement to indicate prices apply correspondingly when services are offered for sale to consumers from a fixed establishment, and when such a service is offered to consumers by electronic means and may be ordered. If it is not possible to indicate the overall price of the service, the basis of calculation of this price shall be indicated, if this will make it possible for consumers themselves to calculate the final price. If because of the quantity of services offered, it is not possible

567. Act 1457/2013 on Consumer Contracts *(Forbrugeraftaleloven)*. *See infra* Part II. Ch. 5. §2.V.C.
568. *See* the Unfair Commercial Practices Directive Art. 6(1)(d).

to indicate the price or basis of calculation of all of them, the price or basis of calculation of a relevant and representative sample shall be indicated.

When information about the price of products or services is provided by advertising or other means in marketing material (including verbal price information), such information must comply with the general requirements mentioned above. If a manufacturer, importer or wholesaler suggests a price in printed or other advertising or by other means for resale to consumers, it must be stated explicitly that this price is advisory.

D. Administration: The Danish Consumer Ombudsman

562. In connection with the introduction of the Danish Marketing Practices Act, a consumer ombudsman institution was established – The Danish Consumer Ombudsman is both a person and an institution consisting of him (currently 'her') and his staff. It is the responsibility of the Consumer Ombudsman to monitor compliance with the Danish Marketing Practices Act and the executive orders issued pursuant hereto. The supervision has to be carried out particularly with regard to the interests of consumers. The Minister has in accordance with section 25(5) laid down more detailed regulations governing the activities of the Consumer Ombudsman.[569] The Consumer Ombudsman is appointed by the Minister for a period of six years and may be discharged without application only if such discharge is for health reasons, or if the individual concerned is unfit to remain in the post as a result of criminality, misconduct in service or fraud. A Consumer Ombudsman must fulfil the general conditions for appointment as a judge.

563. The Consumer Ombudsman may require the disclosure of all details considered necessary for his activities, including a decision as to whether a matter falls within the purview of the Act. Such disclosure may be required within a short time limit where comparative advertising is concerned or when considered necessary under the circumstances. The Consumer Ombudsman seeks according to section 28 by negotiation to influence traders to act in accordance with the principles of good marketing practice and to observe this Act in other respects. If a trader disregards an undertaking given to the Consumer Ombudsman after negotiation, the Consumer Ombudsman may impose such injunctions on the trader as may be considered necessary to ensure compliance with the undertaking (section 36). Following negotiation with the consumers and the relevant trade and industry organizations, the Consumer Ombudsman seeks to influence the conduct of traders by the preparation and issue of guidelines for marketing in specified areas that must be considered essential, especially in the interests of the consumer (section 29).

According to section 30, the Consumer Ombudsman will, upon request, give a statement regarding his view of the lawfulness of contemplated marketing arrangements, unless an opinion would be subject to unusual doubt or other special circumstances exist. An advance indication does not amount to an actual opinion of the lawfulness of the arrangement concerned. Once the Consumer Ombudsman has

569. Executive Order 1249/2014.

delivered an advance indication to a trader to the effect that he thinks a prospective arrangement would be lawful, the Consumer Ombudsman cannot interfere on his own initiative with an arrangement covered by the advance indication and implemented within a reasonable time of its delivery. Even though the relevant minister may lay down more detailed rules concerning advance indication fees, it has remained free to ask for an advance indication.

According to section 27, the Consumer Ombudsman may carry out inspections for the purpose of processing complaints forwarded from enforcement authorities in other EU countries pursuant to Regulation (EC) No. 2006/2004 on consumer protection cooperation, and which concern infringements of directives for which the Consumer Ombudsman has been appointed the competent authority. The Consumer Ombudsman may request oral explanations of the facts in connection with the inspection.

564. Anyone with a legal interest therein may bring a case concerning prohibitions, injunctions, damages and remuneration under section 32 (discussed below). The Consumer Ombudsman may bring a case concerning prohibitions and injunctions, and the Consumer Ombudsman may issue an injunction if an action is clearly in conflict with this Act and cannot be changed by negotiation. A party upon whom an injunction is imposed may require that it be considered by the courts. A request to this effect shall be submitted to the Consumer Ombudsman in writing within four weeks of notification of the party concerned of the injunction. The Consumer Ombudsman shall bring the case to court under the rules governing civil administration of justice within one week of receiving the request. If a charge is preferred for infringement of this Act, the prosecution of the charge will be assigned to the Consumer Ombudsman if he so requests.

Where there is an obvious danger that the purpose of a traditional prohibition will be lost if the court's decision must be awaited, the Consumer Ombudsman may impose a provisional prohibition. A case to affirm the prohibition must according to section 36 be brought not later than the next working day.

E. Sanctions

565. Actions in conflict with the Danish Marketing Practices Act may according to section 32 be prohibited by judgments. Concurrently with this or subsequently, such injunctions may be imposed by judgments as may be considered necessary to ensure: (1) compliance with the prohibition, including through provision that agreements entered into in conflict with a prohibition are invalid; and (2) restitution of the state of affairs existing before the unlawful action, including destruction or recall of products and issue of information or correction of statements. Actions in conflict with the Act incur liability to pay damages under the general rules of Danish law. Any person who infringes or unwarrantably takes advantage of another's rights in conflict with this Act shall pay reasonable damages for this.

566. Non-observance of a prohibition or injunction imposed by the court or an injunction imposed by the Consumer Ombudsman are liable to a fine or imprisonment of up to four months. However, non-observance of an order to repay a payment received does not carry a penalty. A party who omits to provide information required by the Consumer Ombudsman or under circumstances covered by this Act gives the Consumer Ombudsman incorrect or misleading information, is liable to a fine unless a more severe penalty is prescribed under other legislation.

The infringement of a number of provisions is subject to fines unless more severe penalty is prescribed under other legislation. Infringement of sections 20 and 21 is subject to private prosecution. It should be emphasized that the general clause in sections 3 and 4 is not penalized under criminal law, but infringement may result in injunctions and damages.

Companies, etc. (legal persons) are subject to criminal liability under the rules of the Danish Penal Code.

III. Specific Regulation

567. In addition to the Danish Marketing Practices Act, there are a number of more specific acts concerning in particular certain products and media. It falls outside the purpose of this publication to provide a comprehensive presentation of this specific legislation. Hence the relevant acts are only briefly presented in the following parts.

A. Particular Products

568. The marketing of alcohol is comprised by the scope of the Danish Marketing Practices Act, but the industry has together with *inter alia* the Danish Consumer Council issued self-regulatory guidelines for the marketing of alcoholic beverages.[570] The guidelines from 2000 were revised in 2010, and there is an established complaint board (*Alkoholreklamenævnet*) which treats cases of infringements of the guidelines. The Board has no real power of enforcement but may express critique of particular acts of marketing.

569. Advertising for medicinal products is regulated in Chapter 7 of the Danish Act on Medicinal Products.[571] More detailed rules are provided in an Executive Order on Marketing of Medicinal Products[572] which is supplemented by official guidelines.[573] The EU's provisions on this subject are found in the Directive on the

---

570. <https://alkoholreklamenaevn.dk/> (visited Mar. 2018).
571. Consolidated Act 99/2018 *(Lægemiddelloven).*
572. Executive Order 1153/2014.
573. Guidance 10356/2014.

Community code relating to medicinal products for human use,[574] which is implemented in the Danish Act on Medicinal Products. The Danish Act covers in contrast to the directive medicinal products for both humans and animals.

570. There is a very broad ban of marketing of tobacco products found in Act. 608/2016. The Danish Act follows the lines of Directive 98/43 which was annulled by the European Court of Justice and later replaced by Directive 2003/33 on the approximation of the laws, regulations and administrative provisions of the Member States relating to the advertising and sponsorship of tobacco products.

B. Particular Media

571. Chapter 11 of the Danish Radio and Television Act[575] establishes rules for *inter alia* marketing, sponsoring and product placement. More detailed rules on marketing are laid out in an executive order.[576] The Danish Radio and Television Board (*Radio-og tv-nævnet*) can enter administrative decisions in cases relating to this Act. Advertising and sponsoring are dealt with in Chapter 11 of the Act. The main rule is found in section 72 which provides that advertisement must be clearly identifiable as such, and in a way that distinguishes them from editorial programmes, etc.

The Danish E-Commerce Act[577] regulates information society services as defined in the e-commerce directive.[578] The Danish Act follows the directive in structure and content. In section 9 is found the requirement of Article 6(1) that the commercial communication shall be clearly identifiable as such, and that the natural or legal person on whose behalf the commercial communication is made shall be clearly identifiable. There is a general information obligation on providers of information society services to provide information about *inter alia* name, geographic address, e-mail address, etc. when they provide such services.[579]

574. Directive 2001/83/EC of 6 Nov. 2001.
575. Se Consolidated Act 115/2019.
576. Executive Order 801/2013.
577. Act 227/2002 (*e-handelslov*).
578. Directive 2000/31/EC of 8 Jun. 2000 on certain legal aspects of information society services, in particular electronic commerce, in the Internal Market (Directive on electronic commerce).
579. *See* s. 7 of the Act and Art. 5 of the directive.

Chapter 5. State Regulation of the Conditions of Commercial Transactions

§1. Price and Supply Regulation

I. Price Regulation

572. Public price regulation is not commonly taking place[580]. However, general contract law regulates price in case of disputes, competition law poses certain restraints on pricing, and transparency with regard to pricing is regulated in the Consolidated Act on Marketing.

573. The Consolidated SGA only applies if no contract has been entered into concerning the specific disputed incident;[581] i.e., it is background law. The Consolidated Sales of Goods Act provides that if an agreement on purchase/sale of a good has been entered into, but the price is not stipulated in the contract, the buyer has to pay the price demanded by the seller unless the price demanded is unfair.[582] In business to business (B2B) sales, the buyer is required to pay invoices addressed to him, unless he immediately objects to the price documenting that a lower price had been agreed upon, or if the price is obviously unfair.[583] In B2C sales, where the price is not explicit in the contract made, the consumer is required to pay a fair price, taking into account the character and condition of the purchased item, the general price level at the time of the agreement and other relevant circumstances.[584] In all cases, the Consolidated Contract Act provides for regulation of unfair contract terms, including price.[585]

574. In situations where trade between EU Member States is not affected,[586] the 2018 Consolidated Competition Act contains the same restrictions on price setting as Articles 101 and 102 of TFEU. Agreements between undertakings *inter alia* with regard to price (horizontally in the form of cartels, and vertically in the form of resale price maintenance) are prohibited.[587] Dominant undertakings are not allowed to use rebates unless such rebates are cost-based, and predatory pricing is also prohibited.[588]

575. Section 11b of the 2018 Consolidated Competition Act concerns pricing of private supply of welfare services. In some municipalities, the citizens are offered a choice between a public and (several) private suppliers of basic care services/

580. Author: Grith Skovgaard Ølykke.
581. Section 1 of Consolidated Act 140/2014 *(Købelov)*.
582. *Ibid.*, s. 5.
583. *Ibid.*, s. 6.
584. *Ibid.*, s. 72.
585. Section 36 of Consolidated Act 193/2016 (*Aftalelov*).
586. Cf. Part II, Ch. 4., §2, III.
587. Consolidated Competition Act 155/2018 *(Konkurrenceloven)*, s. 6, stk. 2, no. 1 and 7.
588. *Ibid.*, s. 11.

household services, such as: cleaning, personal care, food services. If a private supplier is chosen by the citizen, the municipality pays the private service provider a price equivalent to the public supplier's costs of providing the relevant service. The Competition Council may intervene and order the municipality to use certain methods of calculation for the price, and payment of the price difference owed to the private supplier.

576. In B2C sales of goods, transparency with regard to selling price is required by the Marketing Practices Act.[589] It is required that the advertised price includes VAT, fees, costs and other additions to the total price the consumer has to pay. In B2C sales of services, where it is not possible to give the total price for the individual consumer, the advertised price must make the consumer able to calculate the total price. If services are provided at a price per hour, the invoice must inform the consumer of price per hour, time used and price of materials, or other relevant information which makes the consumer able to assess the price. For B2C sales where the good may optionally be bought on credit, the cash price, the cost of the credit and the annual cost in per cent must be available.[590]

II. Supply Regulation

577. If, in extraordinary circumstances, scarcity occurs or is expected, the Minister for Energy, Utilities and Climate may, if necessary, issue orders on use, allocation, settlement of prices and location of the national stock of the relevant good.[591]

578. Dominant undertakings (public or private) in all sectors may be ordered to supply, if a refuse to supply constitutes an abuse of dominance, which does not affect trade between Member States, contrary to the 2018 Consolidated Competition Act.[592] Refusal to supply may materialize as refusal of access to information, refusal to give licence, refusal of access to infrastructure, delivery delays, unreasonable pricing, conditions of exclusivity or bundling.

579. For certain sectors, public/universal service obligations are assigned in order to ensure security of supply, compare below.

A. Public Supply

580. In the electricity sector, which is liberalized at EU level, the network is owned by the State, in order to ensure equal access for electricity producers.[593] This

589. Marketing Practices Act 426/2017 *(Markedsføringslov)* ss. 14 and 15.
590. *Ibid.* s. 18.
591. Consolidated Act 88/1986.
592. Consolidated Competition Act 155/2018 §11.
593. Consolidated Act 52/2019 on Electricity Supply *(Elforsyningsloven)*, s.35.

also applies for the natural gas sector (heating), which has also been liberalized at EU level.[594] Suppliers of natural gas can apply for assignment of a license to supply natural gas.[595] License is granted for five years by the Minister of Energy, Utilities and Climate.[596] Public service obligations, requiring the company to supply all consumers (who do not choose another supplier) in a specified geographical area are awarded subsequent to the conduct of a public tender, and the award is made to the provider offering the lowest price.[597]

581. Water supply is also regulated at EU level, as implemented by *inter alia* the Consolidated Act on Water Supply, and Act on the Water Supply Sector.[598] Ownership to water supply facilities is divided between municipalities and private suppliers.[599] The Act on the Water Supply Sector regulates the large water supply facilities, primarily the facilities owned by municipalities.[600] The Act imposes price-ceilings on the water supply facilities, based on historic costs and expected efficiency gains.[601] The price-ceiling is fixed by the Water Division *(Forsyningssekretariatet)* hosted by the Competition and Consumer Authority.[602]

B. *Supply Regulation Within the Private Sector*

582. The sector regulation is typically based on EU legislative measures and applies irrespective of public or private ownership. *See supra* Part II, Chapter 5, §1.II, A. for further information.

§2. CONSUMER LAW

I. Institutional Aspects, General Principles and Representation of Consumer Interests

A. *Consumer Law in General*

583. The overall purpose of the consumer policy is to find the right balance between the reasonable interests of the consumers on the one hand and business interests on the other hand.[603] The freedom of trade must be limited in order to

594. Consolidated Act 1127/2018 on Natural Gas Supply *(Naturgasforsyning)*.
595. *Ibid.*, s. 26.
596. *Ibid.*, s. 24.
597. *Ibid.*, s. 27.
598. Consolidated Act 118/2018 *(Vandforsyningslov)* and Act 469/2009 (*Vandsektorens organisering og økonomiske forhold*) as amended most recently by Act 662/2017.
599. In 2008, seventy-five water supply facilities owned by municipalities existed supplying two-thirds of the total water consumption.
600. Cf. Act on Water Supply Sector, s. 2.
601. *Ibid.*, ch. 3.
602. http://www.kfst.dk/vandtilsyn/.(accessed Feb. 2019).
603. Author: Peter Møgelvang-Hansen. *See* in general Børge Dahl, *Danish Law*, 2nd ed. 2002, Ch. 18.

secure a reasonable level of consumer protection and control the trade and marketing conditions of the enterprises. On this background and increasingly the development of the EU consumer law, the Danish consumer legislation has developed in a pragmatic way within areas where the need for regulation has appeared.

The general aim of consumer protection law is to balance the business interests of the enterprises of remaining competitive on the market against safeguarding of the consumers' interest in getting safe products of quality on reasonable terms as well as to safeguard the societal interest in maintaining order and decency in market activities and to safeguard the public health.

584. A substantial part of the current legal consumer protection consists of public law legislation regarding measures of market control and product requirements as well as rules aiming at facilitating the access for consumers to enforce their rights. The public law legislation is generally directed at protecting the consumers as a collective, for example, by preventing the marketing of unsafe products and the use of unreasonable contract terms in future contracts. The consumer protection regulation under public law is typically enforced by a public authority, most notably the Consumer Ombudsman.[604]

Comprehensive, general rules, including General Clauses requiring the observance of good practices regulating the activities and market behaviour of the enterprises are laid down in the Marketing Practices Act (*Markedsføringsloven*).[605] The Act applies not only to B2C relations but also to B2B relations. In the B2C context, the rules of the Act are primarily of a public law nature. The Act is supplemented by special regulation dealing in more detail with certain aspects, e.g., safety,[606] and/or special sectors, for example, financial services marketed by banks, etc.[607]

585. Within private law mainly, rules protecting individual consumers' contractual rights have been passed, often in order to implement EU-directives. The private law rules may be invoked by the consumers as individuals[608] typically in concrete cases, for example, where unreasonable contract terms are imposed on the consumer as the weak party.

Special acts on specific consumer contracts lay down mandatory rules which provide a minimum protection of consumers by declaring contract terms that place the consumer in a less favourable position than according to the act, not binding on the consumer. Provisions to this effect are laid down in, for example, the SGA (*Købeloven*), the Act on Certain Consumer Contracts (*Forbrugeraftaleloven*) and the Act on Credit Contracts (*Kreditaftaleloven*).[609] The protection under the various special acts is supplemented by the protection against unreasonable contract terms under the General Clause of the Contracts Act section 36.[610]

604. *See* Part II. Ch. 4, §3. III.D.
605. *See* Part II. Ch. 4, §3.
606. *See infra* III. on consumer safety legislation.
607. *See* Part II. Ch. 2, §3. on the supervision of financial institutions.
608. Compare *infra* VII. concerning group actions.
609. *See infra* V.
610. *See* Part I. Ch. 9, §1. IV. E. and *infra* V. B.

B. Institutions and Consumer Representation

586. The interests of consumers are safeguarded by private organizations as well as by State institutions. For a general overview of some of the organizations active in the area of consumer information, *see infra* Part II, Chapter 5, §2.II. As far as the Consumer Ombudsman *(Forbrugerombudsmanden)* is concerned reference is made to Part II, Chapter 4, §3. III, D. *See also infra* Part II, Chapter 5, §2.III concerning the Safety Technology Authority (*Sikkerhedsstyrelsen*), and *infra* Part II, Chapter 5, §2.VII concerning the Consumer Complaints Board *(Forbrugerklagenævnet)* and the approved private complaint boards.

587. Consumer representatives nominated typically by the independent Consumer Council *(Forbrugerrådet TÆNK)*[611] are members of the consumer complaint boards and participate (together with business representatives and a professional judge) in the decision of the cases. Furthermore, lay judges nominated by independent consumer organizations participate in cases brought before the Maritime and Commercial Court *(Sø-og Handelsretten)*[612] by the Consumer Ombudsman under the Marketing Practices Act, etc. Representatives of consumer interests also participate in the decision-making of various administrative bodies dealing with questions of importance to consumers. Consumer representatives nominated by the Consumer Council *(Forbrugerrådet TÆNK)* are also on a regular basis member of committees preparing legislation concerning consumer interests.

II. Consumer Information

588. Some of the general assumptions underlying Danish consumer protection are *that* the relatively weak position of consumers vis-à-vis business is closely related to lack of information, mainly concerning the specific properties of goods and services, and *that* consumers are able to deal in accordance with their own interests and preferences if they have sufficient information. Accordingly, many of the initiatives taken in order to improve the protection of consumers are comprised of measures which in different ways promote the dissemination of information concerning goods and services to consumers.

589. Legislation to this effect typically takes the shape of public law regulation ordering businesses to inform consumers on certain facts as part of a more or less detailed regulatory scheme often supervised by a public administrative agency.[613] Detailed rules on information (disclosure) are also found in the special acts on specific types of consumer transactions, such as distance sales, credit contracts, package travel contracts, etc., implementing EU-directives.[614]

---

611. *See infra* II.
612. *See* ss 94 and 225 of the Consolidated Administration of Justice Act 1284/2018 *(Retsplejeloven).*
613. *See* Part II. Ch. 4. §3 on the Marketing Practices Act (*Markedsføringsloven*) concerning *inter alia* price information and *infra* III. on safety information.
614. *See infra* V.

Besides a non-statutory principle of loyalty in contractual relations in the form of a general duty to disclose material facts,[615] there are relatively few private law rules imposing information duties on business. It is, however, worth noticing that the public law rules in practice interplay with the general principles of civil law in that violation of a duty to inform may trigger private law remedies according to general contract law principles or statutory rules on non-conformity of goods and services and/or according to general tort law principles on negligence.

590. Consumer information is one of the main tasks of the Competition and Consumer Authority *(Konkurrence- og Forbrugerstyrelsen)* which is a governmental agency under the Ministry of Industry, Business and Financial Affairs *(Erhvervsministeriet).* One of the principal aims of the Competition and Consumer Authority is to create a foundation for a coordinated and active contribution in the field of consumer affairs through information and service activities. Another main task is to contribute to the creation and maintenance of a high level of consumer protection as regards quality, safety, health and financial and legal rights by means of mediation and the exercise of influence. As far as information activities are concerned, the work is a continuance of the former Danish Government Home Economics Council (*Statens Husholdningsråd*) which was established in 1935.

591. Consumer information concerning food and nutrition is one of the tasks of the Veterinary and Food Administration *(Fødevarestyrelsen)* under the Ministry of Food, Agriculture and Fisheries *(Fødevareministeriet).* There are, for example, specific rules on public disclosure of food inspection results and smiley-reports.[616] The inspections are unannounced and cover relevant regulations concerning hygiene and other areas such as food contamination and labelling. The inspection results are stated in brief inspection reports and summarized in one of five categories by smiley symbols. Inspection reports (positive and negative) must be posted by the enterprise at the entrance to all food retail stores and restaurants, etc. The smiley report has to be displayed in such a way that consumers can read it from outside before deciding to enter a shop or a restaurant. The report must also be disclosed by the enterprise on its homepage. The reports are also accessible under the name of the shop, restaurant in question for the general public on a website run by the Danish Veterinary and Food Administration *(Fødevarestyrelsen).*

592. A special feature of the public consumer information efforts is found in section 31 of the Marketing Practices Act and in the Foodstuffs Act[617] section 10(3). These provisions authorize the Competition and Consumer Authority *(Konkurrence- og Forbrugerstyrelsen)* and the Veterinary and Food Administration *(Fødevarestyrelsen)* to conduct and publicize on the internet comparative test results

615. The principle is embodied in s. 76,(1)(3) of the Sale of Goods Act (*Købeloven*).
616. Rules issued under s. 56 of the Foodstuffs Act *(Fødevareloven)* are found in Executive Order 660/2018 on Food Inspection and Disclosure of Inspection Results (*Fødevarekontrol og offentliggørelse af kontrolresultater*).
617. Consolidated Act 999/2018 *(Fødevareloven).*

based on i.e., anonymous data collection (i.e., the data collector posing as an 'ordinary consumer'). In practice, test methods, etc. are laid down on the basis of talks with the relevant business and consumer organizations.

593. Consumer information, including publication of comparative tests of goods and services, is also one of many activities of the Consumer Council (*Forbrugerrådet TÆNK*) which is an independent organization articulating consumer interests and acting as watchdog in the interest of consumers. The Consumer Council (*Forbrugerrådet TÆNK*) dates back to 1947. Its activities are financed by the sale of consumer magazines and State funding decided by Parliament as part of the annual budget. The activities of the Consumer Council (*Forbrugerrådet TÆNK*) are not controlled by the State.

594. There is a wide range of private and/or voluntary labelling schemes. One of the best known logos is the so-called Ø-mærke signifying that the conditions according to the Danish legislation on organic farming are met under the supervision of the Danish Agri Fish Agency *(NaturErhvervsstyrelsen).*[618]

III. The Safety of Goods and Services

595. Public law regulation concerning a wide range of products provides for products to be safe, so that they are not capable of causing injury to persons or damage to property when handled or consumed in a normal way. Within private law the contract determines the product requirements in accordance with the agreement of the parties. When injury or damage has occurred in spite of the consumers' compliance with the product instructions, the rules of product liability may be invoked.

A. Regulation of Safety

596. General safety rules are found in the Product Safety Act[619] which implements the Product Safety Directive.[620] The scope of the Act is the same as the Directive's, i.e., consumer products. The Act constitutes the basic safety regulation of all consumer products and forms a supplement to the product safety rules in specific sectors.

597. The producer is the one who is mainly responsible for the product. Only safe products may be brought on the market.[621] The distributors who resell the product without influencing the safety qualities of the product must endeavour to resell only safe products and have to look after the products dealt with by the distributor. Both the producer and the distributor have the duty to monitor the product brought

618. Section 6 of Consolidated Act. 21/2017 on Ecology (*Økologiloven*).
619. Consolidated Act 3/2019 *(Produktsikkerhedsloven).*
620. Directive 2001/95/EC.
621. Section 5.

on the market and to interfere if safety fails.[622] A product is safe when it is applied in conformity with its purpose and handled in a way to be expected for use without danger to health or safety.[623] A product is considered to be safe when it complies with the legal requirements, the harmonized European or Danish standards and the actual technical level.[624]

The public authorities of control that safeguard the product safety may order issuance of public warnings and withdrawal or destruction of products.[625] In case of order of withdrawal or destruction, the seller of the product may not invoke the limitation rules under the SGA[626] according to which the buyer loses contract law remedies if she/he does not give the seller notice of the lack of conformity of the goods within two years after the date on which the goods were handed over to the buyer. The producer and the resellers are required to contribute to accomplish the orders and to make the product safe.

598. The Product Safety Act is administered by the Safety Technology Authority *(Sikkerhedsstyrelsen)* which is the coordinating authority concerning product safety, including responsibilities under the EU rapid alert system (Rapex) that facilitates the rapid exchange of information between Member States and the Commission on marketing or use of products posing a serious risk to the health and safety of consumers.

599. Furthermore, the Safety Technology Authority has the overall responsibility as far as gas safety,[627] electrical safety[628] and the safety of fireworks[629] are concerned. The control functions according to the Product Safety Act within other various product lines are assumed by different authorities, including specialized bodies of control established by legislation providing for safety regulation of specific risks related to special products or groups of products.[630] Normally it is assigned to the appropriate minister to work out detailed orders on the basis of EU-legislation and general guidelines. Not only safety but also other elements of quality are frequently taken into consideration in order to ensure a reasonable level of reliability concerning the product in question.

622. Sections 10 and 11.
623. Section 4, 1.
624. Section 6.
625. Section 20.
626. Sections 54 and 83 of the Sale of Goods Act *(Købeloven).*
627. Act 61/20184 on gas security.
628. Consolidated Act26/2019 on electrical equipment security (*Elsikkerhed*).
629. Consolidated Act 2/2019 on fire works and other pyrotechnical products *(Fyrværkeriloven).*
630. For example, The Veterinary and Food Administration *(Fødevarestyrelsen)*, The Environmental Protection Agency *(Miljøstyrelsen)* according to the Consolidated Act 26/2017 on chemical substances and products (*Kemikalielov).*

600. Services are not subject to a general safety legislation. The level of security is regulated by requirements on professional skill and authorization to the persons who have undertaken to perform services. Within special areas, for example, the medical sector, requirements are laid down for the enterprises which exercise professional activities.

601. In private law, the contracting parties are free to agree on the requirements which the product has to fulfil. When nothing else is agreed upon, it constitutes non-conformity of the goods, i.e., breach of contract, if the product sold cannot be used in the usual manner or fulfil its usual or specified purpose without a significant risk of injury to person or damage to property, unless the buyer was made aware of the risk.[631]

B. Product Liability

602. Under Danish law, personal injury and damage caused to property (other than the defective product itself) are outside the scope of the seller's liability for breach of contract. No explicit rule to this effect is found in the SGA but the Act has been and still is understood in this way by the courts.

603. According to non-statutory principles of tort law, the liability of producers and suppliers of dangerous/defective products and services is based on fault (*culpa*) with the supplement that professional suppliers have a vicarious liability for product liability incurred by previous links in the chain of production or distribution. The principle of suppliers' vicarious liability is developed by the courts and its main justification is generally sought in the fact that the professional supplier is regularly in a better position than the injured party to influence and to seek recourse against the producer and other previous links in the chain of distribution.

604. In addition to the court developed principles, rules on product liability are found in the Product Liability Act[632] implementing the Product Liability Directive[633] and imposing a strict (no fault) defect liability on the 'producer' and codifying the pre-existing principle of professional suppliers' vicarious liability for product liability. The rules of the Directive were added 'on top' of the existing court developed rules. As is the case with the Directive, the Danish Product Liability Act is limited to personal injury and damage to consumers' property. Consequently,

631. Sections 75 a and 76 of the Sale of Goods Act *(Købeloven). See supra* Part I. Ch. 9, §2.V. and *infra* Part II. Ch. 5. V.C.
632. Consolidated Act 261/2007 as amended by Act 523/2007.
633. Directive 85/374/EEC on the approximation of the laws, regulations and administrative provisions of the Member States concerning liability for defective products as amended by Directive 1999/34/EC.

liability for personal injury and damage to consumers' property is regulated by two sets of rules: the original ones developed by the courts and the rules implementing the Directive.[634]

605. The Act imposes, in accordance with the Directive, a general strict (no fault) liability on producers[635] for products that are defective.[636] The Act accepts the development risk defence, i.e., that producer is not liable if the state of scientific and technical knowledge at the time when she/he put the product into circulation was not such as to enable the existence of the defect to be discovered.[637]

606. Originally, the Product Liability Act stipulated that suppliers were vicariously liable for also the producers' strict liability. In *Skov Æg v. Bilka Lavprisvarehus,*[638] the European Court of Justice found that the supplier's vicarious liability for the producer's no-fault liability was in conflict with the Product Liability Directive. The vicarious liability rule of the Danish Act was amended accordingly to the effect that suppliers are now vicariously liable for the producer's (and other previous links') fault-based liability only, compare section 10 a of the Act.[639] According to section 11 paragraph 3, thc distributor has the right of recourse against the previous sellers and the producer when he has paid indemnity or compensation. Section 12 of the Act provides that a claim for indemnity or compensation is mandatory, to the benefit of a vicariously liable supplier.

607. An amount of DKK 4,000 (ECU 500) is to be deducted from the amount of compensation for damage to consumer property.[640] However, if the injured person is able to prove that the damage was caused by negligence, the court-developed rules may be invoked to the effect that the consumer is entitled to full compensation for any damage to items of property.

The Act does not include any maximum concerning the amount of the indemnity or compensation.

608. The Product Liability Act is mandatory not only to the benefit of the injured party but also to the benefit of a supplier who has paid damages to the injured party according to § 10 a of the Product Liability Act, i.e., on the basis of the supplier's vicarious liability for fault-based liability of a previous link.[641] This means that a contract term excluding or limiting liability claims between commercial parties is

634. Whereas product liability to business property is dealt with only by the court developed rules.
635. Section 4 of the Act and Art. 3 of the Directive.
636. Section 5 of the Act and Art. 6 of the Directive.
637. Section 7.1.4 of the Act and Arts 7(e) and 15.1(b) of the Directive.
638. Case C-402/03 (2006) ECR. I-199.
639. Amendment Act 541/2006.
640. Section 8 of the Act and Art. 9(b) of the Directive.
641. Cf. ss 12 and 11.3 of the Act.

not binding on suppliers seeking recourse against a previous link in the chain of distribution. The mandatory rule applies only within the scope of the Product Liability Act, i.e., in cases of personal injury and damage to consumer property.[642]

IV. The Quality of Goods and Services

609. Public law regulation of quality requirements is found in the special legislation within the various areas of law. Frequently, there is no sharp distinction between safety requirements and other conditions. Within the foodstuff sector, the provisions on quality laid down in the general and the special legislation, for example, very detailed rules issued under the Act of Foodstuffs[643] implementing numerous EU-directives provide for a so-called positive list *(positivlisten)* which indicates the additives which are approved, and the purposes for which they may be used, and the list brings information on the identity and purity of the additives. Only the registered additives may be added to foodstuffs.[644] Section 7 of the Foodstuffs Act lays down general access to regulation of additives in order to secure the presence of nutritious substances and to regulation of the combination, content and condition of foodstuffs. The Act, Chapter 5, regulates the designation and marking of foodstuffs in order to avoid misleading information and to lay down rules concerning the declaration of the content, the durability and storage as well as rules on advertising.

610. As far as services are concerned quality requirements concerning professional skills are often part of authorization or registration schemes[645] and public supervision.[646]

V. Consumer Contracts

A. *General Survey*

611. Consumer contracts are subject to the general rules laid down in the Contracts Act and the SGA, which include mandatory provisions exclusively concerning consumer relationships. Furthermore, a special legislation concerning contracts of practical interest for consumers has been established. These special areas have, to an increasing extent, been subject to harmonized rules within the EU. In the following, some important general and special consumer contract rules are briefly discussed.

---

642. Peter Møgelvang-Hansen *The Nordic Tradition: Application of Boilerplate Clauses under Danish Law,* in *Boilerplate Clauses: International Commercial Contracts and the Applicable Law* 233–253 (Giuditta Cordero-Moss ed., Cambridge U. Press 2011).
643. Consolidated Act 999/2018 *(Fødevareloven).*
644. Executive Order 1247/2018 (*Tilsætningbekendtgørelsen).*
645. For example, Act 526/2014 concerning real estate agents, *see supra* no. 427.
646. *See* for example, Part I. Ch. 8 §2. on stockbroking.

612. The definition of a 'consumer' varies from the concept usually used in EU-legislation.

Under the Danish SGA,[647] the buyer does not have to be a natural person in order to be a 'consumer' protected by the mandatory rules of the SGA. Thus, also an association (e.g., a homeowners' association and a (non-professional) sports club, etc.) can have the status of a consumer and be protected as such by the mandatory rules of the SGA, provided that the association is not engaged in commercial activity. This definition of a consumer is the very same in a variety of consumer statutes under Danish private law. Furthermore, in cases where the seller, etc. is a non-professional, but the contract has been established for the seller by a person engaged in business, the resulting contract is also considered to be a 'consumer contract'.[648]

B. Unfair Contract Terms

613. In order to make sure that Directive on unfair terms in consumer contracts[649] was implemented properly the general clause in section 36 of the Formation of Contract Act[650] was slightly adjusted[651] and section 38 c of the Contract Act was added providing some minor rather technical modifications.

614. The general clause of section 38 c, compare section 36, protects consumers to a greater extent than does Directive 93/13/EEC. The criterion of the general clause is 'unreasonable or contrary to principles of fair conduct' without the qualifications of the Directive[652] and the general clause is applicable to all terms without any restrictions concerning the price, etc.[653] Furthermore, in contrast to the Directive,[654] also subsequent facts may be taken into account in favour of the consumer (but not to the detriment of the consumer).[655]

615. Rules on preventive control of unfair contract terms were introduced in 1975 with the first Danish Marketing Practices Act.[656]

The scope of the general clause of section 1 (good marketing practices) includes the use of contract terms in consumer contracts. Although the wording of section 1 does not specifically deal with the question the provision, in accordance with the preparatory works of the Act, is interpreted as a means to regulating *inter alia* unfair contract terms in consumer contracts.[657]

---

647. SGA s. 4 a defines the term 'consumer contract'.
648. *Ibid.*, and for example, Act 1457/2013 on Consumer Contracts (*Forbrugeraftaleloven*) s. 2.
649. Directive 1993/13/EEC.
650. *See supra* Part I. Ch. 9, §1.
651. Amendment Act 1098/1994.
652. That is, the Directive requires that the term is contrary to the requirement of good faith and that there is a significant imbalance, cf Art. 3 of the Directive.
653. Cf. Art. 4(2) of the Directive.
654. Article 4(1) of the Directive.
655. Cf. §38c(2).
656. The rules are now found in the Marketing Practices Act 426/2017.
657. *See* for details on the Marketing Practices Act, *supra* Part II. Ch. 4. §3.

C. Sale of Goods

616. The SGA'[658] lays down the general rules on all sales other than sales of real property. Many of the rules applicable to all types of sales are made protectively mandatory in consumer sales. Furthermore, special rules on mainly non-conformity are applicable to consumer sales only, and they are nearly all mandatory in favour of consumers.[659]

617. The non-conformity rules of the Act implement the directive on certain aspects of the sale of consumer goods and associated guarantees.[660] In some respects, the Act protects the consumers to a wider extent than does the directive. One example is the rule providing that it constitutes non-conformity if seller does not on his own initiative disclose information to the consumer information which were relevant to the consumer's assessment the goods and which the seller knew or should have been aware of.[661] Another example is that the consumer, in cases where the seller does not fulfil an offer (or a claim) to cure (repair/replace) non-conforming goods, is entitled to rescission also in cases where the lack of performance is minor. Purchase of water, gas and electricity and goods sold by way of execution, etc. is within the scope of the Act.

D. The Act on Consumer Contracts

618. The Act[662] implements the directives on consumer rights,[663] and on distance contracts for financial services.[664]

619. In addition, the Act protects consumers also in other respects. Thus, the Act lays down a general prohibition against door-to-door selling and telephone advertising. Persons engaged in business may not, without prior request, contact a consumer in person or by telephone at its residence, place of work or other place not open to the public in order to conclude a contract.[665] And in cases where a person engaged in business has sent or delivered goods to a consumer without prior request, and where this is not due to error, the consumer is entitled to keep the goods free of

658. Consolidated Act 140/2014 *(Købeloven). See supra* Part I. Ch. 9. §2. on the general rules of the Act.
659. Section 1 and 1a.
660. Directive 1999/44/EC.
661. Section 76.1, no. 3.
662. Act 1457/2013 *(Forbrugeraftaleloven).*
663. Directive 2011/83/EU.
664. Directive 2002/65/EC.
665. Section 4.

charge.[666] Furthermore, consumers are protected against terms in contracts concerning the continuing delivery of goods or services for an indefinite period in that consumers has a general right to terminate the contract with one month's notice when five months have passed since the conclusion of the contract.[667]

E. Credit Contracts

620. Consumer credit is regulated by the Act on Credit Contracts[668] which implements the EU Directive on consumer credit agreements.[669] The scope of the Act is rather wide and includes, for example, mortgage debt, repossession of goods. Excluded from the Act are *inter alia* short-term contracts that must be paid off within three months and credit agreed by court settlement.

621. The right of repossession or retention of the goods is valid only if an agreement to this effect was made at the latest when the goods are handed over to the consumer; the total payment has to exceed DKK 2,000; and the credit sale may not be related to a credit agreement with a variable amount of loan. Thcsc conditions also apply to non-consumer sales. Furthermore, a special condition, applicable only to consumer sales, is that at least 20% of the price must be paid when the goods are handed over to the purchaser.[670] In case of repossession in consumer sales, the seller is not entitled to claim any part of the debt exceeding the value of the repossessed goods unless the consumer acted negligently.[671]

622. For consumer credit sales without right of repossession or retention of the goods, it is not permitted for the creditor to seek satisfaction by establishing a mortgage on the contractual goods.[672]

F. Real Estate Transactions

623. The Act on Real Estate Agents[673] applies to offers, mediation and counselling concerning real property exercised by real estate agents and by other persons engaged in business in relation to consumers. The principle of transparency is laid down in the Act which contains rather detailed rules. For promoting the ability to compare prices, the Act provides that the value of the real property has to be estimated in cash price for a certain period, and the cash price is to be applied in the advertisements. The consumer also must receive specific information on the amount

666. Section 6.
667. Section 28.
668. Consolidated Act 1336/2015 (*Kreditaftaleloven*).
669. Directive 2008/48/EC on credit agreements for consumers as amended by Directive 2011/90/EU and Directive 2014/17/EU
670. Sections 34 and 50 of Consolidated Act 1336/2015.
671. Section 41 of the Act.
672. Section 21 of the Act.
673. Act 526/2014 (*Ejendomsformidling*).

which shall be at his disposal after the settlement of the sale, and on the yearly expenses. According to section 21, the agent is obliged to inform the consumer of any particular interest that the agent may have concerning the consumer's choice of financing, insurance, etc. Further detailed information requirements are laid down in an executive order.[674]

624. According to section 47, the consumer is entitled to claim damages according to the general compensation rules in cases where the intermediary has not complied with its duties. In case of incorrect calculation of the proceeds of sale or of the charges imposed on the proprietor, the bona fide consumer is entitled to an amount as compensation for the difference between the wrong and the right calculation. If the wrong calculation concerns the valuation of the property, the consumer may claim a reasonable compensation for the difference.[675]

625. The Act on Consumer Protection by Purchase of Real Property[676] contains rules on *inter alia* a right of withdrawal from the purchase under certain conditions.

VI. Sales Promotion and Commercial Practices

626. *See supra* Part II, Chapter 4, §3.

VII. Consumer Redress

627. The Consumer Complaint Board Scheme was established in 1975 in order to offer consumers easy, quick and inexpensive dispute resolution in cases concerning complaints against goods or services. The present rules are found in the Consumer Complaints Act.[677] The system consists of a number of approved private complaint boards financed by business and the public Consumer Complaint Board (*Forbrugerklagenævnet*) dealing with the residual of complaints that cannot be brought before one of the private complaint boards approved by the Minister of Business and Growth. Only cases concerning purchase of real property and health services are exempted from the scheme.[678]

628. The Consumer Complaint Board (*Forbrugerklagenævnet*) is an independent public body. It consists of a chairman and consumer and business representatives. The chairman must be a professional judge without any particular relations to consumer or business organizations. The Competition and Consumer Authority

674. Executive Order 1230/2014.
675. Section 47 does not reflect the general principles of Danish law insofar as it allows compensation of unfulfilled expectations, *see* Peter Møgelvang-Hansen *Danish Law* 268–271 (Børge Dahl et al., eds., 2d ed. Thomson 2001).
676. Consolidated Act 1123/2015 *(Forbrugerbeskyttelse ved erhvervelse af fast ejendom).*
677. Act 524/2015 *(Forbrugerklageloven)* implementing Directive 2013/11/EU on Consumer ADR.
678. Act 528/2014 s. 2.

handles the secretariat functions. The Consumer Complaint Board deals with consumer complaints if the price for the goods or service in question exceeds DKK 1,050 (approximately EUR 140) but not DKK 100,000 (approximately EUR 13,300).[679] The board procedure is optional for the consumer. Contract terms to the effect that a legal dispute shall be dealt with by arbitration or by another special forum of mediation does not bar the complaint from being brought before the board.[680] The complaints board procedure is in writing, and the consumer can choose to contribute to the case on an online basis.

629. A private complaint board can obtain approval by the Minister of Industry, Business and Financial Affairs if it comprises a specific trade or other well-defined areas and if its bylaws contain provisions regarding the composition of the board and a review procedure that is satisfactory for the parties. In 2019, there were seventeen approved private compliant boards covering, for example, the energy sector, telecommunication, banking, insurance, package travels, parking and technical installations.

630. A decision made by the Consumer Complaint Board and the approved private complaint boards does not prevent the parties from bringing the matter before the courts. However, a decision in favour of the consumer becomes binding and enforceable if the business party does not inform the Board within thirty days that she/he will not accept the decision.[681] If the decision made by a complaint board in favour of the consumer is not complied with, the Competition and Consumer Authority may bring the matter to court at the request and on behalf of the consumer. If a decision in favour of the consumer is brought before the courts, the Competition and Consumer Authority may on request cover the costs of consumer (as plaintiff or defendant).[682]

631. A small claims court procedure was introduced in 2008 as part of comprehensive reform of the court system.[683] The scope of the procedure is claims not exceeding DKK 50,000 (approximately EUR 6,660).

632. According to the Arbitration Act[684] section 7.2, the consumer is not bound by an arbitration agreement entered into before the dispute arose. Section 7.2 of the Arbitration Act applies also to arbitration to take place outside Denmark and also in cases where the agreement stipulates that Danish law shall not apply.

679. Executive Order 65/2019.
680. Consumer Complaint Act s. 14(3).
681. Consumer Complaint Act s. 32.
682. Consumer Complaint Act ss 36–38.
683. Sections 400–410 of Consolidated Administration of Justice Act 1284/2018 *(Retsplejeloven)*.
684. Act 553/2005 (*Voldgiftsloven*) as amended by Act 106/2008.

633. The group action is a new civil procedural device that was introduced in 2008[685] in order to enable the courts to deal with disputes concerning a large number of uniform claims in a more effective way than under the traditional rules and to improve access to the courts in cases concerning small claims belonging to a large number of individuals. The basic conditions for bringing a group action are *that* the group action is deemed to be the best method of dealing with the claims, *that* the group members can be identified and notified about the proceedings in an appropriate manner *and that* a group representative can be appointed. As a main rule, a group action includes only group members who positively request to participate. If this is not an expedient way of dealing with the claims, the court can decide that the group action shall include group members who do not opt out of the group action, provided it is evident that the claims because of their limited size cannot be expected to be brought in individual actions (the opt-out model). In an opt-out group action, only the Consumer Ombudsman can act as group representative. So far,[686] only a few group actions, none of which has been on an opt-out basis have been brought.

685. Sections 254 a–254 k of the Consolidated Administration of Justice Act 1284/2018*(Retsplejeloven).*
686. April 2019.

Selected Bibliography

Books in English

Dahl, Børge, Torben Melchior & Ditlev Tamm (eds). *Danish Law in a European Perspective*. 2nd ed. Copenhagen: Thomson, 2002.

Iversen, Bent & Lindencrone Petersen. *Danish Business Law*. 6th ed. Copenhagen: DJØF, 2015.

Lando, Ole, et al. (eds). *Restatement of Nordic Contract Law*. Copenhagen: DJØF Publishing, 2016.

Letto-Vanamo, Pia, Ditlev Tamm & Bent Ole Gram Mortensen. *Nordic Law in European Context*. Springer, 2019.

Nielsen, Ruth. *Contract Law in Denmark*. The Hague: Kluwer Law International, 2011.

Articles in English

Dahl, Børge. 'Danish Law'. In *Contract Law and Practice: The English System, with Scottish, Commonwealth, and Continental Comparisons*, edited by Michael H. Whincup. 5th rev. and enl. edn. Alphen aan den Rijn: Kluwer Law International, 2006.

Edlund, Hans Henrik. 'Termination of Commercial Contracts by Giving Notice'. *European Review of Contract Law* 4(1) (2008): 15–30.

Edlund, Hans Henrik. 'Imbalance in Long-Term Commercial Contracts'. *European Review of Contract Law* 5(4) (2009): 427–445.

Fogt, Morten Midtgaard. 'Direct Liability of Previous Seller, Supplier and Producer in Danish Law'. In *European Perspectives on Producer's Liability: Direct Producer's Liability for Non-conformity and the Sellers' Right of Redress,* edited by Martin Ebers, André Janssen & Olaf Meyer. Munich: Sellier, 2009, 223–254.

Møgelvang-Hansen, Peter. 'The Nordic Tradition: Application of Boilerplate Clauses under Danish Law'. In *Boilerplate Clauses: International Commercial Contracts and the Applicable Law,* edited by Giuditta Cordero-Moss. Cambridge: Cambridge University Press, 2011, Chapter 11.

Østergaard, Kim. 'Denmark'. In *Unexpected Circumstances in European Contract Law,* edited by Ewoud Hondius & Hans Christoph Grigoleit. Cambridge University Press, 2011, 109–117.

Selected Bibliography

Index

The numbers here refer to paragraph numbers.

Accountant, 75, 206, 485. *See also* Auditor
Agricultural sector, 492, 501
Air transport. *See* Carriage by air
Annual account, 62, 63, 64, 110, 296, 485
Auditor, 110, 111, 485, 530. *See also* Accountant
Aviation, 421, 471

Bankruptcy
  assets, 215, 217, 222, 258, 260, 262
  beneficium of need *(trangsbeneficium)*, 222
  claims on estate, 247-259
  close relations, 242
  composition scheme, 251, 258, 261-267
  date of notice, 205, 212, 230, 231, 233, 234, 237, 239, 240, 240, 241, 243, 244
  disposal of property, 218
  illiquidity, 216
  inheritance, 224, 241
  insolvency, 216, 230
  security rights, 234
Bill of exchange, 278
Biotechnical inventions
  plant breeders rights, 197
Board of New Plants *(Plantenyhedsnævnet)*, 197
Broadcasting. *See* Radio; Television
Broker, 293, 374, 388, 496. *See also* Stockbroking

Carriage
  combined transport, 427
  by rail, 4119, 447, 468
  by road, 405, 412
  by sea, 405, 407
Carriage by air, 421
Central Securities Depositories, 277, 445
Cheque, 285
Commercial agency, 327, 375
Company

Danish company structure, 32
  private limited company *(anpartsselskab* (ApS)), 56, 104
  public limited company *(aktieselskab* (A/S)), 56, 105

Competition
  clause, 366, 371, 383
  distortion, 534, 536
  harmful effects, 543
  merger control, 532
  selective distribution, 373
Competition and Consumer Authority *(Konkurrence-og Forbrugerstyrelsen)*, 80, 536-546, 581, 590, 592
Competition Council *(Konkurrencerådet)*, 80, 537, 540, 545, 575
Complaints Board for Competition *(Konkurrenceankenævnet)*, 80, 537, 541, 546
Computer chips
  copyright, 187
Construction contracts, 428
Consumer Complaints Board *(Forbrugerklagenævnet)*, 80, 628
Consumer concept, 612
Consumer contracts, 611
Consumer Council *(Forbrugerrådet TÆNK)*, 568, 587, 593
Consumer credit, 327, 620
Consumer Ombudsman *(Forbrugerombudsmanden)*, 80, 562, 584, 586, 633

Index

Consumer sales, 340, 348, 352, 616
Contracts
  culpa in contrahendo, 336
  in dubio contra stipulatorem, 328
  electronic transmission, 326
  implied terms, 333
  standard terms, 325
  theory of promise *(løfteprincippet),* 320
  unfair contract terms, 334, 401, 555, 573, 613
Contracts for the International Sale of Goods (CISG), 318, 338, 339, 360
Cooperative association *(andelsforeninger),* 62
Copyright
  photograph, 146, 158
Cut-off clause, 401, 404

Danish Association for Indemnity Liability (*Dansk Forening for Skadesforsikring,* SKAFOR), 392
Danish Bar and Law Society *(Advokatsamfundet)*), 75, 404
Danish Financial Supervisory Authority (DFSA) *(Finanstilsynet).See* Financial Supervisory Authority
Danish Guarantee Fund for Depositors and Investors *(Garantifonden for indskydere og investorer),* 396
Danish Industry (*Dansk Industri* (DI)), 71
Danish Standard (*Dansk Standard* (DS)), 89
Dematerialized instruments, 277
Design
  copyright, 179
Direct marketing. *See* Unsolicited communication
Distance sales, 589
Distribution contracts, 361
Doorstep sales, 619

E-commerce, 80, 551, 571
Environment, 507, 527
EU-citizens, 47, 49, 50
European economic interest groupings (EEIG), 67, 106
Exclusive distribution, 362, 363
Exemption clause, 349, 406
Export credit, 84, 513

Factoring, 402
Faroe Islands, 1, 4, 8, 36, 37
Financial Supervisory Authority (*Finanstilsynet,* DFSA), 79, 106, 285, 395, 495
Fisheries sector, 504
Flexicurity, 462
Foreign exchange of capital, 458
Franchise contracts, 372

Gifts, 228, 240, 255, 271, 320
Good marketing practices, 615
Goodwill, 121, 382
Greenland, 1, 4, 8, 36, 37
Group actions, 633
Guarantee, 45, 283, 304, 350, 353, 396, 429, 430

Insider dealing, 311-317
  Insurance, 390.394
Intellectual property rights. *See* Biotechnical inventions; Computer chips; Copyright; Design; Know-how; Patent; Trademarks

Know-how, 123, 372, 454

Leasing, 398
Letter of intent, 324
List of Products *(Produktregisteret),* 112

Maritime and Commercial Court *(Sø-og Handelsretten),* 44, 95, 96, 97, 538, 587
Marketing Practices, 555. *See also* Consumer Ombudsman *(Forbrugerombudsmanden);* Good marketing practices
Mortgage
  book of persons *(Personbogen),* 440
  the general ship register (Det almindelige Skibsregister), 440
  institutions, 65
  the land register *(Tingbogen),* 442
  on movable property, 439
  on real property, 442
Municipalities, 7, 93, 446, 454, 455, 475

NASDAQ Copenhagen, 286-292, 299
Negotiable instruments. *See* Bill of exchange; Dematerialized instruments; Promissory notes
Nordic citizens, 48, 50

Offer, 319-326

Ombudsman of the Folketing *(Folketingets Ombudsmand),* 40, 91

Patent. *See also* Biotechnological inventions
European patent, 159, 161
international cooperation, 159
medical patents, 160
sanctions against violations, 167
secret patent, 159
Patent and Trademark Appeal Board *(Patent-og Varemærkeankenævnet),* 166, 173, 185, 190
Patent and Trademark Authority *(Patent-og Varemærkestyrelsen),* 81, 135, 136, 139, 159-163, 166, 173, 175, 182, 185, 188
Payment cards, 397
Petrol distribution, 371
Planning, 448, 451, 465, 466
Pledge, 214, 259, 436-438
Pollution, 112, 451
Postal service, 33, 453, 474
Price indications, 561
Price regulation, 476, 572
Principle of legality *(legalitetsprincippet),* 446
Product liability 602
insurance, 392
Product safety, 602
Promissory notes *(gældsbreve)*
negotiable (omsætningsgældsbreve), 269
ordinary (simple gældsbreve), 269
Protection of the environment. *See* Environment
Public procurement, 452, 469
Public sector, 29, 76, 446, 447, 482
Public supply, 580

Radio, 477, 571
Railways, 447, 467, 499
Real estate agents, 486-488, 623
Reconstruction, 200, 201, 205-214
Refusal of supply, 367
Roads, 472-473

Safety Technology Authority *(Sikkerhedsstyrelsen),* 82, 586, 598, 599
Sale and lease back, 399
Sale of goods
generic purchase, 341, 342, 349, 351, 353, 360

INCOTERMS, 132
transportation clauses, 344

Sea transport, 407. *See also* Carriage
Secrets. *See* Trade secrets
Shipbuilding, 520
Sponsoring, 571
State ownership, 452, 530
Stockbroking, 293-295
Stock Exchange. *See* NASDAQ Copenhagen
Supervisory Authority of Financial Affairs. *See* Financial Supervisory Authority (*Finanstilsynet,* DFSA)

Telecommunication, 476
Television, 571
Tobacco advertising, 570
Trademarks
collective marks, 134
common marks, 134
comparative advertising, 551, 559
guaranty marks, 134
Kodak doctrine, 140
licence, 143
Trade names, 114-120
Trade practices. *See* Marketing practices
Trade secrets, 125-130, 195, 556
Trade unions, 20, 63, 73
Transportation clauses, 344
Transport terms. *See* Carriage

Unsolicited communication, 560
Utility models, 172-178

Veterinary and Food Authority (*Fødevarestyrelsen*), 591, 592,

Wage Earners' Guarantee Fund *(Lønmodtagernes Garantifond),* 252

Index

www.ingramcontent.com/pod-product-compliance
Ingram Content Group UK Ltd.
Pitfield, Milton Keynes, MK11 3LW, UK
UKHW020139290926
15471UKWH00003B/591

9 789403 516219